Help Me to Find My People

THE JOHN HOPE FRANKLIN SERIES IN AFRICAN AMERICAN HISTORY & CULTURE

WALDO E. MARTIN JR. & PATRICIA SULLIVAN, EDITORS

HEATHER ANDREA WILLIAMS

help me
to find my people

The African American Search *for*
Family Lost *in* Slavery

THE UNIVERSITY OF NORTH CAROLINA PRESS

CHAPEL HILL

This book was published with the assistance of the John Hope Franklin Fund of the University of North Carolina Press.

©2012 THE UNIVERSITY OF NORTH CAROLINA PRESS

Designed by Sally Fry
Set in Minion and Jenson by Rebecca Evans

Manufactured in the United States of America
The paper in this book meets the guidelines for permanence and durability of the Committee on Production Guidelines for Book Longevity of the Council on Library Resources.

The University of North Carolina Press has been a member of the Green Press Initiative since 2003.

Library of Congress Cataloging-in-Publication Data
Williams, Heather Andrea.
Help me to find my people : the African American search
for family lost in slavery / by Heather Andrea Williams.
p. cm.—(The John Hope Franklin series in
African American history and culture)
Includes bibliographical references and index.
ISBN 978-0-8078-3554-8 (cloth : alk. paper)
ISBN 978-1-4696-2836-3 (pbk. : alk. paper)
ISBN 978-0-8078-8265-8 (ebook)
1. Slavery—Social aspects—United States—History.
2. African American families—History. 3. Slaves—Family
relationships—United States—History. I. Title.
E443.W63 2012
306.3'620973—dc23
2011050216

In memory of my father,

ANDREW E. WILLIAMS,

and for CLAY, *again*

Contents

Illustrations

Help Me to Find My People

I learned about grief that night, the kind of bottomless, yawning grief that can find nothing upon which to anchor itself, that stretches itself out into a long howl ending in a hollow silence.

ELIZABETH NUNEZ, *Beyond the Limbo Silence*

Introduction

This is a book about slavery and family and loss and longing. It is a book about emotions. It is about love and loneliness and grief, about anger, and about fear, joy, hope, and despair. It is about the forced separation of thousands of African American families, about their grief, and about their determined hope to someday see each other again. The feelings are grounded in the material conditions of slavery in the American South, so the book places emotions within a historical context that includes the domestic slave trade, the expansion of the United States, the Civil War, and emancipation. It considers legal structures that governed slaves and slavery, relationships between enslaved men and women, relationships between enslaved people and their owners, parenting in slavery, uses of literacy among enslaved African Americans, and networks of communication among African Americans both during slavery and following emancipation.

Several years ago while doing research in the black newspapers that began publication after the American Civil War, I came across advertisements in which African Americans searched for family members whom they had lost during slavery. I had read examples of these notices in Leon Litwack's *Been in the Storm So Long* and Herbert Gutman's *The Black Family in Slavery and Freedom*, but when I began encountering them in the newspapers, just as they had appeared in the 1860s and 1870s, I was compelled to stop and pay attention; I could not simply move on. Soon I started to search them out, and over the years I have found approximately 1,200 "Information Wanted" or "Lost Friends" advertisements, like this one that Thornton Copeland placed in the *Colored Tennessean* in Nashville on October 7, 1865, six months after the Civil War ended and twenty-one years after he was sold away from his mother:

> INFORMATION is wanted of my mother, whom I left in Fauquier county, Va., in 1844, and I was sold in Richmond, Va., to Saml. Copeland. I formerly belonged to Robert Rogers. I am very anxious to hear from my mother, and any information in relation to her whereabouts will be very thankfully received. My mother's name was Betty, and was sold by Col. Briggs to James French.—Any information by letter, addressed to the Colored Tennessean, Box 1150, will be thankfully received.

Or this one, also from the *Colored Tennessean* one week later on October 14, 1865:

> INFORMATION is wanted of my two boys, James and Horace, one of whom was sold in Nashville and the other was sold in Rutherford County. I, myself, was sold in Nashville and sent to Alabama, by Wm. Boyd. I and my children belonged to David Moss, who was connected with the Penitentiary in some capacity. CHARITY MOSS.
>
> P.S. Any information sent to Colored Tennessean office, Box 1150 will be thankfully received.

A son searching for his mother; a mother searching for her sons. Thornton Copeland, Charity Moss, and their relatives had been entangled in the forced sales and migrations that African Americans experienced between the 1600s and 1865, and which escalated beginning in the 1830s as white Americans moved farther south and west. Thornton Copeland does not say how old he was when he was sold from his mother; he could have been a child, an adolescent, or a young man. He was, though, old enough to remember the details of where he was from, his owners' names, and his mother's first name. Whatever his age, he likely joined one of the numerous coffles of people chained together to prevent escape as they walked to their next destination. Decades later, he thought he had a chance of finding his mother. He had only known her as Betty, and even that name, he acknowledged, was unstable and may have changed. Charity Moss had been taken from Tennessee to Alabama, but her sons could have been anywhere. Their purchasers may have remained in Tennessee, or they may have been part of the American expansion that had taken her farther south and west to Alabama.

When I first came to the ads, I was struck by the pain and the longing that these few lines of a family's history contained. Then I also began to see and feel the resilience and the hope encoded in the messages. Thornton Copeland searched for his mother more than twenty years after he last saw her, and Charity Moss hoped she could find her sons across the miles of their separation. The power of simultaneous pain and hope held me entranced, and I wanted to think more about these people, and to know more about them. I wanted to explore the emotions that their words conveyed. I wanted to know how it felt to be sold away from your family or to have your mother or father suddenly disappear. I wanted to know how a mother coped with losing her children, and what happened when she could not cope. I wanted to know how a husband and wife parted with each other when the parting was forced and final. I wanted to know what people did with the grief and the fear and the anger that I thought must be part of these experiences of loss.

The Information Wanted ads inspired this book, and in it I am very much interested in exploring the interior lives of African Americans in the nineteenth-century South, as historian Nell Irvin Painter has urged.[1] Like people in any place or time, enslaved people and former slaves experienced a vast range of emotional responses, a range so multilayered that no scholar, whether sociologist, anthropologist, psychologist, or historian, could completely retrieve or catalog it. *Help Me to Find My People* is an effort to explore the thoughts and feelings of enslaved people as they tried to make sense of their status as slaves and as they reckoned with their feelings of love, powerlessness, and loss. At the same time, white people were ever present and implicated in the vast majority of decisions to sell people or to move them from one part of the country to another. As I am also interested in their emotions, I examine sympathy, indifference, hostility, empathy, and the seemingly purposeful blocking of empathy on the part of a range of whites, including slaveowners, slave traders, abolitionists, and visitors to the South.

Writing about emotions can be daunting. It is difficult enough to be aware of and to understand one's own emotions; attempting to understand the emotions of people who lived several lifetimes ago is a true challenge. As I work with the sources, I feel around in the world of feelings, trying hard to get an accurate sense of what these people's experiences were like. I listen closely to them, reading their words over and over, hearing their sighs and their silences, wanting to pick up their meaning, wanting to know what they are telling me. I interpret their expressions of feeling, but I do not attempt to psychoanalyze these people from the past. First, I am not qualified to do so, and second, the fragments of their lives that are preserved in the historical record would not enable meaningful psychoanalysis. That said, I have found some current psychological concepts helpful in thinking about the experiences of enslaved people, among them disenfranchised grief and ambiguous loss.

In the twenty-first century some may wonder if people, specifically black people who were slaves, felt in the nineteenth century as we do today. That actually can become two questions, one of time and one of race. Some white contemporaries of black slaves believed they felt more deeply than black people, that somehow, losing one's child or mother or father hurt a white person more than it hurt a black person. So there is the question of race. And there is the question of time: Did people, specifically black people, feel less intensely than we do today? Anthropologists have taken up the consideration of emotions across cultures and seem to be split between constructionists, who view emotions as locally and culturally constructed, and psycho-cultural anthropologists, who see broad underlying commonality in human emotions.[2] In my exploration of feeling among enslaved and freed African Americans, both ways of thinking may actually be helpful. The sources offer clear evidence of deep pain on the part of those who lost family members, and they also suggest that the expression of this pain in the presence of whites was sometimes muted, silenced, or buried because whites would not tolerate it, and perhaps also because blacks thought that expressing their grief openly would avail them nothing. The emotions, then, appear to fit into what may be called a universal model, but local restrictions sometimes limited their expression. To further complicate the analysis, enslaved people lived their lives both in the presence and out of the sight and hearing of whites. How they wept and grieved and hoped in their cabins, in their quarters, and in their hearts could never be completely controlled by their owners.

Doing this work of reconstructing the histories of slaves and freedpeople requires methodological fluidity. As the Information Wanted ads demonstrate, evidence often comes in small bits, so I put the pieces together to examine lives and experiences. I call on census data, journals, letters written by whites, and documents generated by the Freedmen's Bureau and other governmental agencies to tell stories of slaves, slaveowners, slave traders, visitors, and once the Civil War ended, freedpeople. I rely most heavily, though, on the narratives that former slaves, often those who had escaped slavery, wrote or dictated during the mid- to late 1800s. These slave narratives and the interviews of former slaves provide the most sustained accounts of separation and its repercussions. Using all of these sources, I attempt to explore both the expression of grief and the mechanisms that enslaved people used to cope with or at least to adjust to loss.

In addition, I draw from letters that African Americans wrote. In my earlier work on education among enslaved people and freedpeople, I learned a great deal about how important it was to some African Americans to acquire literacy. I discovered the lengths to which they went to "steal an education" during slavery when most were legally prohibited from learning to read or write, and to establish and attend schools once slavery ended. Yet, in this project I was frankly shocked to find the letters that people wrote to loved ones from whom they had been separated. For all the time that I had spent working on education and literacy, and as well as I thought I knew what literacy meant to enslaved people, I had never dreamt of finding a love letter from an enslaved man to his former wife. I advise my students to make a wish list for the types of sources they would like to uncover in their research, but a love letter was never on my wish list because I had failed to imagine that such a thing existed.

Three other types of sources emerged as particularly significant in constructing this history: newspaper advertisements, music, and fiction. Advertisements run throughout the book and become near-characters, flagging the status of African Americans at particular moments during the nineteenth century. They are important sources for seeing the way the slave trade operated as well as how African Americans responded to their conditions of enslavement. Sellers and purchasers advertised their offerings and desires in the papers. Owners advertised when slaves ran away from captivity. And following the war, African Americans advertised their urgent desire to reconstruct their families. Each ad is a short, concise artifact intended for a specific purpose, but each also has a great deal to tell us about the business of slavery and about the personal impact of slavery on the lives of African Americans.

Music appears in several chapters in the form of the religious songs that people called on in moments of crisis and fear. These hymns and spirituals provided a balm for some enslaved people's emotional pain. Usually sung in communal settings, whether in formal congregations or in the secret meetings and services that slaves held out of the sight of owners and slave patrollers, the songs also came forward when people were alone and felt as though all was lost.[3] The lyrics, the rhythms and tones, and the faith that produced the songs, as well as the memories of the people with whom they had been learned and sung, offered a promise that the enslaved person who sang them would never truly be alone.

Finally, I work with fiction by writers Mark Twain and Charles Chesnutt, who lived during slavery and wrote afterward about the significance of family separation. Their short stories raise a host of compelling questions and portray the poignancy of loss and longing among African Americans. In comparing the value of fiction and historiography for telling history, particularly histories of trauma, historian Dominick LaCapra suggests that fiction contains a capacity to help us to understand history. "One might argue," LaCapra writes, "that narratives in fiction also involve truth claims on a structural or general level by providing insight into phenomena such as slavery or the Holocaust, by offering a reading of a process or period, or by giving at least a plausible 'feel' for experience and emotion which may be difficult to arrive at through restricted documentary methods." In this instance, the works of fiction by Chesnutt and Twain complement and illuminate the already powerful documentary sources.[4]

Writing history is an act of interpretation. The sources speak, but what we hear is filtered through our own experiences, values, beliefs, expectations, and even desires. I pay close attention to the voices of the people about whom I write—mostly enslaved African Americans, but also the white people who interacted with or observed them. Examining the complexity of the experiences and feelings of enslaved people may seem reasonable today, but historians did not always think nuance and complexity possible among enslaved African Americans. Ulrich B. Phillips, one of the earliest historians to study slavery, saw very little depth of feeling. Phillips, who was born in Georgia in 1877 at the end of Reconstruction and who became a professor at the University of Michigan and Yale University, had no doubt that blacks were both biologically and culturally inferior to whites on every measure, including their emotional capacity. Writing in 1918, Phillips, the white southerner, downplayed the brutality of slavery and slaveowners, claiming that American slavery was "essentially mild," and that by virtue of being black, slaves were docile and submissive, thereby inspiring their owners to be patriarchal "teachers and guardians as well as masters and owners." Phillips paid scant attention to the emotions of enslaved people, and even when he discussed family separation brought on by the domestic slave trade, his characterization of slaves as docile and backward certainly implied a diminished capacity to develop deep emotional ties. Although he acknowledged that slavery sometimes involved physical cruelty, "on the whole," he wrote, "the plantations were the best schools yet invented for the mass training of that sort of inert and backward people which the bulk of the American negroes represented." In Phillips's view, slavery served a positive purpose by civilizing what he considered to be a backward and barbarous people.[5]

Historians and other scholars eventually acknowledged that slavery had indeed been a cruel and sometimes torturous institution that took an emotional toll on individual enslaved people. But this awareness brought its own challenges as scholars attempted to understand how black people had managed to survive the physical brutality and emotional traumas of slavery. If slaves were wrenched from families and traded, could they continue to form caring relationships? If they worked from before day to after dark, how could they create a culture? Once they shifted away from Phillips's reasoning that slavery was not so bad, some scholars worked with the other side of the equation—how enslaved people responded—and they concluded that the horrors of slavery had dulled and even erased the sensitivities of the enslaved.

Writing in 1939, two decades after Phillips, E. Franklin Frazier, an African American sociologist at the University of Chicago, took on the subject of black families in slavery. Beginning with what he considered "disorganized" black family structures in the 1920s and 1930s, he looked back to slavery to find the antecedents. Unlike Phillips, Frazier acknowledged the cruelty of slavery but thought that this very cruelty may have dulled the emotional sensibilities of African captives and African American slaves. Frazier sometimes struggled to explain the effects that slavery *must* have had on slaves, more so than demonstrating with documentary evidence what *had* in fact occurred. For example, he claimed that women began to undergo a process of being dehumanized as traders marched them to the African coast. "Maternal feeling was choked and dried up in mothers who had to bear children, in addition to loads of corn or rice on their backs during marches of eight to fourteen hours," he wrote. In his estimation, the ordeal of the Middle Passage only made matters worse as "the last spark of maternal feeling was probably smothered in the breasts of many mothers who were packed spoon fashion between decks and often gave birth to children in the scalding perspiration from the human cargo." For Frazier, then, the horrors of capture and the Middle Passage began a process in which African women lost feelings of affection and caring for their children. Frazier did not offer sources to support these claims; this was just what seemed to make sense. How, after all, could a woman care about her child when the child was a physical burden? Still, Frazier did acknowledge a range of responses on the part of enslaved mothers. Although he thought the march to the African coast must have destroyed maternal affection, he also claimed that some women's love for their children survived this movement as well as the Middle Passage, and he drew from the slave narratives to support his claim that enslaved women in America displayed affection for their children and suffered when they were separated.[6]

Like Frazier, historian Stanley M. Elkins parted from the Phillips school to acknowledge that American slavery had indeed been physically and emotionally violent. Elkins, however, theorized what must have happened as a result, more than he demonstrated the actual effects of the slave trade and slavery on Africans and African Americans. "We may suppose," he wrote, "that every African who became a slave underwent an experience whose crude psychic impact must have been staggering and whose consequences superseded anything that had ever previously happened to him. Some effort should therefore be made to picture the series of shocks which must have accompanied the principal events of that enslavement."[7] American slavery, he argued, operated as a "closed" system in which slaves, who were pitiful and without culture or civilization, interacted with the outside world infrequently and were therefore completely dependent on white owners, who wielded absolute power.[8]

This closed system, Elkins conjectured, created a unique American personality type of the "Sambo," someone who was lazy, infantile, dependent, and lacking in manhood. Sambo was a stereotype, but Elkins wanted to uncover whether there was any truth to the characterization. In search of Sambo, he retraced Frazier's steps, following African captives to the coast through a process of "shock and detachment" and through the Middle Passage into American slavery.[9] Stripped away from their African values and standards, the captives and slaves now became dependent on owners. "He could now look to none but his master," Elkins wrote, "the one man to whom the system had committed his entire being: the man upon whose will depended his food, his shelter, his sexual connection, whatever moral instruction he might be offered, whatever success was possible within the system, his very security—in short, everything."[10] Elkins likened slavery to a German concentration camp in which, he claimed, prisoners became infantile and mimicked their captors. Elkins criticized historian Kenneth Stampp, who argued in his book *The Peculiar Institution* that enslaved people had resisted domination by owners. He asserted that Stampp was unrealistic in claiming that some slaves had been rebellious and courageous, "all the characteristics," Elkins said, "one might expect of white men who knew nothing of what it meant to be reared in slavery."[11] Elkins then, while making some exceptions for house servants and skilled workers, thought the "typical slave on the plantation" resembled the Sambo personality, infantile and dependent.

On the face of it, Elkins's theory may appear logical—slavery was terrible and it led people to detach emotionally and to become totally dependent upon their owners. It seems like common sense. The problem is that people are much more complex and multifaceted than he was able to conceive and than his Freudian analysis of the concentration camp would allow. Like other humans, enslaved people had many types of personalities and engaged in many types of behaviors. Even one individual could be inconsistent, obsequious at one moment and assertive or aggressive in another. How much more likely, then, that millions of people, living in various situations over a period of more than 200 years, could not be encompassed within the "mass behavior and mass manifestations of personality" that Elkins theorized.

Even though Frazier and Elkins rejected Phillips's argument that slavery was a positive good, both scholars harbored some sense of blacks in slavery as pathetic beings. Frazier, for example, while not as crude as Phillips, intimated that assimilation of white "ideas, sentiments, and beliefs" elevated enslaved people, so that the house servant who had direct contact with whites was rendered fundamentally different from the "semibarbarous field hands."[12] Still, Elkins and Frazier did important work for those of us who would come after them. They challenged the notion that slavery had been a benign institution, and they began a process of contemplating the possibility of an emotional life, however limited, for the African Americans held in slavery. But Elkins certainly was not able to see the possibility of greater depth in enslaved African Americans. He could not see the possibility of resilience, intellect, courage, determination, will, or creativity. He could not conceive of a world in which slaves both encountered brutality and had hope. And the primary reason why he could not see these possibilities is that he remained in the realm of theory rather than examining what former slaves had to say about their experiences and their feelings. Frazier had started down that road of detachment and insensitivity, but when he turned to the sources that former slaves produced, he had to acknowledge a depth of feeling on the part of enslaved mothers. Two generations of historians have since engaged in research that relies on, among other sources, material generated by enslaved people and former slaves. By looking at documents left by whites as well as African Americans, these historians have found evidence of agency and resistance among enslaved people, and they have identified spaces of negotiation despite the great imbalance in power between slaves and slaveowners.[13]

Frazier and Elkins greatly influenced the field of African American history and public policy. In 1965, for example, Daniel Patrick Moynihan, a sociologist who worked in the Lyndon Johnson administration, turned to Frazier's work on enslaved families to explain what Moynihan perceived as family dysfunction among poor and working-class African Americans. In Frazier's work he found support for the prevalence of female-headed households and agreement that such families were, by definition, dysfunctional. Moynihan blamed what he perceived as the contemporary dysfunction of black families on the model set forth in slavery and, in turn, blamed this family structure for unemployment and other social and economic problems. He proposed that the federal government intervene to help stabilize families in order to avert the social disruptions, or "Negro Revolution," he feared would unfold when blacks failed to attain equality despite the passage of the 1964 civil rights bill. "In this new period," Moynihan wrote in his report for the Department of Labor, "the expectations of negro Americans will go beyond civil rights. Being Americans, they will now expect that in the near future equal opportunities for them as a group will produce roughly equal results, as compared with other groups. This is not going to happen. Nor will it happen for generations to come unless a new and special effort is made."[14] Moynihan's negative prognosis was grounded in two factors, he said: persistent racism in the country and the history of oppression of African Americans. Yet he placed the problem squarely at the door of the black family. In his view, the fundamental problem responsible for the widening gap between blacks and whites was the structure of the black family, and here he agreed with Frazier that female-headed households were at the heart of the problem.

In 1976 Herbert Gutman's book *The Black Family in Slavery and Freedom, 1750–1925* constituted a response not only to Moynihan but also to Phillips, Frazier, and Elkins. Gutman's study of the records of several large plantations challenged a number of the earlier interpretations of slavery and its impact on enslaved people and family structure in particular. Where Frazier and Elkins suggested that the movement from Africa to America and subsequent generations of bondage had wiped away all cultural memories of Africa, Gutman found otherwise. Where Phillips and Elkins thought that blacks had been entirely dependent upon white owners to shape their values, beliefs, and behaviors, Gutman found numerous examples of contradictory behavior, such as naming practices and the refusal of slaves to marry their cousins as their owners did. Most significantly, Gutman saw strong evidence that although slavery routinely destroyed African American families through sale of family members, many people exhibited a resilience that enabled them to form new families. Gutman, then, was able to hold at once the cruelty of slavery and the capacity of most enslaved people to deploy a range of strategies to withstand it. Historian Brenda E. Stevenson, in her study of families in Loudoun County, Virginia, has challenged Gutman's assertion of nuclear family stability as well as the suggestion that the nuclear family was even an ideal in the minds of enslaved people.[15] The enslaved people and freedpeople whom I discuss in this book placed emotional value in their nuclear families. People who described their experiences of family loss emphasized the fact that their children, parents, and spouses were important to them, although in some instances they also reference the significance of extended family and a broader community. These differences among scholars of slavery who have worked with sources generated by enslaved people and who have taken their expressions into consideration only serve to demonstrate how varied a spectrum of values and emotions enslaved people occupied.

As Daniel Patrick Moynihan's report suggests, it has been popular to trace any perception of African American family dysfunction directly to slavery and its forced separation of African American families. In *Help Me to Find My People* I attempt to get inside separation to see how it came about, to take notice of enslaved people's awareness of impending loss, and to see how they prepared for it, how they attempted to stave it off, how they grieved over it, and how they worked to reverse it. Unlike Frazier, Moynihan, and even Gutman, I do not take up the question of whether the separation of families in slavery accounts for the prevalence of female-headed black households today or for the absence of fathers from these households. So much has intervened between even the last years of slavery in the 1860s and the present that it is nearly impossible to draw a single direct line between slavery and any contemporary African American practice. Indeed, the racism that slavery produced and that, in turn, shored up slavery has persisted and has continued to reproduce itself from 1865, when slavery ended, to the present. Racism has spawned all sorts of discrimination and inequalities that have affected every aspect of African American life, including the family. The racial violence of the Ku Klux Klan and other organized groups, lynching, Jim Crow segregation, migrations to escape discrimination and terror, industrialization, redlining, welfare, growth of the prison industrial complex, illegal drugs in black communities, and so on have all had their impact on individual black people and on black families. It is true that some aspect of each of these phenomena can be traced to the enslavement of black people and to the construction of racial hierarchies and inequities in this country between 1619 and 1865, but ignoring these social factors as important intervening elements that have affected families risks erasing the significance of a great deal of African American and American history of the late nineteenth, twentieth, and early twenty-first centuries. Add to these examples of social inequities the dramatic changes that have occurred since the mid-1960s in American attitudes toward family makeup, single parenthood, and childbirth out of wedlock, and we have even more possible explanations for the female-headed black families that Frazier and some critics today would label disorganized or dysfunctional.

What my research does demonstrate is that despite painful losses during slavery, large numbers of African Americans continued to invest emotional capital in creating new families as well as finding those whom they had lost. In other words, losing a family member did not necessarily mean that people came to see family bonds as insignificant. Certainly some people would have become numb and chosen not to take the chance of being hurt again.

But most people continued to care. They risked severe punishment and sale when they ran away to be reunited with their relatives. Some pleaded with owners to purchase relatives in order to avoid separation. Some spent many years searching for their family members even long after slavery had ended. These were not people who thought family was superfluous or insignificant, or impossible to maintain. They were people who, despite most slaveowners' disregard for their emotional ties, continued to maintain the desire to be with loved ones and to establish and maintain emotional bonds.

But as historian Nell Painter asserts in her essay "Soul Murder and Slavery," not everyone survived the emotional torment that slavery wrought through family separation and other offenses such as sexual abuse or violent, sometimes sadistic punishment.[16] Not everyone was strong and resilient, and certainly no one was strong all of the time. Some people broke under the pain of separation, became depressed, considered suicide, or lost their minds because they could not clear their heads of the cries of their lost children. What I have found most striking in writing this book is how so many African Americans were able to create new families—marry again, have children—while at the same time keeping an emotional space for those whom they had lost. Within these chapters we encounter people as they clung to one another to avoid separation; then as separation became fact, we see their efforts to make sense of their loss and to figure out how to handle it, and we see them making choices about how to move on emotionally.

The work of several historians helps me to place individuals and families into a broader historical context. The domestic slave trade stands as the most significant cause of disruption of African American families; historian Michael Tadman estimates that between the years 1820 and 1860, 200,000 black people per decade were sold and or moved from the Upper South to the Lower South and West.[17] Historians have produced extremely important work on this trade, starting with Frederic Bancroft in his 1931 book *Slave Trading in the Old South*, to Michael Tadman's *Speculators and Slaves: Masters, Traders, and Slaves in the Old South*, to Robert Gudmestad's *A Troublesome Commerce: The Transformation of the Interstate Slave Trade*, to finally, Walter Johnson's brilliant and inspiring *Soul by Soul: Life inside the Antebellum Slave Market*. This book builds on their work and focuses on the implications of sale and movement for black families and individuals.[18]

Although the trade of people from north to south and west brought about the most disruption, it is important to be aware that separation also occurred *within* states and regions. Further, not all enslaved people experienced family separation through sale or other means. Yet sale and separation always hovered as a possibility. People were property. They had owners who had the right to sell them, to move them across the country, or to gamble or mortgage them away. The specter of separation was ever present. It could happen at any time, and the separation could move people just a few or hundreds of miles away.

After many debates with myself about what structure would best suit the stories I wanted to tell, I divided the book into three parts with six chapters and an epilogue. Part 1 has three chapters that treat separation: Chapter 1 examines separation from the perspective of children who lost their families, Chapter 2 focuses on the separation of husbands and wives, and Chapter 3 looks at sale and separation through the eyes of a range of white people from both the North and the South. Part 2 contains two chapters that pay attention to the search for family. Chapter 4 looks at people's efforts to locate or connect with family members while slavery was still in place, and Chapter 5 takes up the search once slavery ended with the conclusion of the Civil War. This chapter presents the full text of several Information Wanted and Lost Friends ads just as they appeared in newspapers in the 1860s; I would like readers to see them together and to get a sense of the outpouring of desire to find family members. Part 3 consists of one chapter that considers the complicated and conflicted emotions that arose when family members found one another. It is not by happenstance that separation and the search for family dominate the book; they dominated people's lives, and the sources suggest that reunification took place only rarely. The book ends with an epilogue that draws connections between African Americans' search for family members in the nineteenth and early twentieth centuries, and African Americans' continuing search for family history in the twenty-first century.

Deciding how to structure the book did not resolve all of the organizational options. Emotions, for example, do not always emerge in a straightforward manner in a slave narrative; for example, a writer may speak of one event then jump to another. Sometimes I cannot be certain of the precise chronology, or I may know that one thing came before another, but I am not sure how long before. These former slaves wrote or dictated their stories much as they may have spoken them to audiences. They had limited time and space in which to describe a life, and they had important points to make that sometimes do not correspond to my questions exactly. So, I feel around. I try to sort it out, but the narratives do not always fit neatly into the themes of my yellow file folders or my Word files. Further, feelings cut across time and space and individuals and events, so I have had to figure out how to work them into my structure and how to arrange my structure around them. I treat a number of themes that have overarching relevance beyond the confines of the categories of people who constitute the focus in any one chapter. For example, I chose to address mourning, hope, or the repression and expression of grief within a specific chapter, although these themes actually cut across several chapters. Other themes emerge throughout the book, including identity, empathy, domination, resistance, and of course, memory.

As I worked on this book, I gave several talks, and each time I was fascinated and moved by the connections that members of the audience made between African American separation and loss during slavery and the experiences of other groups in other historical moments. The linkages point to a universality of family loss and separation and, arguably, to some universal features of emotional life. People in these audiences have, for example, pointed to the orphan trains that took children from New York to western states beginning in the early twentieth century, or to the poignant stories of Aboriginal Australian children who, up to the 1960s, were forcibly taken from their families and sent to institutions and white homes to be assimilated into white Australian culture. Native American children in the United States, in keeping with government assimilation policies, were sent from western states to schools in the East that aimed to "kill the Indian and save the man."[19] At a conference in Sweden, an Israeli woman told me that every afternoon you can still hear personal announcements on an Israeli radio station. The practice, she said, began after the Holocaust as people searched for dislocated and lost family members. After my talk at the University of Tokyo for Foreign Studies, several faculty members offered interesting insights into family separation in the places and eras they study.

My own observations have identified examples of severe disruptions of families and relationships, and I have noted strategies that would have seemed familiar to, and some that would have been coveted by, the nineteenth-century African Americans about whom I write. We have all seen the images of a child on a milk carton placed there by parents who are searching for him or her. In 2009 I received an advertising circular that I would normally have considered junk mail, but given the subject of this book, I paid attention. The ad included a photograph of a young boy beside the image of a man whose face had been constructed through digitized age progression of the child's photograph. The child, Leigh Savoie from Revere, Massachusetts, disappeared in 1974 at age eleven. Thirty-five years later, someone still remembered him and was still searching for him. The ad directed anyone with information to call 1-800-THE-LOST.

In 2008, the CNN website featured a story about a brother and sister who had been separated during World War II. The story read, "Dateline Donetsk, Ukraine: A frail Irene Famuluk clutched her brother on the airport tarmac, her arm wrapped around him in a tight embrace, tears streaming down their faces. It was the first time since 1942 they had seen each other, when she was 17 and he was just 7." Invading Nazis had taken Famuluk and her older sister to a labor camp in Munich, Germany, where Irene spent the war working in kitchens, the report said. "She never saw her parents again after that day in 1942 when Nazis separated her from her family. She and her brother still have no idea what happened to their mother and father. Some of their siblings lived through the war, but later died; others, they never heard from again after being separated." Famuluk had migrated to the United States in 1956, and her brother found her in 2008 with the help of the American Red Cross Holocaust and War Victims Tracing Center. "I don't believe anyone has ever known such happiness," Famuluk's brother said. "Now I truly believe I can die satisfied."[20] With only a few edits, this could easily have been the story of enslaved siblings who had been sold apart in America.

In Hiroshima, Japan, I visited the Fukuromachi Elementary School, where still visible are the messages people wrote on the walls in the days following August 6, 1945, when the atomic bomb deployed by the United States devastated Hiroshima. The school is now a museum, and the walls are exposed for visitors to read the original Japanese inscriptions. Here are some rough English translations:

Kumiko Hisago a junior high school student of 12 or 14 years got burns and received treatment in a rescue station. She lost her family. She doesn't have any relatives in Hiroshima so she went to an island nearby.—written by Kato, a teacher at the school.

To my sister. I am moving to the Meiji Life Insurance building. I may come back to the school again. I hope we will find each other.

If you know the person named Suzue Tanaka please inform us.[21]

These are the type of messages that I can imagine captives carving in Arabic into the stone walls of the dungeons at Elmina in Ghana, or Goree Island in Senegal, before exiting the "Door of No Return," headed for the Americas; or in English on the bricks of the slave mart in Charleston, South Carolina, as they headed to cane or cotton or rice or indigo fields. I imagine messages that contained the thoughts and fears and hopes of the moment. But my imagination is strained by the realities of the past. I know that African captives were chained in the dungeons for most of their stay and lived under surveillance. People in the slave markets also lived under great scrutiny, finding it difficult to convey even a disapproved feeling or thought through facial expressions. I know, too, that there was no toll-free number for African Americans to call, no national data bases, no milk cartons or Red Cross mission to help them to find family members. Still, they did leave messages in their letters and advertisements and in the stories that they passed down to their children.

Family separation and the resulting longing, grieving, and searching, then, are universal occurrences brought on by war, famine, political strife, and more generally, what the eighteenth-century Scottish poet Robert Burns called "man's inhumanity to man." I am intrigued by the connections that can be made between the experiences of African Americans and of other people around the world, and I can even foresee comparative work in this area. In this book, however, I am concerned with exploring the particularities of the separation of African Americans during slavery in the American South. I want to explore what methods African Americans were able to devise to enable a search for family members. I am interested in an experience that shares elements with those of other people in other places and times yet remains uniquely African American.

Sometimes the stories I recount are raw, emotional, and dramatic. That's what these people's lives were. It was dramatic, painful, and outrageous to be sold, and even more so to be sold away from family members. I cannot downplay it. It is sometimes difficult to face the pain, the anger, the outrage, and the love. It sometimes takes courage to look at the humiliation and the loss that people suffered. And sometimes, though rarely, a reunification provides relief. During that first summer when I began looking for the Information Wanted ads, I hoped that they would never lose their power for me. I remember hoping that I would never become immune to the poignancy of people's searches. After several years of working on this book, I am still moved by the depth of emotion in the ads, letters, and accounts of family separation and loss. I am still touched by the stories of people's stubborn efforts to find their families. And I remain in awe of people's ability to remember and to care.

It is worth saying one more time: Not all enslaved people experienced separation, but this is a book about those who did. It is a book that seeks to explore and understand separation and the material conditions that triggered it. It is a book about resilience and survival. It is a book about the texture and contours of loss and grief, and despair, and hope. In the end, it is a book about human beings who lived with a broad spectrum of emotions, including love, grief, anger, hope, and joy. It is a journey into their lives and their feelings.

PART ONE
Separation

ONE

I was growed up when the war come. And I was a mother before it closed. Babies was snatched from their mothers' breasts and sold to speculators. Children was separated from sisters and brothers and never saw each other again. Course they cry; you think they not cry when they was sold like cattle? I could tell you about it all day, but even then you couldn't guess the awfulness of it.

DELIA GARLIC, former slave, Montgomery, Alabama

Fine Black Boy for Sale
Separation and Loss among Enslaved Children

A vague fear came over me, but I did not know why.

THOMAS LEWIS JOHNSON, former slave

Early in the fall of 1836, N. A. Hinkle of Snickersville, Virginia, wrote a letter of five lines to slave trader William Crow in Charles Town, Virginia. "A friend of mine," the letter said, "has a fine Black Boy that is now in the market for Sale and I told him that I would write to you about him he is about 12 years old not tall for his age but verry stout. You had better come over or send some word immediately about him if you want to get him."[1] The brief communication was layered with significance: A child for sale—a sense of urgency—the need to act immediately to stave off competition or perhaps to get this boy to a purchaser in time for the harvest. The boy was twelve years old, ready to be put to work in the fields or in a craftsman's shop to learn a trade. He was not tall, but his strong, sturdy body rendered him capable of doing the hard labor that a new owner would require. Hinkle wrote to a likely purchaser. William Crow was in the business of purchasing people in Virginia and imprisoning them in the basement of his house until he had enough to send to New Orleans, where his agent sold them at market.[2] Seething silently between the lines of Hinkle's business proposition is a layer that concerns the child's feelings, his thoughts, and his emotional ties to parents, siblings, friends, and place. Sale of this child would almost certainly result in separation from his family, but Hinkle, acting as the middleman in this proposed transaction, gave no apparent consideration to such concerns.

In contrast to Hinkle's silence, this chapter examines the emotional lives of those African American children who experienced separation from families either through their own sale or through the sale of parents or siblings. Although we may never learn any more about this specific unidentified black boy who for a fleeting moment anonymously entered the historical record, sources produced by former slaves, slaveowners, and slave traders provide a degree of access to the lives of young people who had similar experiences. We do not know if this particular boy found himself chained in William Crow's basement before making the trek to New Orleans, but others who left records of their lives help us to gain some sense of what it was like for a child to be sold and taken far away from home and family.

Scholars who write the history of children or childhood note that children leave behind few records with which historians can work.[3] Enslaved African American children left even fewer than most. What we know of their thoughts, feelings, and experiences is refracted through the memory of the adults they became. We must rely, then, on adult memories of childhood, however flawed memory may be, or leave these lives unexamined. The narratives that African Americans wrote or dictated in the nineteenth century as well as the memories they shared with government-employed interviewers long after slavery had ended are key sources of insight into how enslaved children experienced family separation.[4] These autobiographies and interviews allow us into the world in which children came to understand that they could be treated as commodities, that they could be sold, and that frequently, sale meant their families would be broken apart. These sources also divulge how parents responded to the loss of their children. Through accounts of a mother's anguished wail or a father's lapse into depression, we are able to see the impact of separation on enslaved parents. The reactions of both parents and children reveal deep emotional bonds among family members and a variety of methods of coping with the pain brought about by separation. Former slaves' accounts of highly charged separations contrast with owners' and traders' calculations as they carried out the business of slavery, and these accounts by the enslaved contradict the analyses of historians who thought these people were either satisfied with their condition or incapable of emotional depth.

Former slaves who wrote the narratives of their lives described the shock and sense of loss that accompanied the separation they experienced as children. What amounted to a business transaction for owners could be a traumatic and defining experience in an enslaved child's life. In the narrative of her life, Kate Drumgoold captured the innocence, grief, and faith of a small girl whose mother was suddenly taken away. Drumgoold was born in Virginia close enough to the start of the Civil War that she might have missed the pain of slavery altogether. Instead, the war itself became the source of her grief when her mother was sold to pay a substitute to serve for their owner in the Confederate army. As Drumgoold recalled it, "My mother was sold at Richmond, Virginia, and a gentleman bought her who lived in Georgia, and we did not know that she was sold until she was gone; and the saddest thought to me was to know which way she had gone, and I used to go outside and look up to see if there was anything that would direct me, and I saw a clear place in the sky, and it seemed to me the way she had gone, and I watched it three and a half years, not knowing what that meant, and it was there the whole time that mother was gone."[5] In a sky as vast as her grief, the child fixed her mind on a clear place to help her to grapple with the dislocation brought on by her mother's abrupt disappearance. In that spot, she could summon a nearly tangible connection with her absent mother. Drumgoold designed her own mourning ritual, a practice infused with hope and a touch of magical thinking that allowed her to believe her mother was in the sky and would return just as suddenly as she had disappeared. Drumgoold had not attended a funeral for her mother, had not said goodbye, and had no gravesite to visit, but her mother was as much gone as if she had died. She reasoned in her child's mind that if she could keep finding that place in the sky, she could find solace and perhaps, someday, see her mother again. This child's story speaks to the experiences of many enslaved people: the jolt of sudden loss, holding on to a faint hope of reunification, and the searing, lasting memory of confusion and pain.[6]

Former slave Charles Ball's family members did not suddenly disappear; instead, four-year-old Ball watched as purchasers tore the family apart. The incident was painful and memorable. When Ball's owner died in Maryland, the estate put all the slaves up for sale at auction, and each member of Ball's family was sold to a different bidder. His new owner, Jack Cox, put the child on a horse and prepared to take him home, but according to Ball, "My poor mother, when she saw me leaving her for the last time, ran after me, took me down from the horse, clasped me in her arms, and wept loudly and bitterly over me. My master seemed to pity her, and endeavored to soothe her distress by telling her that he would be a good master to me and that I should not want any thing." Still grasping her child, Ball's mother begged Cox to purchase her and her remaining children so that they would not be taken from the area, but her new owner intervened and ordered her to "give that little negro to its owner." According to Ball, this man "snatched me from her arms, handed me to my master, and seizing her by one arm, dragged her back towards the place of sale. My master then quickened the pace of his horse; and as we advanced, the cries of my poor parent became more and more indistinct. At length they died away in the distance, and I never again heard the voice of my poor mother." Ball recalled clinging to his new owner "as an angel and saviour, when compared with the hardened fiend into whose power [his mother] had fallen." The traumatized four-year-old having just witnessed his mother's distress sought comfort from his new owner, who had at least spoken kind words to her. Writing many years later, Ball reflected, "Young as I was, the horrors of that day sank deeply into my heart, and even at this time, though a half a century has elapsed, the terrors of the scene return with painful vividness upon my memory."[7]

Neither Drumgoold's nor Ball's mother had anyone, any institution, or any authority to whom she could turn for protection of her family. Only Louisiana and, belatedly in 1852, Alabama ever sought to protect mothers and children by adopting laws that regulated the ages at which children could be sold separately from their mothers.[8] The vast majority of enslaved children belonged to people who had complete discretion to sell them or to give them away at will. Indeed, approximately one third of enslaved children in the Upper South experienced family separation in one of three possible scenarios: sale away from parents, sale with mother away from father, or sale of mother or father away from child.[9] Slaveholders and, by extension, slave traders particularly desired adolescents, as they were immediately productive, and their youth promised a lifetime of service to the purchaser. The value of boys lay primarily in their physical strength; owners desired girls aged twelve to fifteen years both for their strength as laborers and for their potential reproductive capacity. Still, many owners sold much younger children alone as well.

Practices of sale and purchase varied, but for enslaved people, the single most important fact was that owners had the power to decide what they would do with the people they owned. They decided whom and when to sell. They decided which children would be sold with their mothers and which would be separated. They decided whether to keep families together or to ignore familial bonds, and their actions held great consequences for enslaved people. Every death of an owner, every auction, and every sale portended separation for the enslaved child and parents; every transaction could bring about loss and grief.

Sometimes owners and traders announced their intention to sell a woman and her children together, as was the case, for example, when the administrator of an estate in Fauquier County, Virginia, advertised that he would "offer for sale by public auction a negro woman and her four children consisting of two boys and two girls."[10] Or when an ad in Charleston offered, among many other enslaved people, "5 likely Families, with from 2 to 7 in number." The sellers here suggested to potential purchasers that the families came as a package; however, the purchaser usually stood to make the final decision as to whether to take the whole group or only part. Other advertisers made it clear from the start that they gave no consideration to family relationships by openly declaring that children would be sold alone. A seller in Virginia, for example, offered forty to fifty slaves for sale, among them "six or seven young Men, about the same number of young Women an excellent Semptress [*sic*] a most dexterous House Servant about 18 years old, some Boys and Girls, and several Children, healthy and generally between two and four years of age."[11] These very young children seemed to be thrown in almost as an after-thought, with no evident attention to their connections to parents or siblings. In 1858 when a Virginia slave trader compiled the assessed value of enslaved people, he included categories of boys aged twelve to fourteen and girls aged as young as ten and eleven. The "demand was good for likely Negroes," he wrote, but at the bottom of his list he noted, "families rather dull and hard to sell," meaning that the boys and girls would in all likelihood be sold individually without siblings or parents.[12]

Nursing children generally had the best chance of remaining with their mothers because it made economic sense to both traders and purchasers to include them as part of a bargain for their mother. Sometimes the infant had a price attached, as when appraisers assigned a value of $150 for six-month-old Minnie in 1860.[13] At other times, the child was included as part of the mother's sale. In Orangeburg, South Carolina, a seller wrote out a bill of sale for $1,005 for the purchase of "a negro woman called Salley about 24 years old, and two children the oldest called Lear 2 years and ten months old, the youngest called Deanah 9 months old, to have and to hold the said Negro woman and children forever."[14] In Augusta, Georgia, Samuel B. Clark sold "a negro woman named Clarissa, her child Eliza one and a half year of age and her infant one month old."[15] And when a Virginia slave dealer provided quotes for the value of slaves, he included a category of "good young woman and first child."[16] The decision to sell mothers and young children together usually meant there was some benefit to the dealer and the purchaser; a lactating mother was in the best position to take care of an infant who would be a burden to anyone else. Additionally, sale with an infant indicated to the buyer that this woman was fertile. Indeed, a woman with a first child might be even more valuable, as she was both fertile and presumably young enough to give birth to several more children, who, by law, would inherit their mother's status and became the property of her owner.

But former slave Jim Allen's recollection of his childhood is an important reminder that even when a mother was sold with her infant, she and her other children still lost one another. As Allen recounted it, "Before I could remember much, I remember Lee King had a saloon close to Bob Allen's store in Russell County, Alabama, and Mars John Bussey drunk my mother up. I mean by that, Lee King took her and my brother George for a whiskey debt. Yes old Marster drinked them up. Then they was carried to Florida by Sam O'Neal, and George was just a baby. You know the white folks wouldn't often separate the mother and baby. I ain't seen them since." Allen's mother got to keep her baby, but she lost her other children.[17]

Slavery was a business, the slave trade the most cold and stark element of it, and the market did not always tolerate even a very young child accompanying his or her mother. In a letter to his employer in central North Carolina, Samuel Browning, a slave trader, hinted at the inconvenience of having an infant along while he transported slaves. Browning was in Greenwood, Mississippi, heading to Milliken's Bend, Louisiana, and complained that there was no "spirit of trade" anywhere he had been because people were "extreamly anxious to buy but have not got the money to pay." He had expected to keep moving, he said, "but a girl that I have along had a child yesterday which I shall have to wait on a few days if I cannot make some disposition of her—." By disposition he presumably meant selling the woman and possibly her baby, but with the market so slow, he may have taken other steps to make sure that he and the slaves could move on.[18]

Former slaves told horror stories of what could happen to an unwanted child. Parthena Rollins from Kentucky recalled an incident in which the financial interests of the owner trampled on any concern for mother and child. Once when the slave traders came through, Rollins told an interviewer, "there was a girl, the mother of a young baby; the traders wanted the girl, but would not buy her because she had a child. Her owner took her away, took the baby from her, and beat it to death right before the mother's eyes, then brought the girl back to the sale without the baby, and she was bought immediately." According to Rollins, the child's mother became ill after this agonizing loss. "The thought of the cruel way of putting her baby to death preyed on her mind to such an extent, she developed epilepsy," Rollins said. This angered her new owner, who returned her for a refund of his money.[19] And William Wells Brown, an enslaved man who belonged to a slave trader, told of the trader giving away a woman's five-week-old child because the infant's crying annoyed him. The child's mother, part of a coffle of slaves being taken to market, begged and promised to quiet the child, but the trader had made his decision. His peace of mind was worth more than he could get for this child in the market, and the infant's mother, like many other enslaved people, was powerless to prevent the loss of her child.[20]

Many former slaves recalled the moment when, as children, they first confronted the reality of this powerlessness. It was one of the early awakenings that some children experienced: first the realization that they could be sold, then the awareness that they were slaves, and finally, the dismaying consciousness sometimes brought on by an impending sale and separation, that the parents they loved and looked up to could not shield them from white people's power.[21] Former slave Thomas Lewis Johnson of Virginia conveyed this unfolding awareness and developing sense of vulnerability. "I can well remember," he wrote, "when other children and I were very happy, not knowing that we were slaves. We played merrily together, knowing nothing of the world and of the long oppression of our people. But," he recalled, "as time passed on, first one and then another of those who were as helpless as myself were missed from the company of little slaves." Johnson remembered seeing an older boy named John, with a "small bundle in his hand," saying goodbye to his mother while a white man stood waiting in the hall for him. "His mother and mine, with others, were crying, and all seemed very sad. I did not know what to make of it," Johnson recalled. "A vague fear came over me, but I did not know why."[22]

Johnson and the other children overheard that the man was a Georgia trader, and from then on, he said, whenever they saw a white man looking over the fence while they played, the children ran and hid. Sometimes they went to their mothers, as Johnson put it, "ignorantly thinking they could protect us." But as one after another child was taken away, he came to two realizations. First, "white children were free—'free born'—but black children were slaves and could be sold for money." And second, their mothers could not protect them. In fact, some mothers began to use the threat of sale to teach lessons of behavior that they hoped would protect their children. "Often we were reminded," Johnson wrote, "that if we were not good the white people would sell us to Georgia, which place we dreaded above all others on earth."[23] Already small and physically vulnerable, these children came to realize that their parents, the adults who cared about them, were unable to protect them.

Thomas H. Jones learned of his vulnerability and his mother's powerlessness when he was sold to a man in Wilmington, North Carolina, forty-five miles from his home. His new owner sent a black man named Abraham to take Jones to Wilmington. As Jones recalled, the man was ugly and his voice frightening. "I was very much afraid and began to cry, holding on to my mother's clothes, and begging her to protect me, and not let the man take me away," Jones recalled. According to him, "Mother wept bitterly and in the midst of her loud sobbings, cried out in broken words, 'I can't save you, Tommy; master has sold you, you must go.' She threw her arms around me, and while the hot tears fell on my face, she strained me to her heart. There she held me, sobbing and mourning, till the brutal Abraham came in, snatched me away, hurried me out of the house where I was born, my only home, and tore me away from the dear mother who loved me as no other friend could do." His mother, Jones said, followed them, "imploring a moment's delay, and weeping aloud, to the road, where Abraham turned around, and striking at her with his heavy cowhide, fiercely ordered her to stop bawling and go back into the house."[24]

The reality of being sold baffled children. It took time to sink in. They were stunned to realize that they could be taken from their parents, or that a parent or sibling could be taken away. Over and over the language of the adult narrators conveys this sense of only dimly perceiving what was happening to them. In Maryland, Josiah Henson remembered that when his drunken owner fell from a horse and died, all the property was divided and Henson and his siblings were sold away from their mother. "My bothers and sisters were bid off one by one," he recalled, "while my mother, holding my hand, looked on in an agony of grief the cause of which I but ill understood at first, but which dawned on my mind, with dreadful clearness, as the sale proceeded." His mother was put up for sale by herself. "She was bought by a man named Isaac R., residing in Montgomery County, and then I was offered to the assembled purchasers," Henson said. "My mother, half distracted with the parting forever from all her children, pushed through the crowd, while the bidding for me was going on, to the spot where R. was standing. She fell at his feet, and clung to his knees, entreating him in tones that a mother only could command, to buy her baby as well as herself, and spare to her one of her little ones at least." However, her new owner kicked and hit her, forcing her to crawl away. Within days Henson had become so ill that his new owner convinced Isaac R. to purchase him and keep him with his mother, who nursed him back to health.[25]

Children such as Johnson, Jones, and Henson learned slowly that slavery meant vulnerability and lack of control. They watched the people around them for clues as to what words and actions meant. Reading lips, interpreting expressions, sensing the tension among adults, and watching their mothers' agitation, some came to understand that strange white men might signify sale, that sale meant separation, and that the black adults in their lives were unable to disrupt the plans their owners had put into play.

In the face of inevitable separation, some enslaved people retreated to their slave community to seek both information and solace from people they trusted. The account of former slave John Brown offers access to the private spaces that the enslaved people in his orbit occupied, describes the process by which their lives were disrupted, and offers a glimpse at the emotions of fear and grief and the secondary emotion of anxiety with which they grappled. When he was eight and a half years old, Brown, a slave in Southampton County, Virginia, realized that his life might change dramatically. Pursuant to his owner's will, all the slaves were to be divided equally among his wife and three daughters. About a month later, Brown recalled, "it began to be talked about that the distribution was going to take place. I remember well the grief this caused us to feel, and how the women and the men used to whisper to one another when they thought nobody was by, and meet at night, or get together in the field when they had an opportunity, to talk about what was coming." The adults understood that the world they had known could be completely disrupted. "They would speculate, too," Brown said, "on the prospects they had of being separated; to whose lot they and their children were likely to fall, and whether the husbands would go with their wives. The women who had young children cried very much. My mother did, and took to kissing us a good deal oftener," Brown recalled. "This uneasiness increased as the time wore on, for though we did not know when the great trouble would fall upon us, we all knew it would come, and were looking forward to it with sorrowful hearts." One afternoon James Davis, the son-in-law of the deceased owner, arrived. "This man," Brown said, "had a dreadful name for cruelty. When we young ones saw him, we ran away and hid ourselves. In the evening the orders came to the negroes, at their quarters, to be up at the big house by nine the next morning."[26]

In the morning all the slaves gathered in the yard under a sycamore tree. Here the division would be made. The widow held back one fourth of the slaves, including Brown's brother and sister, Silas and Lucy. Then the executors divided the remaining people into three lots of about twenty-five or thirty each, taking into consideration the relative monetary worth of each person, not their kinship connections. According to Brown, "As there was a great deal of difference in value of the slaves, individually, some being stronger than others, or more likely, the allotments were regulated so as to equalize the value of each division. For instance, my brother Silas and my sister Lucy, who belonged rightly to the gang of which I and my mother and other members of the family formed a part, were replaced by two of my cousin Annikie's children, a boy and a girl."[27] The husbands of the inheriting daughters then drew slips from a hat, thus determining to whom each lot of people would belong. Brown described a "heart-rending scene" with "crying and wailing," when the people got together in the slave quarters following the division. "I really thought my mother would have died of grief at being obliged to leave her two children, her mother, and her relations behind. But it was of no use lamenting, and as we were to start early next morning, the few things we had were put together that night, and we completed our preparations for parting for life by kissing one another over and over again and saying goodbye till some of us little ones fell asleep again."[28]

John Brown's narration of the destruction of kinship and friendship ties is illuminating in many regards. He describes awareness on the part of the enslaved adults that the death of their owner would result in their separation from one another. He gives a sense of the mounting anxiety among the people as they whispered to each other, trying to predict the fates over which they had no control, anticipating "the great trouble" they knew would come. Brown and the other children became part of this grieving process as they noticed the changes in their parents' behavior and picked up from the adults the implications of division. Parents transmitted their apprehensions to their children, kissing them more, looking worried, whispering to one another. The children learned to be fearful; they ran and hid when James Davis rode into the yard. They internalized, too, the message that even as their community expressed its grief through crying and wailing, "it was of no use lamenting." People more powerful than they made the decisions that would affect them forever.

Now the property of James Davis, Brown and his mother traveled nearly fifty miles away from their old home. Although he lost his siblings, Brown was fortunate to have remained with his mother.[29] Still, he was vulnerable, always subject to sale. One day his owner took him into town to a tavern where he attempted to sell Brown to a speculator. The deal did not go through, and when he told his mother, Brown recalled, "she cried over me, and said she was very glad I had not been sold away from her." Eighteen months after the division, when Brown was ten years old, he faced the prospect of sale again. "Owing to a considerable rise in the price of cotton," Brown said, "there came a great demand for slaves in Georgia." When a speculator named Starling Finney arrived on James Davis's plantation with a coffle of enslaved people, Davis offered Brown for sale. The men haggled over the price, and Finney agreed to purchase Brown by the pound. They rigged a scale, placed the boy in it, and concluded their arrangement.[30] Brown's mother was overcome by the sale of her son. "I looked round and saw my poor mother stretching out her hands after me," Brown recalled. "She ran up, and overtook us, but Finney, who was behind me, and between me and my mother, would not let her approach, though she begged and prayed to be allowed to kiss me for the last time, and bid me goodbye." This mother had now lost her last child, and at age ten Brown had lost his last relative.[31]

If the bond between mother and child mustered only the most limited protection, the relationship between father and child was not protected at all, except for a short time in Louisiana. While many enslaved children lived in homes with both mother and father, or had a father who lived nearby, for others, fathers were only vague memories. It was common for fathers to belong to an owner different from that of mothers and children, so one owner's decision to sell or give away a mother and her children frequently meant separating them from their husband and father. As a consequence, some former slaves had only hazy recollections of their fathers. Sam Broach, for example, recalled being moved from South Carolina to Alabama with his mother and siblings. But he said that his father, "named Isaac, belonged to another family that lived pretty close in South Carolina, but I don't remember nothing about him. He didn't come with us when we come to Alabama."[32] Likewise, when Nettie Henry recalled that their owner gave her and her mother and sisters to his daughter, who moved them from Alabama to Mississippi, she also remembered, "My pappy didn't go with us to Meridian. He belonged to one set of white people, you see, and my mammy belong to another."[33] Josiah Henson's father was sold from Maryland to Alabama after he received a severe beating for fighting a white man. Henson was three or four years old at the time.[34] Fanny Hodges never knew her father at all because he was sold before she was born. He barely even appeared in her account of her family history: "They said my pappy's name was George," she told an interviewer. "I don't know."[35]

Still, in spite of owners' disregard of enslaved men's relationships with their children, some former slaves managed to have strong recollections of their fathers. Hannah Chapman from Mississippi recalled, "My father was sold away from us when I was small. That was a sad time for us. Master wouldn't sell the mothers away from their children so us lived on with her without the fear of being sold. My pa sure did hate to leave us. He missed us and us longed for him." Chapman had memories of visits from her father after he had been sold. "He would often slip back to us cottage at night," she told her interviewer. "Us would gather round him and crawl up in his lap, tickled slap to death, but he give us these pleasures at a painful risk. When his master missed him he would beat him all the way home. Us could track him the next day by the blood stains." Despite the risk and reality of punishment, Chapman was able to visit his family because they remained in close proximity to him.[36]

Robert Glenn remembered that his father, a skilled tradesman in Hillsborough, North Carolina, who belonged to a different owner than that of Glenn and his mother, was frustrated in his efforts to purchase his son. According to Glenn, after his owner died, a speculator, or slave trader, named Henry Long purchased him, and "Mother went to Father and pled with him to buy me from him and let the white folks hire me out. No slave could own a slave. Father got the consent and help of his owners to buy me and they asked Long to put me on the block again." The father's owner acted as a surrogate for Glenn's father, but when Long learned who the true purchaser was, he reneged on the deal and put Glenn on the auction block once more at an even higher price. Again, Glenn's father, through his surrogates, won the bid, but according to Glenn, "Long then flew into a rage and cursed my father saying, 'You damn black son of a bitch, you think you are white do you? Now just to show you are black I will not let you have your son at any price.' Father knew it was all off. Mother was frantic, but there was nothing they could do about it. They had to stand and see the speculator put me on his horse behind him and ride away without allowing either of them to tell me good-bye." Glenn's father enjoyed some liberties within the system of slavery; he was able to work on his own and to keep some of his income. Yet he failed in his efforts to purchase his son and thereby prevent the destruction of his family.[37]

Glenn left his family behind, so he could not recount how his father coped with his loss, but Charles Ball, the young boy who clung to his new owner as an "angel and saviour," described his own father's descent into depression when he lost his wife and most of his children. Ball's mother and siblings had been sold to a Georgia trader, but Ball's new owner did not live far away, so he was able to maintain contact with his father. He was struck by the effect on his father of losing his family. "My father never recovered from the effects of the shock, which this sudden and overwhelming ruin of his family gave him," Ball recalled. "He had formerly been of a gay, social temper, and when he came to see us on a Saturday night he always brought us some little present, such as the means of a poor slave would allow—apples, melon, sweet potatoes, or, if he could procure nothing else, a little parched corn, which tasted better in our cabin, because he had brought it." During these visits his father told the children stories and sang songs with them. All this changed suddenly. According to Ball, after the sale of the family, "I never heard him laugh heartily, or sing a song. He became gloomy and morose in his temper, to all but me; and spent nearly all his leisure time with my grandfather." Ball's father changed dramatically in his grief, and he isolated himself from social engagement with other slaves. In turn, his owner interpreted this profound grief as "discontent with his position as a slave," concluded that he must be planning to escape, and arranged with a slave trader for his sale. Ball's father got wind of the imminent sale and did, in fact, escape, leaving Ball with only his grandfather, a man nearly eighty years old, to show him any affection.[38] Even so, he had more than most. With neither law nor custom to keep them with their parents, children often went away alone or remained behind alone after a parent's sale.[39]

What for these children and their parents amounted to a tragedy translated into good business practice for owners and traders. By age eight or nine, childhood effectively ended on plantations and farms as enslaved children went to work alongside adults inside the master's house, in artisans' shops, and in tobacco, cotton, rice, indigo, or corn fields. They nursed white babies, rubbed white women's feet, walked white children to school, ran errands, slept at the foot of an owner's bed to keep her company, dug ditches, picked cotton, wormed tobacco, stitched shoes, and fanned flies from owners' tables.[40] Black children such as Kate Drumgoold, Charles Ball, John Brown, Robert Glenn, Thomas Johnson, Thomas Jones, and innumerable other boys and girls, with their potential for long years of labor, constituted valuable commodities in the slave market. Over the course of the nineteenth century, southern newspapers regularly advertised them for sale.

Traders and owners spelled out supply and demand in the texts of these advertisements. In 1828, for example, Franklin and Armfield, a northern Virginia slave-trading firm, unabashedly proclaimed its desire to purchase slaves in Virginia for resale in the Lower South.

CASH IN MARKET

The subscribers having leased for a term of years the large three-story brick house on Duke Street, in the town of Alexandria, D.C. formerly occupied by Gen. Young we wish to purchase one hundred and fifty likely young negroes of both sexes between the ages of 8 and 25 years.

Persons who wish to sell will do well to give us a call, as we are determined to give more than any of the purchasers that are in market, or that may hereafter come into market. Franklin and Armfield.[41]

Ethan Allen Andrews, an abolitionist from Connecticut, visited the Franklin and Armfield property in 1835 and provided a description of the "slave pen" in which the traders held black children and adults until they were sent hundreds of miles away. The establishment, he wrote, was "easily distinguished as you approach it, by the high, white-washed wall surrounding the yards, and giving to it an appearance of a penitentiary." It had separate yards for males and females, and the gate had strong padlocks and bolts. John Armfield told Andrews that they sent some slaves to New Orleans on ships the firm had built for this purpose. From there they headed to Natchez, Mississippi. Other slaves walked to Natchez. Andrews observed that security ranked as a high concern for the trading firm. In addition to noting that Franklin and Armfield held the enslaved people in what looked like a prison, he observed, "[it] is true that they are often chained at night, while at the depot at Alexandria, lest they should overpower their masters, as not more than three or four white men frequently have charge of a hundred and fifty slaves." Then he described the coffles in which people were taken farther south. "Upon their march, also, they are usually chained together in pairs, to prevent their escape; and sometimes, when greater precaution is judged necessary, they are all attached to a long chain passing between them. Their guards and conductors are, of course, well armed."[42] It took force and restraints to subdue and control the men, women, and children the trading firm purchased and sold.

Another trader placed an ad in a Virginia newspaper that listed the type of labor children and young people would be expected to perform.

CASH FOR NEGROES

We wish to purchase a number of likely YOUNG NEGROES, from twelve to twenty-five years of age, of both sexes; field hands, house servants and mechanics of every description, of which we will give liberal prices. — Persons wishing to dispose of slaves would do well to give us a call. LEWIS & JORDAN[43]

As William Crow did, these traders simultaneously tapped into and expanded a thriving domestic slave trade. A number of factors contributed to this growth. First, the abolition of the Atlantic slave trade in 1808 made it illegal to bring captives from Africa into the United States. This virtually aborted the supply on which American planters had depended for nearly two centuries. Second, for a number of reasons, including exhaustion of lands by tobacco farming, planters in Virginia and Maryland had less need for large numbers of slaves to work their plantations. Third, at the same time that Upper South planters owned excess numbers of people, the United States was expanding into territories such as Alabama, Texas, and Louisiana, where planters would use enslaved people to develop immense cotton, rice, and sugarcane plantations on land newly taken from Indians and Mexicans, and purchased from France. With the development of the cotton gin in 1793, the processing of short staple cotton became more lucrative, and within years, planters and others came to think of the South as cotton country. To meet the needs of the Lower South, traders purchased children, young adults, and adults in Virginia, Maryland, and other parts of the Upper South and moved them hundreds of miles to waiting markets. In the period between 1790 and 1865, more than 1 million slaves were sold in this interstate domestic slave trade, and this figure does not include people who were sold locally or those who were displaced and separated from families as a result of the migration of owners.[44] The demand for slaves fluctuated with the market for crops such as cotton, but in the antebellum period, demand was frequently high.

The children, young people, and adults that traders needed to meet this demand came from private sales by individual owners, from the estates of deceased owners, or from other traders who had purchased them for re-sale. John Brown's family and the other enslaved people on his Southampton County, Virginia, plantation, for example, could easily have been included in a notice such as this one of an estate sale in Virginia after their owner died: "All the Personal Property of which the said [Willis] Parker died possessed, including STOCK of all kinds, many valuable NEGRO SLAVES among which are Men, Women, Boys and Girls, together with the last year's crop of Corn, Fodder and Peas as also considerable Household and Kitchen Furniture."[45]

In Charleston a "Broker, Auction'r and General Agent" advertised "Ne-groes at Private Sale." He held a mortgage on a parcel of real property, as well as on human property, and he hoped to recoup his investment by selling the land and the people. He offered "2 active and intelligent BOYS, 12 and 14 years of age, accustomed to housework." His inventory also included "3 active and intelligent Girls, of the same age, house servants," and "a family consisting of a Woman and 3 children, to be sold low."[46] Another seller, John Gibson, of-fered a tract of land consisting of 411 acres along with eight slaves, "consisting of one man, one woman, and the residue boys and girls. They constitute a lot of valuable slaves," he assured potential purchasers. The "residue" of boys and girls were children who would surely be sold without mother or father, and possibly without their siblings.[47]

Eager to raise money, these sellers would not have been much concerned about keeping children with their families. A trader interested primarily in moving his human stock and making a profit did not care about keeping a child with his or her mother. After all, a customer just beginning to build his wealth in slaves might only be able to afford to purchase one child who cost less than an adult.[48] Or a man might want to purchase a young girl as a gift to his wife to help with household chores. The market demanded young children—"*Wanted to Purchase—A Negro Girl, ten or twelve years of age*"—and traders and slaveowners prospered by filling the demand.[49]

As John Brown learned from the whispers of his mother and other members of his slave community, the death of an owner often brought about sale or division of property, both of which could result in separation. But owners had innumerable additional reasons for selling children or adults, and they spoke of these transactions in the language of law and finance. To pay a debt, "a Likely Negro Boy, about 12 years old [would] be sold at Public Auction for Cash" in front of the auction stores of Mr. Edward Lee.[50] "For the purpose of division" of property among heirs, an advertisement offered "several likely Negroes, to wit: One Fellow, Woman, and child, one Young Woman and one old Woman" for sale.[51] In partial payment for 108 acres of land, William Preston agreed to hand over "Greene, the mulatto boy."[52] "For the sake of peace," H. T. Weatherly gave up "a negro slave Viney and her two youngest children Frances and Aaron to be disposed of among the heirs" of the deceased.[53] But it was not always about business; owners held ultimate and arbitrary power, so a sale could also come about because of shame or embarrassment. Thus, at age four, William Singleton was sold by his owner from Newbern, North Carolina, to Atlanta because the owner was embarrassed and annoyed that his brother was the child's father.[54]

The businessmen and planters who participated in the domestic slave trade offered legal warranties for the children involved in these transactions. For the sum of $300, William Bennett warranted "good and lawfull title to the said negro boy Henry against the claim of all and every person and persons whatsoever." Henry was about fourteen years old.[55] For $600, James Schiller sold and warranted "a Negro Girl named Mary aged about nine years" to be "sound and sensible" and "a slave for life."[56] Jacob Cable and Erwin Hamer received a warranty that Aron, the ten-year-old boy they purchased,

Ad of boy for sale, *Norfolk and Portsmouth Herald*, January 29, 1821

Ad of mother and child for sale, *Hillsborough Recorder*, May 26, 1824

was "sound and healthy" so far as the sellers knew.[57] James Sale warranted the title of "one negro girl slave named Sally and her future increase, if any," to the man who purchased her. And Mahada Bowie sold to Hugh McDonald, "the following negro slaves, To wit. One negro woman named Bitty of a copper color aged about Twenty two years. One Boy of a dark color aged about three years and named Kirt, also one Boy child aged about Ten months of a copper color named Burt. To have and to hold the said Slaves unto him the said W. McDonald his heirs and assigns forever."[58] Sometimes these warranties proved to be defective, and purchasers took legal action when a person who had been sold proved not to be sound or sensible or healthy.[59]

Traders and owners spoke in the language of the slave market: property, warranties, mortgages, deeds, valuable, stock, inventory. They described the children they sold as "likely," meaning that they were strong, growing, and capable of years of hard labor. They commented upon the "good character" of a young boy or girl, described the child as being "tractable," or held out that he had been "brought up in a good family," meaning that he belonged to owners who knew how to teach a slave his role in society. "Good character," "tractable," and "good family" all signaled to buyers that they would have no difficulties with this new acquisition. This young person, the seller promised, would work, would not run away, and would understand and maintain his or her place within the slave society. Included in all of this was the implied promise that the disruption of the child's emotional life would not negatively influence the child's behavior and performance. After all, being tractable demanded the ability to project outward signs of a quick adjustment to losing one's family.

The language former slaves such as John Brown used to describe the experience of being sold lived a world away from the legal and financial terms that owners and traders used. Deeds of trust, debts, and property division resulted in separation and loss. Financial transactions translated into shock, wrenching pain, fear, and anger. Brown said that he was so "stupefied with grief and fright" when sold away from his mother that he could not shed a tear though his heart was bursting. "I walked on before Finney, utterly unconscious of any thing," he wrote of this experience; "I seemed to have become quite bewildered."[60] In her narrative, a woman known only by the name Elizabeth wrote of her separation from her family at age eleven: "I grew so lonely and sad I thought I should die, if I did not see my mother. I could do nothing but weep. I lost my appetite, and not being able to take enough food to sustain nature, I became so weak I had but little strength to work; still I was required to do all my duty."[61]

As new owners loaded these dazed, bewildered children into wagons, placed them atop horses, or forced them to walk miles to unknown destinations, the children sought to understand what had befallen them and tried to find some relief from the pain. These children were being uprooted from the only homes they had known at the same time that they began to perceive that their role in society was to be powerless and inferior, and they struggled in their parents' absence to make sense of this new world into which they were so abruptly thrust.

Robert Glenn from Hillsborough, North Carolina, sold after his father's unsuccessful efforts to purchase him, turned to two white women for help. "Missus when will I see my mother again?" Glenn asked the women, who were spinning flax in a room where his new purchaser left him. "I don't know child," one woman replied, "go and sit down." But Glenn overheard one of them say, "Almighty God, this slavery business is a horrible thing. Chances are this boy will never see his mother again." Even these seemingly sympathetic white women appeared unable to help him. The remark, he said, "nearly killed me, as I began to fully realize my situation." Here was another child experiencing the slow dawning of awareness that he could lose his family forever. As it happened, Glenn did see his mother again. She found out through the "grapevine telegraph" that the trader had sold her son in an adjacent county and that his new owner was soon to take him to Kentucky. She received permission to visit him, and when she had to leave, the owner allowed Glenn to walk part of the way with her. But he also sent two enslaved girls to monitor the visit, threatening that if they allowed Glenn to run away, they would be whipped every day until he was caught. Glenn recalled the pain he experienced as an eight-year-old when he left his mother for the last time. "When the time of parting came and I had to turn back, I burst out crying loud. I was so weak from sorrow I could not walk, and the two girls who were with me took me by each arm and led me along half carrying me."[62] Glenn traveled with the trader and several other enslaved people by train and on foot, moving farther and farther away from his parents and his home until they reached Kentucky, where he lived and worked on a plantation for several years until the end of the Civil War.

When children lost their parents, some found surrogate caregivers, as African American men and women stepped in to take care of those "orphaned" by the domestic slave trade. Robert Glenn made a fleeting reference to the woman who took care of him and another enslaved boy. This woman was likely assigned by their owner to take care of the children.[63] Former slave Laura Clark recalled that the man who purchased her in North Carolina when she was seven also purchased ten other children and an old woman named Julie Powell to look after the children on the road and once they arrived in Alabama. According to Clark, "None of them ten children no kin to me, and he never bought my mammy, so I had to leave her behind. I recollect Mammy said to old Julie, 'Take care of my baby chile (that was me) and iffen I never sees her no more raise her for God.' Then she fell off the wagon where us was all setting and roll over on the ground just a crying." But Clark was eating the candy that the trader had given the children to keep them quiet, and according to her, "I didn't have sense enough to know what ailed Mammy, but I knows now and I never seed her no more in this life. When I heard from her after surrender she done dead and buried. Her name was Maybell Powell. My pappy's name I don't know because he done been sold to somewhere else when I was too little to recollect."[64]

Although the owner appointed Julie Powell to take care of the children, Clark did not remark on what type of a caretaker she was. She gave no indication of whether Powell had nurtured her or tried to console her and the other children. As their owner had purchased Powell with her two sons but left their father behind, she may have been distracted by her own grief. According to Clark, the overseers on the plantation eventually beat Powell to death.[65]

As she recounted her story to an interviewer decades after her sale, Clark, now an old woman, sang a verse of a hymn from her church:

A motherless chile sees a hard time
Oh, Lord, help her on the road.
Sister will do the best she can
This is a hard world, Lord, for a motherless child.[66]

The words of this hymn, sung in a congregation of former slaves like herself, resonated with Laura Clark, mirroring as it did her own "hard time," her own traumatic experiences of losing first her family and then her caretaker.

Louis Hughes, sold from his mother in Charlottesville, Virginia, at age eleven, found someone who nurtured him. "I grieved continually about my mother," Hughes said. "It came to me, more and more plainly, that I would never see her again. Young and lonely as I was, I could not help crying, oftentimes for hours together. It was hard to get used to being away from my mother." In the depths of this grief another enslaved person reached out to him. "I remember well, 'Aunt Sylvia,' who was the cook in the Reid household," Hughes said; "she was very kind to me and always spoke consolingly to me, especially if I had been blue, and had had one of my fits of crying. At times she would always bake me an ash cake for supper, saying to me: 'My child, don't cry; "Aunt Sylvia" will look after you.'"[67] Aunt Sylvia, a stranger to Hughes, recognized and perhaps empathized with his distress, and she reached out to comfort him. As time passed, Hughes wrote, "I thought of my mother often, but I was gradually growing to the idea that it was useless to cry, and I tried hard to overcome my feelings."[68] This was yet another lesson African American children had to learn: how to move on despite the pain.

African American adults also stepped in to comfort Mingo White, who was born in Chester, South Carolina, and remembered being sold at age four or five. "I remembers that I was took up on a stand and a lot of people came round and felt my arms and legs and chest and asked me a lot of questions. Before we slaves was took to the trading post Mars Crawford told us to tell everybody what asked us if we'd ever been sick to tell them that us never been sick in our life. Us had to tell them all sorts of lies for our Master or else take a beating." After the auction, White recalled, "I was loaded in a wagon with a lot more people in it. Where I was bound I don't know. Whatever become of my mammy and pappy I don't know for a long time." White lamented many years later, "I was just a little thing took away from my mammy and pappy just when I needed them most."[69] White ended up in Alabama, where, he said, "the only caring that I had or ever knowed anything about was given to me by a friend of my pappy. His name was John White. My pappy told him to take care of me for him. John was a fiddler and many a night I woke up to find myself asleep twix his legs whilst he was playing for a dance for the white folks." In addition to John, Mingo had another surrogate caregiver, Selina White, a woman on the new plantation whom everyone called "Mammy." Mingo believed for a long time that she was his mother.[70]

While some children turned to adult surrogates for comfort, others turned to the God their parents had promised would take care of them. In anticipation of sale and to help children to cope with the difficulties of living as a slave, some parents bolstered their children with a belief that no matter how painful or desperate the situation, they could turn to God for support. When Laura Clark was sold, her grandmother said to her, "Pray, Laura, and be a good gal, and mind both white and black. Everybody will like you and iffen you never see me no more pray to meet me in heaven."[71] And Thomas Lewis Johnson's mother told him "that in heaven there would be no slaves—all would be free. Oh, I used to think," Johnson recalled, "how nice it must be in heaven, 'no slaves, all free,' and God would think as much of the black people as he did the white."[72] Taken from their families into strange new environments, children were supposed to find comfort in believing they were not truly alone, that they always had a protector who would look out for them.

But making this connection and finding relief from their grief through a belief in a loving and caring God did not always come easily. Elizabeth, who was enslaved in Maryland, told of her struggle to stay alive through the cutting pain of losing her parents and siblings.[73] Her mother's lessons about God did not provide an immediate salve. "In the eleventh year of my age," she told the person who wrote her narrative, "my master sent me to another farm several miles from my parents, brothers and sisters, which was a great trouble to me. I grew so lonely and sad I thought I should die if I did not see my mother." The overseer denied permission to visit her mother, so Elizabeth left on her own. She remained with her mother for several days but then had to return to the farm. "At parting," Elizabeth recounted, "my mother told me that I had nobody in the wide world to look to but God. These words," Elizabeth said, "fell upon my heart with ponderous weight, and seemed to add to my grief. I went back repeating as I went, 'none but God in the wide world.'" Upon her return, the overseer whipped her and put her back to work, but the child was overcome with sadness and loneliness. She mourned, she said, "like a dove," repeating words of sorrow whenever she could find a space in which to be alone. "I continued in this state," she recalled, "for about six months, feeling as though my head were waters, and I could do nothing but weep." She lost her appetite and became so weak that she could hardly work. Even constant prayer, it seemed, offered no relief from her despondency. "One evening," she said, "after the duties of the day were ended, I thought I could not live over the night, so threw myself on a bench, expecting to die." Elizabeth, it appears, was ready to give up. She may, in fact, have been ready to will herself to die rather than continue her life as she knew it. But she did not want to die without being saved from her sins. In desperation, she fell on her knees and prayed, "Lord have mercy on me—Christ save me." At this point began a vision in which she was surrounded by angels dressed in white robes. Someone led her toward a fire while she screamed and wrestled, thinking that she would "sink to endless ruin." But a figure stretched out his hands to her and she heard a voice saying, "Art thou willing to be saved? Art thou willing to be saved in my way?" She said she accepted the Lord as her savior that night and immediately felt a great weight lift from her.[74]

Elizabeth's account of her grief over separation and her experience of salvation are quite significant. Her description of her salvation experience resonates with the messages of evangelicals who began preaching in the 1730s to large crowds of blacks, whites, and Indians, to free and enslaved people, to northerners and southerners. The sermons at these widespread revivals condemned sinners to eternal damnation and urged them to seek salvation from an all-powerful God.[75] These messages that had been passed down to Elizabeth by her parents, who attended Methodist Society meetings, came to her aid when she needed them most. Her grief upon losing her mother was so intense that, as many other former slaves also said, she thought she would die. The vision intervened as she lay on the edge, hovering between life and death or perhaps between sanity and insanity. Her mother's last words to her that she had no one but the Lord finally sank in. "If thou are not saved in the Lord's way, thou canst not be saved at all," the voice said to Elizabeth, and she believed she had to turn her mind and heart over to this figure, this force, or die. Once she made the choice to be saved, she appears to have replaced her yearning for her mother with her desire to see her "Saviour," and she transformed her sorrow into an intense seeking. "The next day when I came to myself," she said, "I felt like a new creature in Christ, and all my desire was to see the Saviour." She engaged in private worship constantly: "Everyday I went out amongst the hay-stacks, where the presence of the Lord overshadowed me, and I was filled with sweetness and joy. Many times while my hands were at work, my spirit was carried away to spiritual things."[76] Elizabeth's intense preoccupation with this force helped to take her mind away from the people she had lost and the pain that she could not withstand. It even kept her mind off her labor. Freed at age thirty, she eventually became an evangelist.

Even when enslaved children and adults found ways to survive, some carried grief, sorrow, and a sense of loss with them for a lifetime. Caleb Craig held on to memories of his family into old age. At age eighty-six, when he was interviewed in Winnsboro, South Carolina, he remembered, "My mammy was Martha. Marse John soon give us children to his daughter, Miss Marion. In that way us separated from our mammy. Her was a might pretty colored woman and I has visions and dreams of her, in my sleep, sometime yet."[77] At age eighty-five, Sylvia Cannon told an interviewer in Florence, South Carolina, "I can just remember when I was sold. Me and Becky and George. Just can remember that, but I know who bought me. First belong to old Bill Greggs and that's who Miss Earlie Hatchel bought me from." Cannon was purchased at age six to help take care of an infant. "I see them sell plenty colored peoples away in them days cause that the way white folks made heap of their money," she recounted. "Course they aint never tell us how much they sell them for. Just stand them up on a block bout three feet high and a speculator bid them off just like they was horses. Them was bid off didn't never say nothing neither." Then she cried as she reported, "Don't know who bought my brothers George and Earl." Although she had been allowed to visit her parents every two weeks, decades after being sold Cannon could still come to tears when she tapped into the memory of losing her siblings.[78]

Sylvia Cannon's interview suggests that grief was not all that former slaves held on to; they also carried resentment. Her words were still tinged with resentment of the "white folks" who made their wealth by selling black people as though they were animals. In his narrative, former slave William Singleton, who as a child was sold because he was the son of his owner's brother, suggested that the initial shock, disbelief, listlessness, and grief of separation could also harden into anger and bitterness. "I had been sold off the plantation away from my mother and brothers with as little formality as they would have sold a calf or a mule," Singleton reflected. "Such breaking up of families and parting of children from their parents was quite common in slavery days and was one of the things that caused much bitterness among slaves and much suffering, because the slaves were as fond of their children as white folks."[79]

Former slave Susan Hamilton was particularly bitter and bold in her condemnation of slaveowners and in her linkage of the brutality of slavery with the separation of families. At age 101 years she did not censor herself. "The white race is so brazen," she told her interviewer. "They come here and run the Indians from their own land, but they couldn't make them slaves cause they wouldn't stand for it. Indians used to get up in trees and shoot them with poison arrows. When they couldn't make them slaves then they gone to Africa and bring their black brother and sister. They say among themselves, 'We going to mix them up and make ourselves king. That's the only way we'll get even with the Indians.'" Then Hamilton linked whites' brazenness and desire for power to separation of black families. "All the time, night and day," she said, "you could hear men and women screaming to the tip of their voices as either ma, pa, sister, or brother was taken without any warning and sell. Some time mother who had only one child was separated for life. People was always dying from a broken heart."[80]

Dinah Hayes, born into slavery and interviewed in Mississippi many years after it ended, offered a bit of insight into one method of coping with a broken heart. "When I was a child," Hayes reflected, "I can remember my old Mammy sitting and praying for the children that were sold away from her during slavery and wondering if she'd ever see them again, and then she taught me to be kind to others so that others may be kind to one's blood and kin far away."[81] Hayes's siblings had been dragged into the vortex of the slave trade by owners, traders, and middlemen such as N. A. Hinkle. In response, her mother had devised a strategy for coping with the pain, the uncertainty, and the knowledge that her children were out in the world somewhere without a mother to comfort them. Her mother also passed on memories of her missing children to the remaining child, who in turn uttered the memories into the recorded history, thereby rescuing her family from the anonymity of the "fine black boy" about whom Hinkle wrote.

TWO

And you all remember the home house and the
wife house, how the wife house was often eight or
ten miles from the home house, and we would go there
Saturday night expecting to see the wife we had left and
she would be gone! Sent down South, never to come back,
and the little cabin shut up and desolate; then we would
fold our arms and cry, "O Lord, how long!"
and that was all we could say.

BAYLEY WYATT, former slave

Let No Man Put Asunder
Separation of Husbands and Wives

For this cause shall a man leave his father and mother, and shall
cleave to his wife: and they twain shall be one flesh. What therefore God
hath joined together, let not man put asunder.

WORDS OF JESUS, Matthew 19:5–6

People then used to do the same things they do now. Some marry and
some live together just like now. One thing, no minister never say in reading
the matrimony "let no man put asunder," 'cause a couple would be married
tonight and tomorrow one would be taken away and sold.

SUSAN HAMILTON, former slave

Enslaved people learned as children that they were vulnerable to sale; as
adults they grasped the realization that even their most private and intimate
relationships lacked sanctity in the larger white society and could not be protected from the interference of slaveowners and slave traders. Children lost
their parents, siblings, or extended families to the domestic slave trade; in
adulthood they stood to lose their spouses as well. One of the many challenges that African Americans encountered in slavery took place on this
ground of family separation in a world in which owners possessed the absolute right to sell slaves, to separate children, husbands, and wives. Slave states
denied them the right to marry legally, yet many enslaved people entered into
loving relationships, made commitments to one another, and had children
whom they loved. When faced with impending separation, they negotiated,
begged, pleaded, connived, and even escaped, but power remained weighted
in favor of their owners. Sometimes when they could do no more than watch
as loved ones were taken away forever, enslaved people held their words and
stifled their grief.

"There is no legal marriage among the slaves of the South," fugitive slave Henry Bibb wrote in his 1850 autobiography. "I never saw nor heard of such a thing in my life, and I have been through seven of the slave states. A slave marrying according to law, is a thing unknown in the history of American Slavery."[1] Bibb was right. The large majority of colonial and state statutes did not even mention marriage with regard to enslaved people. There was no need; the law considered enslaved people property and commodities, not legal persons with the capacity to enter into contracts, and marriage was very much a legal contract.[2]

Indeed, marriage was arguably the most fundamental contract into which two people could enter; the legal institution of marriage enabled consolidation of wealth, determined the legitimacy and custody of children, and provided a mechanism for the distribution of property from generation to generation. In the nineteenth-century South, legal marriage created households that, although sometimes headed by widowed white women, most often had white men at the helm. A legally married white man was a husband, a father, and head of a household. Within that structure, all others—white women and children or enslaved black men, women, and children—amounted to dependents who were subsumed under the authority of the white, male head of household. There was no room for more than one dominant figure.[3]

While most other states simply ignored the concept of marriage between enslaved people, Louisiana, with its vestiges of French law and Catholic Church influence, did acknowledge marriage-like relationships, but the state denied slaves any legal marital rights. To judges in the Louisiana courts, slaves' marriages did nothing more than acknowledge emotional desires and needs. In 1819 a Louisiana court concluded, "It is clear that slaves have no legal capacity to assent to any contract. With the consent of their master they may marry, and their moral power to agree to such a contract or connection cannot be doubted; but while in a state of slavery it cannot produce any civil effect, because slaves are deprived of all civil rights." In other words, the court found that enslaved people had the same moral capacity—what some might call the God-given ability—as other people to agree to be faithful to one another, but according to the laws enacted by men, they could not derive any of the legal rights that the state bestowed upon legally married individuals.[4]

The Louisiana legislature affirmed the court's decision with a statute: "Slaves cannot marry without the consent of their masters, and their marriages do not produce any of the civil effects which result from such contract." The Louisiana legislature, which like the court consisted of elite white men, acknowledged that enslaved men and women could come together in something that resembled marriage; however, they needed permission from their owners to do so, and their marriages gave them none of the rights and duties that marriages between free people triggered.[5] Therefore, the chapters of the Louisiana Code that prescribed "mutual fidelity, support and assistance" between husbands and wives, or that determined whether a wife could testify against her husband or how property would be distributed or the legitimacy of children or the terms for dissolution of marriages, did not apply to enslaved couples. States that paid any attention to slave marriage drew clear lines between free people and enslaved people because in a society that relied upon slavery to produce and maintain its wealth, there had to be very clear demarcations between owner and owned. The society could not tolerate any challenge to the power or authority of white slaveowners.[6]

When they considered the specter of enslaved people having the right to legally marry, members of the southern elite envisioned a model of patriarchy with a man at the head of the household entitled to subservience and obedience. Granting enslaved men the right to head households constructed through legal marriage would have set the stage for a collision of interests and power. Any civil rights or connection to the state flowed through the white patriarch only, and slaves could have none of that power.[7] North Carolina Supreme Court Justice Thomas Ruffin, himself a slaveowner, said as much in his 1836 opinion in *State v. Samuel*, a case in which an enslaved defendant claimed that his enslaved wife should not be compelled or allowed to testify against him and sought to exclude her testimony. In denying the appeal, Justice Ruffin reasoned that the spousal privilege applied only to marriages in which the parties had entered into a legal contract to marry, but as enslaved people could not give consent, they could not enter into contracts and therefore could not legally marry. This made sense, he reasoned, because it would be difficult to give legal validity to the marriage "without essentially curtailing the rights and powers of the masters." Legal marriage, then, carried with it important legal rights that could not be afforded to slaves without diminishing the rights of their owners. Challenging the owner's power within the household also threatened to destabilize the broader social order that grew out of these patriarchal households.[8]

This reasoning remained in place as long as American slavery did. As late as 1858, the North Carolina Supreme Court reiterated the ruling that slaves could not legally marry. In *Howard v. Howard*, the question concerned whether children born to enslaved parents were legitimate and therefore able to inherit from their father. The father in question had, after becoming free, legally married a new wife, and they subsequently had children. The children born to him while he was a slave and in a marriage with their mother, an enslaved woman, asserted a right to inherit from their father's estate. Writing for the court, Justice C. J. Pearson explicitly laid out the limitations of marriage as it applied to enslaved people. "A slave, being property, has not the legal capacity to make a contract, and is not entitled to the rights or subjected to the liabilities incident thereto. He is amenable to the criminal law, and his person (to a certain extent) and his life are protected. This, however, is not a concession to him of civil rights, but is in vindication of public justice, and for the prevention of public wrongs. Marriage," he said, "is based upon contract, consequently the relation of 'man and wife' cannot exist among slaves. It is excluded, both on account of their incapacity to contract and of the paramount right of ownership in them as property." Pearson reaffirmed Justice Ruffin's belief that legal marriage for slaves would interfere with their owners' rights. The concern seemed to be that if slaves could marry, they would not be fully slaves, and therefore their owners would have lost some of their property rights.[9]

Justice Pearson also repeated Justice Ruffin's earlier acknowledgment of the fragile and tenuous nature of marriage among slaves. "The relation between slaves," he argued, "is essentially different from that of man and wife joined in lawful wedlock. The latter is indissoluble during the lives of the parties, and its violation is a high crime; but with slaves it may be dissolved at the pleasure of either party, or by the sale of one or both, dependent on the caprice or necessity of the owners."[10] Marriages between slaves carried no legal weight, and owners retained the right to dissolve them at will.

The notion of legal marriage between enslaved people raised thorny issues in societies bent on controlling the bodies and minds of the slaves in their midst. If marriage were held to be legal and binding for the enslaved as it was for the free, owners stood to lose authority and control. Vesting marital right in human property would have resulted in confusion and even chaos in the power relationships between the owned and their owners. An enslaved husband might, for example, have dominion over his household, as free men usually did in the nineteenth century, and this would undermine owners' authority over the adults and children within that black household. Upholding the biblical teaching that husband and wife should cleave unto each other would interfere with owners' prerogatives to sell a husband or a wife. If, as the common law provided, a man were the head of his household with responsibility for supporting his wife and children, he would need to have control over the fruits of his labor and theirs as well. He would also have the right to make decisions as to how and where his family lived. Legal marriage, with the attendant civil rights, would have threatened the very foundations of slavery, obscuring lines that owners continually strived to draw between the powerful and the powerless, the dominant and the subservient, the owner and the owned. From the perspective of elite white men, it was reasonable that owners would not recognize marriage among slaves as having the same meaning as that of their own marriages. If owners admitted or endorsed the sanctity of marriage among slaves, they would have one more moral contradiction to reconcile when they broke husbands and wives apart, and one more barrier to overcome in their struggle to control the labor and behavior of the people they owned.

Considering the certainty with which nineteenth-century legal authorities declared that there could be no legal marriage among slaves, William Goodell, a white abolitionist from New York who edited a collection of state slave codes, could not help wondering what value marriage could possibly hold for enslaved people. "The obligations of marriage are evidently inconsistent with the conditions of slavery, and cannot be performed by a slave," he wrote. Then he enumerated some of the expectations of marriage in the mid-nineteenth century that the law denied enslaved people: "The husband promises to protect his wife and provide for her. The wife promises to be the help-meet of her husband. They mutually promise to live with and cherish each other, till parted by death. But what can such promises by slaves *mean*?" he asked. "The 'legal relation of master and slave' renders them void! It forbids the slave to protect even himself. It prohibits his possession of any property wherewith to sustain her. It bids the woman assist, not her husband, but her owner! Nay! It gives him unlimited control and full possession of her own person and forbids her, on pain of death, to resist him, if he drags her to his bed! It severs the plighted pair, at the will of their masters, occasionally, or for ever! The innocent 'legal relations' of slave-ownership permits all this." Following this litany of impediments, Goodell raised the question, "What, then, can the marriage vows of slaves *mean*?"[11]

Marriage, in fact, meant a great deal to enslaved people. Despite the lack of legal status for a marriage between enslaved persons, despite the absence of civil protections, and despite the ever-looming possibility of forced separation, many enslaved people entered into relationships that they considered marriages. As former slave Thomas Jones explained, "We called it and we considered it a true marriage, although we knew well that marriage was not permitted to the slaves as a sacred right of the loving heart."[12] Henry Bibb also acknowledged that although the laws did not honor them, enslaved people considered their marriages valid. Regarding his own marriage, he wrote,

required the approval of owners. Patriarchy expects dependence, and displays of power and authority by slaveholders demanded displays of obedience and obsequiousness from slaves. On large plantations with hundreds of enslaved people, owners and even overseers likely had less direct influence, but slaveowners nonetheless retained ultimate control over whom and when enslaved people could marry. When the man and woman belonged to different owners, both owners had to agree. Henry Bibb and Malinda needed permission from two men. Malinda's owner, according to Bibb, "was very much in favor of the match, but entirely upon selfish principle. When I went to ask his permission to marry Malinda, his answer was in the affirmative with but one condition, which I consider to be too vulgar to be written in this book." The owner's "selfish principle" likely concerned Bibb's capacity to father children who would then belong to him, as by law, whoever owned the mother also owned her children. In readily giving his permission, Malinda's owner likely assessed Bibb's virility and determined that this marriage would enrich him.[22] On the other hand, also weighing his self-interest, Bibb's owner opposed the marriage because, according to Bibb, "he feared my taking off from his farm some of the fruits of my own labor for Malinda to eat, in the shape of pigs, chickens, or turkeys, and would count it not robbery." Bibb's retelling of his owner's concern makes clear that even though there were no legal strictures requiring enslaved husbands to support their wives and families, some enslaved men did, and some owners feared this. Eventually Bibb's owner relented, and Bibb and Malinda married.[23]

It must have humiliated some enslaved men and women to request permission to marry. This was not a matter of courtesy to a young woman's father; it was obligatory. Nor was it a case of a minor needing permission from a parent. Two fully grown adults had to seek permission to marry; they could never reach an age of consent because their status as slaves nullified the ability to give consent.[24] Lunsford Lane's description of the process by which he sought permission to marry hints at some of the resentment that these adult slaves felt. Lane was enslaved in Raleigh, North Carolina, and sought permission to marry Martha Curtis. "I went to her master, Mr. Boylan," Lane wrote, "and asked him, according to the custom, if I might 'marry his woman.' His reply was, 'Yes, if you will behave yourself.' I told him I would. 'And make her behave herself?' To this I also assented and then proceeded to ask the approbation of my master, which was granted."[25] Lane did not give an explicit account of his feelings, but his frustration with being owned, expressed elsewhere in his narrative, sheds light on how galling it likely was for him to seek permission from his as well as Curtis's owner. Reflecting on when, as a boy, he had seen other children being sold and learned that he, too, was a slave and could be sold away from his family, Lane wrote, "To know, also, that I was never to consult my own will, but was, while I lived, to be entirely under the control of another, was another state of mind hard for me to bear. Indeed all things now made me feel, what I had before known only in words, that I was a slave. Deep was this feeling, and it preyed upon my heart." If this lack of control over his life disturbed him as a child, it is easy to imagine that seeking permission from two owners in order to marry must have troubled him indeed. Martha Curtis's owner had the right to withhold approval of the marriage, and he made that clear by attaching a condition of good behavior to his agreement.[26]

"Behave," for a slave, meant more than anything else "obey," and this is what Lane agreed to do; and he agreed to exercise authority over Curtis to make her behave as well. It is interesting that when Lane approached Martha Curtis's owner, he asked permission to "marry *his* woman." Here he projected the message that he understood and respected the relative positions of owner and owned. By extracting a promise from Lane to make Curtis behave, the owner seemed to delegate to Lane some of his right to control Curtis, but the need for permission from the owner, as well as his ability to attach a condition to his consent, reinforced the fact that the owner still had authority over her. Martha Curtis would be beholden to two men. An enslaved man and woman might set up a patriarchal household in which the husband was dominant, or they might agree to a more companionate marriage; but whatever their arrangement, they remained the property and dependents of owners, and their fragile marriage, as Justices Ruffin and Pearson noted, could be completely changed by "caprice or necessity" of these owners.[27]

A letter from one slaveowner to another in December 1859 starkly demonstrates the rights and privileges owners asserted in the marriages of enslaved people. Charles Locher, proprietor of the James River Cement Works in Balcony Falls, Virginia, wrote with great formality to Captain William Weaver in Buffalo Forge, Virginia: "Greeting, Respected Sir My Col Boy named James Carter, has my free and full permission to marry your Colored Woman Amy, with such privileges as you may see proper to grant having reference allways to his duties as a servant and obedience to his master. Truly your friend Ch. H. Locher."[28] When Locher referred to "such privileges" as Weaver might grant, he likely had in mind another type of permission that married slaves needed: permission for the husband to visit his wife. Locher understood that Weaver would set those guidelines, as Amy lived on his property, but he also wanted her owner to take into consideration Carter's responsibilities to

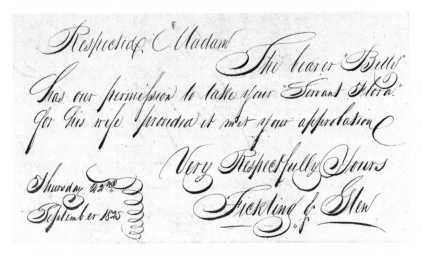

Letter from Fickling and Glen to Mrs. E. Kane, September 22, 1825 (Jared Irwin
Papers, Duke University Special Collections Library, Durham, N.C.)

Locher when he set up a visiting schedule. An overly liberal visiting agreement could interfere with Carter's work for Locher. James Carter and Amy
could marry each other, but their marital relationship was secondary to their
primary obligations to their owners.

Owners such as Locher relished the opportunity that a proposed marriage
between slaves offered them to play the roles of "employer," "father," and al-
truistic yet strict owner. They constructed their identities as masters through
just such power to make critical decisions that affected the lives of their
slaves. An owner in South Carolina, for example, not only granted permission for the man who belonged to him to marry; he also sent a letter of endorsement to the woman's owner as though he were recommending someone
for employment. "My servant Abraham," he wrote, "being desirous of taking
a wife at your place has requested a certificate of character and I take pleasure
in stating that he is remarkably steady and industrious and I want to rec-
ommend him to your favorable consideration."[29] Another owner penned his
permission with calligraphic flourish suited for a formal wedding invitation:

Respected Madam

The Bearer "Billy" has our permission to take your "Servant Flora" for
his wife provided it meet your approbation.

Very Respectfully Yours

Fickling & Glen.[30]

Two significant concerns undergirded owners' involvement in marriage among enslaved people: first, the paternalistic notion that owners, like fathers, had a responsibility to impart morals to their slaves and, second, owners' persistent struggle to obtain and maintain control over the people they owned.[31] Encouraging or allowing marriage enabled owners to believe that they had passed on notions of the morality of monogamy to their slaves, despite the fact that the marriages they permitted did not contain any of the rights they reserved for themselves as well as the fact that some owners violated their own marriage vows. At a meeting of a Georgia agricultural association, planter Nathan Bass reminded fellow slaveowners that slavery was "an institution ordained of Heaven, and that we are the chosen instruments for the melioration and civilization of the downtrodden and oppressed African race. Placed in this position by Providence, we should feel and appreciate the responsibility and importance of our station, and so discharge our duties as to fulfill Heaven's designs towards us." Owners, Bass said, should regard slaves as a "Heaven-sent gift, designed for our rational comfort and profit, at the same time that we are the moral agents through which they are to be moralized, Christianized and saved." As he saw it, encouraging and facilitating marriages was one element of this obligation to save enslaved African Americans.[32]

A Tennessee minister agreed that owners had a moral obligation to encourage marriage among the people they owned. "It is the duty of Christian masters," Rev. H. N. McTyeire wrote in 1860, "to promote virtuous and fixed attachments between the sexes, and, while encouraging marriage, to guard it with all the forms of consent, postponement, preparation, and solemn consummation. A marriage-supper is often given. Beforehand the impediments should be looked into, and if any grave ones exist, they should work a prohibition. Let the institution be magnified. Let religion lend its solemnity to its rites; and when once consummated by the master's permission, all the mutual rights it confers should be protected by his authority. Leaving one wife and taking another should not be allowed."[33] In this minister's configuration, owners would be involved in the slaves' marriage from permission to preparation, to wedding, to consummation, to monitoring of the marriage, to consideration of divorce. Indeed, elite southern white men appeared at their paternalistic best when they intoned about marriage among their slaves. They were in charge, knew what was best for the enslaved people, and would be firm in enforcing the rules they designed.

Marriage, some slaveowners and their advisors also believed, would entice slaves to remain on or near plantations where their families lived. Henry

Bibb feared that marriage would confine him to the plantation, but that was just the outcome owners desired. They revealed their profound desire for control when they argued that slaves should only be permitted to marry "at home" and not "abroad."[34] Planters often pictured themselves as fathers of a large family that included their own relations as well as the children and adults they owned.[35] They had "inside" families and "outside" families: their white wives and children who lived inside their homes and the slaves who lived outside. Owners positioned themselves as the heads of large households, with responsibility for all who lived there, and the law upheld that view. "Home," then, referred to the owner's property, his plantation or farm; "abroad" referred to anywhere else, generally nearby plantations. Enslaved people often wanted to marry someone off the plantation, one reason being that they wanted to make sure they did not marry close relatives. Despite the white elite's endogamous practice of marrying first cousins, for example, African Americans were generally exogamous, refusing to marry people who were so closely related to them. The choice to marry someone abroad framed one more struggle between owners and slaves, one that enslaved people won more often than their owners. Despite owners' opposition, vast numbers of people married abroad. Perhaps this is why owners spent so much time spelling out their objections.[36]

Planters told each other that abroad marriages should be prohibited and that slaves should only be permitted to marry at home. An essay in a southern agricultural magazine argued, for example, "Marriage at home, should be encouraged among them. The practice of taking wives abroad, should as much as possible be prevented. It engenders a habit of rambling, which is injurious to the constitution of the negro, besides removing him frequently, and at important times from the influence of the domestic police, which should be always strict. 'Give the negro an inch, and he will sure take an ell.'"[37]

These owners harbored a great deal of anxiety about black people "rambling," or moving about, as any movement presented challenges to the persistent desire to control them. As a result, legislatures in slave states enacted codes that imposed all sorts of restrictions on enslaved people and sometimes on free black people. They regulated, for example, how many slaves could be in any place at the same time or required that slaves carry a written pass whenever leaving their plantation. These codes also instituted patrols and other mechanisms for policing the movement of enslaved and free black people. Some planters feared that the visits resulting from abroad marriages would amount to a loophole in their efforts to control how enslaved people moved about the southern landscape.[38]

A South Carolina planter presented a lengthy argument for why slaves should be forced to marry "at home." His letter appeared anonymously in the *Southern Agriculturalist*, but the editor endorsed the writer as someone who was "eminently distinguished as a planter, who practices what he communicates and is peculiarly successful in all of his operations."[39] Control of enslaved people's movements as well as control of their attitudes emerged as this planter's primary concerns. "The slave should know that his master is to govern absolutely and he to obey implicitly. That he is never for a moment to exercise either his will or judgment in opposition to a positive order," he wrote. Then he gave a list of rules: Rule number 1, slaves should never leave the plantation without permission from the owner or the driver; rule number 2, the driver, who was responsible for watching the slaves, should leave the plantation only on "very urgent business"; and rule number 3, "No negroes should be allowed to marry out of the plantation." There were others, but, the planter wrote, "no rule is of more importance than that relating to negroes marrying out of the plantation. It seems to me, from what observations I have made, it is utterly impossible to have any method or regularity where the men and women are permitted to take wives and husbands indiscriminately off the plantation. Negroes are very much disposed to pursue a course of this kind, and without being able to assign any good reason." Still, he argued, though they might not offer any reasons, he knew what their true motives were. He listed six reasons why slaves wanted abroad marriages and why owners should not approve them: First, allowing men to marry off the plantation gave them an "uncontrollable right to be frequently absent." Second, the men tended to think of their wives' homes as theirs and were therefore "indifferent to the interest of the plantation to which they actually belonged." Third, "It creates a feeling of independence from being, of right, out of the control of their master for a time." Fourth, they were exposed to temptations from other slaves as they traveled about. Fifth, the husbands of women you owned could be a bad example to your slaves. Men, he said, who have permission to leave their owners' plantations when their work is done, "come into yours about midday when your negroes are at work and the driver engaged; they either take possession of the houses in which their wives live and go to sleep, or stroll about in perfect idleness, feeling themselves accessible to everything. What an example to those at work at the time! Can any circumstances be more subversive of good order and contentment!"[40]

It is simply astounding to consider the perpetual struggle that slaveowners waged to maintain order. Just when they thought they were in control, an enslaved man, having completed his task for the day on his plantation, could stroll in and upset the balance that planters, overseers, and drivers had worked so hard to put in place. This South Carolina planter and others spelled out several concerns, most having to do with the problem of keeping their involuntary workforce in subjection both physically and mentally. Enslaved men who had freedom of movement for visiting their wives might think that they had an unlimited right to move about. Both the movement itself as well as the belief that they had the right posed problems for slaveowners. The movement threatened good order, making it difficult for owners and patrollers to keep track of who was supposed to be where. Moving about also made it much easier for these men to enter into plots against owners. But even without plotting, their very attitudes could be subversive. If a man could exercise some freedom, he might begin to take steps to become truly free. If a man went onto a plantation in the middle of the day and made himself at home, his very presence could pose a threat to an owner's control over his own slaves, whom he expected to be hard at work. Despite having the law and policing authority behind them, slaveowners had to wage a constant battle for domination over enslaved people, and marriage was one ground on which these daily contests played out.

Some owners also raised the possibility of separation as the reason for forbidding abroad marriages. Separation through sale was more likely, they claimed, if the husband and wife belonged to different owners. The sixth reason why owners should not allow marriages abroad, according to the South Carolina planter mentioned above, spoke to this concern. Having husbands and wives on separate plantations could result in separation if an owner sold one member of the couple, he argued. And he urged fellow owners to equalize the number of men and women they owned in order to avoid any necessity of abroad marriages.[41] "I never allow them to have husbands or wives abroad—think it better for them to mate at home, so that there may be no separation in case of removal," wrote a small planter in Alabama in 1860.[42] Another planter urged, "Let it be settled principle that men and their wives must live together. That if they cannot be suited at home they must live single, and there will be no further difficulty. If a master has a servant and no suitable one of the other sex for a companion, he had better give an extra price for such a one as his would be willing to marry than to have one man owning the husband and another the wife. It frequently happens," he asserted, "where husband and wife belong to different persons that one owner sells out and wishes to move. Neither is willing to part with his servant, or if one will consent the other is not able to buy; consequently the husband and wife must part. This is a sore evil, surely much greater than restricting to the plantation in making a selection."[43]

These men spoke as though being owned by the same person somehow protected husbands and wives from being sold apart. It did not. Owners separated wives and husbands through sale, inheritance, division of property, and movement from one part of the country to another. The provisions of the last will and testament of William Geddy of New Kent, Virginia, in 1816 exemplified such potential for separation. When he contemplated his mortality, Geddy was concerned with providing for his family, not with whether an enslaved couple would be separated.

> I loan to my beloved wife during her natural life, a yellow girl sister and twin to the yellow girl now in the possession of Henry Smith; also a negro man by the name of Charles, a black smith and the smiths tools, also Charles's wife by the name of Eliza and at the death of my wife, said Charles the aforesaid black smith is to go free, but his wife Eliza and her increase to be sold and the money arising from the sales to be equally divided into three parts, my son Edward Geddys children to have one part, and my daughter Sally Smiths children another part, and Elizabeth Lindsey's children the other part.[44]

Eliza and her children would be sold, perhaps separately, to enrich Geddy's grandchildren. Charles, Eliza, and their children would be separated without consideration of their status as a family. Slaveowners wrote numerous such provisions into wills, and innumerable families were sold apart during the life of the owner. For all their posturing about ensuring morals among the people they owned, owners always reserved the right to break up enslaved families.

Enslaved men and women realized that no matter what their owners proclaimed in southern journals, whether they married "at home" or "abroad," separation was a persistent possibility. According to Thomas Jones, the prospect of separation was an integral part of his marriage to Lucilla. "When we knelt in prayer," he said, "we never forgot to ask God to save us from the misery of cruel separation, while life and love were our portion." Together they had three children, which only seemed to heighten their fear and anxiety that they would lose each other.[45]

Bethany Veney, too, entered marriage with the awareness that forced separation could destroy the relationship. Even on her wedding day, the fear of loss was on her mind. Veney agreed to marry a man named Jerry who lived seven miles from her home in Virginia. They had been attending church services together, so she insisted that a minister perform the ceremony. What they got instead was a black peddler who stepped in to marry them. Veney understood that the ceremony and words had no binding meaning. "He asked us a few questions," she said, "which we answered in a satisfactory manner, and then he declared us husband and wife. I did not want him to make us promise that we would always be true to each other, forsaking all others, as the white people do in their marriage service, because I knew that at any time our masters could compel us to break such a promise." Perhaps she had wanted a minister to perform the ceremony so that she could at least know that theirs was a marriage in the eyes of God if not of their owners.[46]

It was clear to slaves that the vows white people took in their own wedding ceremonies did not apply to the enslaved, precisely because owners made certain there could be no confusion about the impermanence of marriages between enslaved people. In December 1854, Charles J. McDonald, two-time governor of Georgia, justice of the Georgia Supreme Court, and slaveowner in Marietta, advised his sisters how to avoid the complications of trying to keep husbands and wives together when economics mandated separation. "I have a negro preacher who marries them," he wrote, "for the union to last as long as they live or until it is the pleasure of their owners to separate them." In this way, the enslaved couple would have no expectation of being together forever, and regardless of the couple's feelings, by being transparent, McDonald and his sisters would have divested themselves of any responsibility in the matter. Some people had to be taught how to dominate and how to distance themselves from the pain that resulted from their actions. This brother took it upon himself to be his sisters' teacher.[47]

Although some owners had an enslaved minister perform the ceremony, others took on the role of officiant themselves.[48] Mississippi slaveowner Francis Terry Leak, for example, left a record of the marriage ceremony he performed for the people he owned. The vows Leak wrote in his plantation journal in early 1857 speak to his mastery and to his attempt at self-deification.[49] He was their owner, he officiated, he decided what should be included and what should be left out of the marriage vows, and he even substituted himself for God in the wording of the vows. Where nineteenth-century wedding vows customarily said, "We are gathered before God and these witnesses," Leak never mentioned God at all. The silences in the ceremony pointed clearly to the possibility of separation. On January 24, 1857, Leak made the following entry in the journal. The quotation marks are his.

"Moses & Pal were married to night. I record the ceremony used on the occasion for future use.

"We are assembled here together again on an interesting occasion. It is another marriage occasion that has brought us together. The parties to be married to night are Moses & Pal, who now stand before us hand in hand.

"With this short statement of the nature of the present occasion, we will proceed to solemnize the rites of matrimony between this couple by asking the usual question & exacting the usual vow of the parties separately.

"*Moses*—Do you agree, before me & these witnesses to take Pal as your wife, and do you solemnly pledge yourself to discharge towards her all the duties of an affectionate and faithful husband?

"*Pal*—Do you agree before me and these witnesses to take Moses as your husband and do you solemnly pledge yourself to discharge towards him all the duties of an affectionate and faithful wife?

"As all the parties have thus publicly agreed to enter into the marriage relation with each other and have solemnly pledged themselves to a faithful discharge of all its duties, it only remains for me to pronounce them and accordingly in the presence of these witnesses I do pronounce them married.

Salute your bride"

Moses and Pal had no last names worthy of Leak's recognition. They made their vows before Leak and witnesses. God was nowhere present. And though they pledged to faithfully discharge all the duties of marriage, they did not promise to do so for a lifetime. Leak spoke of the "usual vow," but he purposely left out the traditional declaration, "Those whom God hath joined together let no man put asunder." As Moses and Pal repeated their vows, they, like Bethany Veney and many other enslaved African Americans, knew that their marriage would always be vulnerable to their owner's prerogative to sell them apart.[50]

Enslaved couples and their families, then, lived with the perpetual threat of separation, and when they got wind of an impending sale or move, some negotiated, some pleaded, and some begged a white person to intervene. They implored their owners or whites they considered sympathetic to help keep their families intact. This usually meant requesting that a white person purchase one or both of the spouses. In October 1854, in a poignant and compelling letter written with the hand and spelling of the self-taught, a woman named Delia in Louisville, Kentucky, wrote to her owner, Rice Ballard, begging him to purchase her husband, Henry, so that his new owner would not take him away.[51]

Rice Ballard was not known to be an especially moral, generous, or sympathetic person and had no particular concern for enslaved people. In fact, not only was he a slaveowner, but for many years in the 1830s and 1840s he had been a partner in the large slave-trading firm of Franklin and Armfield, the same firm that purchased a building in Alexandria, Virginia, and offered to pay top price for black men, women, and children. Through his business dealings, Ballard had been responsible for separating hundreds of families. Furthermore, in their correspondence, Ballard and his business partner, Isaac Franklin, joked about their own sexual interactions with the "fancy girls"—mostly light-skinned women and girls who were sold and purchased for sexual purposes—who formed part of their lucrative trade. And in the 1830s when, in response to the Nat Turner rebellion in Virginia, Mississippi passed a law that required a certificate of good conduct for any slave taken into the state and sold, Rice Ballard circumvented the law by moving his sales outside Mississippi to nearby Louisiana. Rice Ballard was deeply immersed in the economy and culture of slaveholding, yet this is the person to whom Delia appealed, because she had no alternative. He was her owner, he was wealthy, and she had once before convinced him to help her. Delia lived in Louisville, Kentucky, with Ballard's wife and daughters. She was a house servant who now drew upon her access to Ballard to keep her husband nearby. Ballard and his wife knew her as they would not have known individual black women who worked in the cotton fields on Ballard's nearly one dozen plantations in Louisiana, Arkansas, or Mississippi.[52]

Delia addressed her desperate letter to Ballard at his plantation in Vicksburg, Mississippi. "Master," she wrote, "I take this liberty to ask you Pleas to bye henry and let him com hom and live with me. Pleas overlook my not asking you to bye him when you was here but I thought that you were angry with him because he did not agree to com to you when you offered to bye him." She attempted to make Ballard understand why Henry had declined Ballard's earlier offer to purchase him. "Master you no [know] the nature of a man when he is got a family it is to make all he can for them henry only objection of living with you was because he could not make anything in a private house." It is likely that Henry was hired out by his owner, which meant that he was allowed to keep a portion of his earnings for himself after handing over most of it to the owner. He was therefore in a position to help support Delia and their children. He evidently feared that belonging to Ballard would mean having to work, as most enslaved people did, without earning any wages. But circumstances had changed, and Henry's owner had sold him to someone who intended to take him elsewhere.[53]

Having explained Henry's earlier reluctance to have Ballard purchase him, Delia addressed an even more serious offense that would have tainted Henry in the eyes of a slaveowner; Henry had recently attempted to run away from his current owner. Delia explained this as an act of desperation born out of his distress at being sold away from her. "When he found that he was forced to leave me it was like taking his life and I suppose he be com despat [desperate] and thought if he could make his escape." Knowing that an attempted escape would render Henry less attractive, Delia described his state of mind in an attempt to reassure a leery slaveowner. Because Henry had attempted to escape only when he thought he would be taken away from Delia, she reasoned that Ballard could be confident that he would remain if he could be near her. Her husband was industrious and proud, and in the system of slavery, these characteristics earned him demerits.

Delia then appealed to Ballard's own feelings and asked him to empathize with Henry. Perhaps at some risk of insulting Ballard's ego by equating him with a slave, she pointed to the fact that both men had similar feelings, fears, family loyalties, and perhaps even mistaken judgments. "Master pleas over look his fault and bye my housband if you pleas," she wrote; "you no how hard it is to leave your family when you no there [they] are all well provided I hope you will think for a moment how hard it is for my housband is take away from me I never expect to see him agen in this world no master please bye him." Rice Ballard traveled a great deal, leaving his family in Louisville, so Delia appealed to his anxieties at being away from his own wife and children. She was aware that Henry's escape attempt, added to his show of pride when he refused Ballard's earlier offer to purchase him, presented serious obstacles to the transaction she now proposed. Owners wanted slaves whom they considered submissive and loyal, not a man who made it a priority to provide for his family or who attempted to take his life into his own hands by escaping ownership. Such a man raised a challenge to owners, who wanted to believe that they, as masters of inside and outside families, took care of all of them. Such a man also represented a threat to a financial investment.

Delia was a resourceful woman who employed several strategies to maintain a relationship with her husband. She had earlier convinced Ballard to purchase Henry. She had obtained a now-broken promise from Henry's owner that he would not sell him away from her. And before she wrote to Ballard, she got his wife to agree to her plan. She ended her letter by invoking Louise Ballard's approval. "I have done all I can if you don't by him please get some body to bye him that will let him com and see me Miss Louiser has promist me that she would ask you to bye him." She closed, "Your resecly [respectfully] humble servent delia." Her letter sits in a collection in an archive with no signs of whether Ballard was moved by her pleas to purchase Henry or whether, as she requested as a last resort, he found someone else to purchase him so that he would remain close enough to maintain his relationship with his family. Delia's frantic desperation is palpable in her letter as she faced the dreaded prospect of losing her husband forever.[54]

Delia's secondary strategy was to find someone other than her owner to purchase her husband. Sometimes a free spouse, usually the husband, attempted to purchase the other. Such was the case in October 1845 when Henry Tatterson, who appears to have been free, wrote to his wife, Amy, urging her to find out how much it would cost to purchase her from her owner. Tatterson had asked the question before but received no response from Amy's owner, so this time he made his own offer of a price he could afford to pay. "Since he has not mentioned any sum," he wrote, "I have thought best in this letter to propose the highest sum that I could possibly raise not only from my own means but also aided by every friend I have which is two hundred and fifty dollars and there fore if Mr. Holliday will take that sum I shall immediately after selling my tobacco and other stuff come in or send for you." Tatterson wanted to be clear with Amy, though, that he would not be able to afford any more than that amount. "If he will not take that sum," he wrote to her, "it will not be in my power to purchase you, which I consider it my duty in plain terms to let you know." He seemed resigned to the possibility that he would not be reunited with Amy and their child and was already making provisions for the care of his son in his absence. "Tell Jack," he wrote, "that I calculate very much upon his assistance in bringing up my son." He closed with these words: "Amy you will please to accept my love and be assured it has not abated in the smallest degree." With only $250, Tatterson was likely unable to purchase Amy and their son. In 1846 Amy would have been valued at about $400. Their child may have borne an additional price, depending on his age and the disposition of the owner.[55]

Though lacking the details of resolution that we crave, these letters pleading for help in maintaining families tell a great deal about both the material and the emotional lives of enslaved people. Husbands and wives experienced a range of dissonant feelings, including love, frustration, pain, hope, and resignation. Through their narratives and letters we are able to get closer to understanding how they experienced loss. The sources themselves can be frustrating, though. Each letter leaves the reader wondering whether the intended recipient—Amy, for example—ever read it; guessing at what that person's feelings may have been; and of course, wondering how things turned out. Still, the letters introduce us to a spectrum of emotions as well as to some of the strategies enslaved people employed to avoid separation.

Despite their pleas and maneuverings and the occasional intervention of a concerned white person, thousands of enslaved couples experienced separation through sale, the movement of owners, or division of property after an owner's death. The process of separation could occur in one of several ways. Sometimes people knew that sale or departure was imminent and had an opportunity to attempt to intervene, as Delia did. Other times sale and separation were sudden and shocking. Moses Grandy, for instance, told the story of the sudden and immediate loss of his wife. "I married a slave belonging to Mr. Enoch Sawyer, who had been so hard a master to me," Grandy wrote. "I left her at home, (that is, at his house,) one Thursday morning, when we had been married about eight months. She was well, and seemed likely to be so: we were nicely getting together our little necessaries." Recently married, they were planning a life together, perhaps forgetting that their lives were not their own. "On the Friday," Grandy wrote, "as I was at work as usual with the boats, I heard a noise behind me, on the road which ran by the side of the canal: I turned to look, and saw a gang of slaves coming. When they came up to me, one of them cried out, 'Moses, my dear!' I wondered who among them should know me, and found it was my wife. She cried out to me, 'I am gone.'" Grandy was shocked at the sight of his wife and realized immediately that she had been sold. He called out to her purchaser, a Mr. Rogerson, "For God's sake, have you bought my wife?" Rogerson said he had and according to Grandy, "He drew out a pistol, and said that if I went near the wagon on which she was, he would shoot me. I asked for leave to shake hands with her, which he refused, but said I might stand at a distance and talk with her. My heart was so full," Grandy recalled, "that I could say very little. I asked leave to give her a dram: he told Mr. Burgess, the man who was with him, to get down and carry it to her. I gave her the little money I had in my pocket, and bid her farewell. I have never seen or heard of her from that day to this. I loved her as I loved my life."[56]

In other circumstances the realization dawned slowly for adults, just as it did for children, that their families were being broken apart. This was the case for a number of enslaved people who belonged to the Brownrigg family of Chowan County, North Carolina. The Brownriggs joined the migration from north to south in search of fertile, cotton-producing land. The increase in the owners' wealth and the expansion of the nation came at a high cost to African Americans who lost kinship ties as well as to Native Americans who lost their homes through forced removal. As a descendant of the Brownrigg family wrote in a genealogical essay, "For better health and richer lands (with about 100 negroes), Gen. Brownrigg moved to Lowndes County, Miss., and settled near Columbus, the county seat on a plantation formerly owned by the chiefs of the Choctaw Indians."[57]

In the early summer of 1835 Richard T. Brownrigg, descendant of Irish immigrants who came to America in the 1700s, traveled to Mississippi and Alabama, where he purchased land. Later that year, Brownrigg sent his sister Sarah Brownrigg Sparkman and her husband, William Sparkman; his brother Thomas Brownrigg; and brother-in-law R. T. Hoskins as the advance team to set up his plantation in Mississippi. The Sparkmans wrote letters from the road to family members back home in Chowan County that documented their journey, providing descriptions of the landscape as well as a sense of Sarah's emotional adjustment to moving away from her home and most of her family members. Some of the letters also included messages from a few of the nearly 100 enslaved people they took with them.

On October 20, 1835, shortly after the group had begun their westward movement across North Carolina, Sarah wrote to her sister-in-law recounting details of her new adventure. "We are thus far on our journey to the far West. I find camping out much better than I expected. We sleep very comfortable in our tents. Our repast is very good we have toast, coffee, ham, eggs, for breakfast and we eat our dinner along the road as we can get it. . . . The roads are very rough so that it is impossible to read or work." Then she commented on the people who would make the establishment of a plantation possible. "The Negroes are all in high spirits," Sparkman reported; "they run and play like children along the road it is remarked by every one that they have never seen so many without being chained and all looked so cheerful and happy last night they were fiddling to night singing hymns, we travel from 15 to 20 miles a day and they set up as late as if they were at home. Sometimes the Negroes a mile before us they stop at every well spring they find so many 91 Negroes, and only 4 whites we are stared at such a caravan, the two jerseys and four wagons 13 horses, and 14 mules including the Jack and Jinny." Then Sparkman returned to her own concerns. "If only I could divest myself of the idea of my seperation from my Dear Dear relatives and friends," she wrote. "I hope to meet with some if not all again and if kind

Providence permits I expect to visit this part of the country again." She ended with her sincere love to her relatives and friends and noted, "The Negroes desire to be remembered to all."[58] In *his* letter to Richard Brownrigg on October 20, William Sparkman wrote, "I am in camp about three miles from Enfield all well not the least accident have happened and you would be pleased to see how chearfull they all are."

By 1835 these scenes of large numbers of black people on the road with owners or slave traders had become fairly common. Sometimes enslaved people traveled by ship from the Upper South to places farther south and west, but more often they moved by foot in coffles with the men chained together, just as the slaves bought and sold by the slave traders Franklin and Armfield did. Women and children usually moved without restraints. Sarah Sparkman pointed out the oddity of their caravan in which the Brownriggs and Sparkmans had decided not to attach chains to the people. This made them stand out, she said, and she implied that the enslaved people, in their childlike innocence, were so happy to make this trip that it was unnecessary to shackle them.

On November 4 the caravan was still on the road. William Sparkman wrote that they were in Wythe, Virginia, having moved through the Allegheny Mountains. The enslaved people had been walking for sixteen days. Sarah Sparkman traveled in a wagon; the white men were on horseback. Sarah Sparkman wrote to her brothers Richard and John that many of the slaves had asked her to write letters home for them. "The servants request me to send many messages to all their friends and relations and your Dave requested me to write a letter to his wife which I will do on the other page and you can read it to her You will see what a medly I have written for the Negroes I hope you will read it to their friends they say it is the very words they want to say to them you would be glad to see them so contented and I hope they may continue so." The words of the enslaved people convey a more complex set of feelings and concerns than Sarah's account of their childlike enthusiasm and sanguine satisfaction with their situation would suggest.[59]

Dave Brownrigg's message read,

My dear wife

I write these few lines to inform you of my health which is much better than it has been I can walk all day and have a good appetite We get fine cabbage and good water and great many apples and I have seen great sights the mountains and a great many towns rocks rivers If I only knew my master was well and had you with [*sic*] I should be quite happy to get my master to say something for you on his letter for it would comfort to me to hear from you all our fellow servants are in good health and spirit and all desire their love to you and accept love and good wishes for you and my children and relations and friends May the Lord Bless you my dear wife and may we meet again is the prayer of your husband Dave Brownrigg.

Coexisting with wonder at the sights, the mountains, the rocks, and the rivers, there was worry in Dave Brownrigg's words. He expressed his concern about his owner's health; he knew that Richard Brownrigg's death could result in the sale of his slaves, bringing about permanent separation of Dave's family. He wanted his owner to be healthy, and he wanted to know that his wife was still with him and had not been sold. He prayed that he would see her again. Dave Brownrigg's only chance to communicate with his wife was through two white Brownriggs, the one who wrote his words and the one who would, he hoped, read them to his wife. He depended on them to make any contact with his wife and other relatives.

Author Holley dictated the following letter to his wife:

This is for my wife Amy to let you know that myself and children are well and I was highly glad to hear from home but was sorry to hear that master kept sick we have good time all well and hearty and all desire their love to you and all our friends I hope to see you and the children in the Spring the children and Polly are well also. The baby grows a little they all send a heep of love to you and the children Your husband Author Holley.

Author Holley was headed to Mississippi without his wife or children. Like Dave Brownrigg, Holley was concerned about their owner's health.

Rose dictated a letter to her husband:

My Dear Husband Hardy

I write to let you know that I think of you often and wish to see you very bad I have good health and the children are too but feel hard a little but I see so many sights and have so many good things I wish you all had some of them I hope yet to see you Maria joins me in love to you and all of friends your loveing wife Rose.

More so than Dave Brownrigg or Author Holley, Rose stated how deeply she missed her husband. He was alone; she had the children. She felt "hard a little," perhaps angry, perhaps bitter, but she did not go further, switching immediately to the sights she had seen and the good things. Such a shift may have served several purposes: to keep herself positive and distracted from her feelings, to assure her husband of her well-being, and of course, to keep her amanuensis convinced of her contentment so that Sparkman would continue to send messages on her behalf.

Sandy sent a message to his wife:

> My Dear Wife Anis I know you would be glad to hear from me and the boys we get along very well the Boys obey me very well I feel very anxious about you but hope to hear you are doing well I long to see all in the Spring we get on very fast in our journey and expect to reach our home in four weeks all join me in love to you and all our friends your affectionate husband Sandy.

Sandy had his sons with him, but his wife had been left behind.

Sarah Sparkman also included a letter from Grace to her mother and sister:

> My Dear Mamy and Sister
>
> I was mighty glad to hear last night and [sic] master was better and sister had her baby our relations are all well that are with us and send a heap of love to you and the children. Uncle Jacob say tell his wife he is well and give his love to her and the children Anis—gives her love to her children and she is very well and all the children keep well they are all satisfied.
>
> Your affectionate Daughter Grace.

The messages reveal a web of friends and relations. Grace missed her mother and sister, and she also sent messages from Jacob to his wife and children, and from Anis to her children. Some of them were fortunate to move with some family members, but all of them left family behind. They left mothers, sisters, children, husbands, wives, and a wider community of friends and neighbors. The messages also conveyed a range of emotions: Rose felt hard, Sandy felt anxious, Author Holley was hopeful, and Dave would be comforted by hearing from his family. Some expressed concern about Richard Brownrigg's health, at least partly because they knew that the death of an owner left slaves more vulnerable to sale or distribution than ever. They were relying on him to come to Mississippi and bring their relatives with him. Some of these husbands and wives belonged to the same owner. They had not engaged in abroad marriages, yet they were being separated. Still, even as they were divided up—some to remain in North Carolina, others to make the journey to Mississippi—they were probably relieved that they had not been sold away. They were going south, but with the family to whom they and many of their closest relatives belonged. This promised a possibility of communication—at least a few of them could impose upon their owners to write on their behalf. Believing their relatives would come in the spring, some saw this as a temporary separation.[60]

Those whose relatives did not already belong to the Brownriggs hoped for a change. From the road, they attempted to negotiate sales and purchases that might reunite them with their loved ones. In a later letter, for example, R. T. Hoskins, one of the white men on the journey, reported, "Dick C sends his love to his wife and children and wishes you to buy them if possible" and "Brommel wishes his wife to come to Miss[issippi] if you can purchase her."[61] Another letter stated, "George Rumbo says please buy his boy of B. White."[62]

On December 9, 1835, the group arrived in Columbus, Mississippi, in Lowndes County. The black people had walked for nearly two months. They arrived expecting to find Richard Brownrigg. Evidently the plan had been for him to travel by ship or to use a shorter route than they had taken with the coffle. William Sparkman was eager to deliver Brownrigg's slaves to him and be done with the responsibility for any problems or injuries, but he learned instead that Richard Brownrigg had hired an overseer who would be in charge of the people. Sparkman was wary of handing them over, not having been given any guidance from Brownrigg; instead, *he* put the enslaved people to work. "I have bought axes for your hands," he wrote. Then, "your hands commenced this morning on the negro houses." They were beginning to build the houses in which they would live. They asked to be remembered to all, Sparkman said; they "appeared to be considerable disappointed in your not coming."[63]

Some weeks later a much more dramatic Thomas Brownrigg sent this pronouncement to his brother: "My Dear Brother, I arrived here after a very bad and disagreeable travel of 54 days and found no letter from you or any person from the Old North State but after a few days I heard with much supprise that your health and that of my Brother John was little or no better and I was at first very much temted to return but since conversing with Mr.

Amis I have concluded to stay and try what I can do." Then he turned to the feelings of the enslaved people: "Your negroes and mine were thunderstruck when I told them that you would not come out untill the summer and they think now that they are to be sold but I have told them to the contrary."[64] The enslaved people were thunderstruck because they knew that so much of what would become of them and the relatives they left behind in North Carolina depended on their owner. The postponement of his arrival was cause for grave concern.

Thomas's assurances did not mollify the slaves. As time passed, they continued to worry about their families in North Carolina. In January, Sarah Sparkman wrote, "I have a great many messages from the servants they are better satisfied than at first. Anis says she never will be until you all come out. She desires her love to her children says they are all well and her love to Phillis Tom is well now and the baby Violet has two teeth India says please to let her know how her mother and children are in fact they have so much to say that *all* give their love to *all* their friends and their best service to Master and Mistress, Cousin Mary and the children." The people's concern did not subside, and later in January, R. T. Hoskins wrote to Richard Brownrigg, "Some of your negroes think that you will never come out to Mississippi." In March, Thomas Brownrigg wrote to Richard, "The negroes appear very much dejected owing to the sickness in part and part in their thinking still that you are not coming out."[65] Someone had promised these ninety-one people that the relatives they left behind in North Carolina would join them in Mississippi in the spring. They were beginning to realize the lie.

In Mississippi as well as back in North Carolina, the Brownriggs appear to have been experiencing financial difficulties, and of course this compromised the security of the people they owned. In North Carolina, Richard and his wife, Mary, boarded with acquaintances, and they were down to one servant girl and no slaves. "We sold our trifeling girl Caroline and family for $808. And now hire a free girl very smart for $4 per month and she clothes herself," he wrote. When Richard asked Thomas to pay a debt in Columbus, Thomas responded that he had no money and was entangled in his own financial problems with the sheriff. "Do not write to me any more about money," he told his brother, "or to authorize me to sell some of your negroes, which authority I would despise to use." The status of the black people was insecure; they were, as ever, vulnerable to being sold, and they knew it.[66]

Richard Brownrigg finally arrived in Columbus, Mississippi, on July 20, 1836. It is not clear who traveled with him, but it is evident that the people whom the slaves had left behind in North Carolina did not. Dave Brownrigg's wife did not arrive; Rose's husband was not there, and neither were Author Holley's wife or Grace's mother or sister. Brownrigg wrote in his travel journal, "My negroes pleased to see me. Many sick and all had been displeased with the muddiness of the county and made many complaints about it." The people were silent about their missing family members. Several of them had been ill since their arrival eight months earlier; some had colds or pleurisy due to working in water. It had been a cold, wet winter, and they had been working to clear the fields to start Richard Brownrigg's new cotton plantation. Perhaps they complained only about the muddiness because that is what their owner would tolerate; he may not have taken their complaints about their missing family members as lightly.[67]

What became of the enslaved people left behind in North Carolina is murky at best. In 1837, two years after arriving in Lowndes County, Richard Brownrigg owned seventy-nine slaves who produced sixty bales of cotton on 400 acres of land in Columbus, Mississippi. This number suggests that the slaves left in North Carolina, including Dave's wife and Rose's husband, had never made it to Mississippi. They and the other enslaved people would have had to come to terms with the permanence of their losses.[68]

As the finality of separation from their husbands and wives set in, enslaved African Americans had to make agonizing decisions about how to cope, how to go on with their lives. They may have negotiated with owners to remain together, they may have relied on owners' false promises, or they may have simply hoped that even with the prevalence of separation they would somehow be exempt. At some point, however, they had to face their circumstances and make choices about how to move forward emotionally. Individuals sometimes found themselves at a crossroads, deciding whether to continue to hold on to the hope of seeing a loved one again or to begin a new relationship. It was likely a process: a period of holding on, a moment of letting go, times of looking back, wondering and hoping. Your husband was not dead, but he was gone. Your wife still loved you, but she had left. It must have been confounding to struggle with the feelings.

Yet people did go on, and somehow African American families continued, even after slaveowners and slave traders tore families apart. Individuals chose to continue living, forming new families and even loving again.[69] A letter from James Tate, an enslaved man in West Point, Georgia, to his wife in Mobile, Alabama, takes us to the particular crossroads where he began his process of capitulating to the permanence of their separation. Her owner had moved her nearly 250 miles away. He was still negotiating, and he was still hoping; but he was also realizing for himself and forewarning her that he could not stand frozen in place forever, but might one day move on.

On February 4, 1863, Tate sent a letter: "My dear Wife, I received your very welcome letter two weeks ago, you must not think hard of me for not answering it sooner." He explained that his owner's wife had been writing for him but the owner found out and forbade it. Tate told his wife that his owner thought "it was just keeping you and me miserable to be writing letters to each other for he said that your Mars John would never let you come to see me and that he never expected to let me go to see you that Mobiel was too far off for him to ever let me go there, and that he was going to persuade me to marry another woman that is living here and that he wants you to marry some other man that is living in Mobiel." Then Tate quickly added, "Now I am just telling you what Master said it is not what I say for I can assure you my dear wife I have not thought or said anything like that yet for I have never seen any other woman here that I could love." Tate wanted to put forth his owner's wishes but attempted to assure his wife that as of now he had no inclination to fulfill them. The "yet" was highly significant, though; it was a signal that things could change. Although he still loved his wife, he had opportunities to become involved with other women. "Since you left me," he told her, "there are several colloured ladies here that I have been told are in love with me and I know that I could get either one of them if I want them— but I do not want any of them, and I don't think master or any body else can pursuade me to marry again, for I think that I would be a very unhappy man to be married to another woman and to always be thinking and studying about *my dear wife* and *dear little children* that are in *Mobiel*."[70] He *thought* he could not be persuaded to remarry; he *thought* he would not be happy with anyone else. He was not sure.

Tate then turned from thinking about future possibilities with another woman back to ways to bring about reunification with his wife and children. He urged her to persuade her owner to hire her out to someone in West Point. He was certain that several families there would be willing to hire her. In fact, he told her, "I am willing to hire you my self and pay your Mars John *ten* dollars a month and clothe *you* and the *children* myself just to have *you* with me for I can not bear to be seperated from you any longer I have been praying every night that some thing would turn up to bring you and me togeather but I am afraid now the way master talks that we will never get to see each other again in this world my dear wife and I am getting more and more unhappy every day." It was difficult for Tate to hold on to hope. He was hired out, working in a grocery store, so he had some income; but $10 per month would have been a great expense for him, and in any event, such an arrangement needed permission from his wife's owner. His wife had probably already pleaded with her owner to no avail. Having his slave working on her own so far away would have raised concerns over how he would control her actions and would have jeopardized his ability to collect his portion of her income. Allowing a slave and her two children to go 250 miles away was tantamount to not owning them at all.

Tate's hope faded into frustration, and his initiative seemed to be losing out to debilitation. He had done everything that he thought possible and seemed to think that any resolution would now have to come from his wife's owner. "It seems," he told his wife, "the longer I am separated from you and my children the worst off I get and I am more unhappy about you now *dear wife* than when you first left me. Master says that if he had of moved off and taken me away from you that he would try and let me go back to see you sometimes but as it was the other way that you were taken away from me— he thinks that your Mars John and Miss Caroline ought to let you come to see me once a year any how." He then offered a proposition to make the visits possible. "I would be always willing to pay your expences here and back if you would only come and I would always give you a nice dress and some money and get something for my children too," he wrote. Tate, it seemed, was willing to settle for even an annual visit. It appears, too, that he thought he had to convince his wife to want to come to see him, and he endeavored to lure her with the promise of material things. Perhaps he thought these promises would induce her to plead more convincingly with her owner.

Tate alerted his wife that she might not hear from him often because his mistress was writing this one last letter without her husband's knowledge. He closed the letter with two important messages. He sent his love to his children: "My dear wife, you must kiss Jimmie and little Mary Olivia for me and tell them their Papa would give any thing he had in this world to see them both." Then he addressed once more what must have seemed more and more inevitable: "If I ever do take a notion to marry again my dear wife I shall write and let you know all about it but I do not think I shall ever take such a notion again directly not if I always feel like I do now, for I can not think of any other woman nor love any other but *you* my dear wife." He ended with "Your devoted husband. James Tate."

As James Tate edged toward a new life, he kept looking back, trying desperately to hold on to the old one he did not want to relinquish. Here lay the power of slavery and slaveholders; two men held control over his life and the lives of his wife and children. His wife's owner had made a decision to move farther south and west, from Georgia to Alabama, a decision that had a momentous effect on the Tate family. His wife was maintaining communication with him; he had received a letter from her recently, so presumably the strong affection was mutual. Still, they did not control their own lives, and neither owner was willing to accommodate their desire to be together as a family. The expectation was that these two people who loved each other would each marry someone else and move on as though they had not experienced this love or this loss. Indeed, slaveholding whites considered enslaved couples' commitments and feelings so trivial that even some of their churches ruled it acceptable for slaves to remarry after being separated by sale.[71]

Some people moved on by both holding on to the memory of a spouse *and* marrying again.[72] A letter from John E. Beck in Pike County, Mississippi, demonstrates how someone who had moved forward could also look back with longing. In July 1856 Beck sent a letter by hand, most likely through a member of the white family to whom he belonged. Although he addressed the letter to his former wife's owner, in truth it was a love letter to Malinda. He first paid his respects to the owner: "Mr Elick Farer Dear friend after a tender of my respects to you, and your mother and all the rest of the family etc. I pen you these few lines to inform you that I am in good health hoping this will find you enjoying the same blessing. I am going to write your negroes a few lines and I will request if yu pleas [*sic*] to write me an answer for them and direct it to Osyka Mississippi Pike." Then he got to the purpose of his letter, the opportunity to reconnect with his former wife: "Give my respects and love to Malinda my former wife, Malinda I wish to know how many children you have and who you have got for a husband and if there is anything in my power that I can do for you let me know and I will do it." Just as slaveowners expected and sometimes demanded that separated spouses remarry, the people involved also anticipated that their loved ones would form new families. Beck expected this of Malinda and indeed had done so himself. "Malinda I maried a very fine looking yellow girl," he wrote. "I thought that I could enjoy my self as well as I did with you but it was a mistake, we lived together about two years and dissolved and quit, we have been quit about six months."[73]

John Beck's letter raises a number of issues. First is the matter of privacy. Although he wrote his letter himself, even apologizing for his spelling and writing, it was being sent via his owner's family and would be delivered to his wife's owner. Beck therefore had to pay his respects to the owner before addressing himself to the true intended recipient, and he wrote his message to his former wife fully knowing that he had to rely on someone else to read it to her. This question of privacy was there for the enslaved Brownriggs as well as for James Tate, all of whom relied on whites to both write and read their letters. Second, this appears to be another example of the division of a plantation, perhaps similar to the Brownrigg situation. Beck and Malinda had once lived in the same place, perhaps had belonged to the same owner. The fact that the letter went by hand strongly suggests that Beck's current owner knew Malinda's owner, and they were quite likely related. Malinda and her owner, Alexander K. Farrar, lived in Adams County, Mississippi, a few counties away from Beck in Pike County. Beck sent regards from a woman named Mary Ann to her husband. He also updated the husband on the fact that Mary Ann now had four children in addition to the one they had had together. Malinda, John Beck, Mary Ann, and her husband had all once belonged to the same community of enslaved people.

Most significant, of course, is the matter of the relationship between Beck and Malinda. Beck thought he had moved on, but he longed for Malinda still. One can't help wondering why he decided to tell her about his failed marriage. They had not communicated for some time, apparently for at least the two and a half years since he married the "very fine looking yellow girl," yet he reached out to her now. It may be that breaking up with his second wife stirred memories of Malinda and forced him to come to terms with his persistent love for her. Perhaps he wanted Malinda to know that emotionally he remained faithful to her. Perhaps even though neither he nor Malinda had the power to reunite, just acknowledging his love brought him a moment of hope, as though the strength of his love could bring them back together.

Some people refused to go on the mandated journeys of separation with white families or traders. As happened with Charles Ball's father, who descended into depression and then escaped after his wife and most of his children were sold away, the threat of imminent sale and separation motivated some people to run. In some instances slaves intended to absent themselves from their owners' premises temporarily; other times they aimed to escape permanently. Some people escaped to return to family members from whom they had been separated; others made the decision to escape from slavery altogether despite the consequence of leaving family behind. Some decided to run after losing their family. Henry Box Brown, whose dramatic escape made him famous, fled slavery after he watched his wife and children leave on the journey that took them away from him forever.

Brown, who lived in Virginia, had been married for twelve years when his wife's owner sold her and their children to a trader. Brown recalled the last time he saw his family: "I stationed myself by the side of the road," he wrote, "along which the slaves, amounting to three hundred and fifty, were to pass. The purchaser of my wife was a Methodist minister, who was about starting for North Carolina. Pretty soon five waggon-loads of little children passed, and looking at the foremost one, what should I see but a little child, pointing its tiny hand towards me, exclaiming, 'There's my father; I knew he would come and bid me good-bye.' It was my eldest child!" Then Brown saw his wife. "She passed, and came near to where I stood," he recalled. "I seized hold of her hand, intending to bid her farewell; but words failed me; the gift of utterance had fled, and I remained speechless. I followed her for some distance, with her hand grasped in mine, as if to save her from her fate, but I could not speak, and I was obliged to turn away in silence."[74]

Having lost his family, Brown focused on finding a way out of slavery. "The first thing that occurred to me," he wrote, "after the cruel separation of my wife and children from me, and I had recovered my senses, so as to know how to act, was, thoughts of freeing myself from slavery's iron yoke. I had suffered enough under its heavy weight, and I determined I would endure it no longer; and those reasons which often deter the slave from attempting to escape, no longer existed in reference to me, for my family were gone, and slavery now had no mitigating circumstances, to lessen the bitterness of its cup of woe." As both owners and enslaved people knew, marriage and family had a tendency to keep people bound to a place. With his family destroyed, Brown no longer had any emotional commitment to quiet his desire to be free. "It is true, as my master had told me," he wrote, "that I could 'get another wife;' but no man, excepting a brute below the human species, would have proposed such a step to a person in my circumstances; and as I was not such a degraded being, I did not dream of so conducting. Marriage was not a thing of personal convenience with me, to be cast aside as a worthless garment, whenever the slaveholder's will required it; but it was a sacred institution binding upon me."[75] Over the next several months, Brown strategized his escape. First he burned his hand with acid so that his overseer would be forced to give him time off from work. Then he devised a plan and enlisted help. His family was sold away in August 1848, and in March 1849 Brown shipped himself by train from Richmond, Virginia, to an abolitionist in Philadelphia in a wooden box measuring 3 feet long by 2 feet wide by 2 feet 6 inches high, with three small holes for air. It was a dramatic move in response to a devastating loss. Brown never found his original family, but he did marry again.[76]

Some people escaped to get back to family members from whom they had been sold. The powerful pull of family and the determination to reunite after separation are evident in the runaway advertisements that slaveowners placed in newspapers.[77] These ads often noted that the owner suspected the escaped slave was heading toward a husband or wife. Owners realized the importance of family in many enslaved people's lives, and when they could, they used the location of relatives as the starting point for their search. The ads ranged from general allusions to relations to more specific references to brothers and sisters, and husbands and wives. When Henry Cobb placed an ad in a Virginia newspaper, he noted that his slave Thornton "was formerly owned by Mr. George Nelson near Warrenton Fauquier County Virginia and is supposed to be lurking in that neighborhood, or Winchester, as he has relatives at or near both places."[78] And when a carpenter named Stephen escaped, his owner suspected that he was likely to be in the neighborhood of Mr. Faber's plantation, as he had relations there.[79]

The ads suggest that a recent sale sometimes provided the impetus to escape. This was a time when people felt dislocated and lonely; they had recently left family behind and had not yet established new connections. Sale could also signal confusion and disruption within the original owner's finances and household, provoking anxiety among enslaved people about what would happen next. Sale to an owner a few miles away could be disruptive but manageable, while sale farther away would change the relationships people had come to rely on. George, an enslaved man in Hampton, Virginia, who, according to his owner, was a house servant and an excellent cook and waiter with "bushy hair which he generally wears platted," escaped shortly after his wife was sold near Craney Island in Norfolk County, Virginia. The owner warned masters of vessels "against harboring or carrying away said negro as the law will be enforced against them."[80] This ad points to one of the interesting aspects of these notices, namely the type of information that owners had about the runaways' families. Not only did they know who and where relatives were; in the case of George, for instance, the owner also knew of current developments affecting his family members—that is, George's wife had recently been sold. Some information owners knew independently—for example, where a slave had been purchased and where he had been raised. As to the sale of George's wife, it may be that George had attempted to enlist the owner's help in purchasing his wife so that they could be together. It is also quite likely that when a slave ran away, owners went to the other people with whom he had lived, to gather leads as to where he would likely go. Within a slave community, someone would know who was important to a fellow slave. As they worked during the day or as they socialized or prayed at night, people would have had conversations about where a sister lived or about a wife being sold in Craney Island. Within that community, people would have told stories of their past and would have shared their memories of lost family members. They would also have shared with someone their dreams for the future, perhaps even their plans for escaping. Depending on whom owners rewarded or threatened, they stood to obtain a great deal of information. They often had a sense of who was attempting to escape slavery altogether and who would remain in the slave states close to family members.

Owners frequently suspected that a runaway slave was "lurking" in the neighborhood of his spouse or other relative. Slaveowner Thomas Davis had those suspicions about Paul, a fifty-year-old man: "I understand Gen. R. Y. Hayne has purchased his wife and children from H. L. Pinckney, Esq. and has them now on his Plantation at Goose Creek, where no doubt, the Fellow is frequently lurking."[81] The ad was still running in the newspaper five months later, nearly a year and a half after Paul had made his escape. A Virginia owner searched for the "headman" of his boat, who absconded when the boat docked in New Canton, Buckingham County, and thought he was "probably lurking about that place, as his wife lives in that neighborhood."[82] In South Carolina, Isaac's owner suspected that he might be "lurking about in some of the neighboring Parishes, where he has a good many acquaintances as he has a wife living in Wraggsborough and sister in Burns's Lane, who are all free he may be harboured by them."[83] Also in South Carolina, Jacob, described as "fond of using high flown language," had recently "absconded without any provocation whatever" from the man to whom he was hired. His owner suspected that "if not lurking about the farms on the Neck, it is most probable he has left the neighborhood of the city, as he has a wife near Mulberry, on Cooper River, and is well known in that neighborhood."[84]

Lurking in the neighborhood went hand in hand with something slave-owners feared: that the escaped slave would be "harbored" by others. Owners expressed concern that a white person or a free person of color might be lending support to the escaped slave. Such was the case with the Barnwell County, South Carolina, owner who offered a $50 reward for the return of his female slave, Tenah, who had escaped some four months earlier. Tenah, he said, "was bought in this city in June last, at a sale of the estate of Vancy's

Negroes, and it is believed from some recent information that she is harbored in this place by a free person." The owner's informants told him "her husband is a free man by the name of William Levy, and resides permanently at Goose Creek, though for two or three months past he has been living in town, and has been seen in her company at the person's house in which she is harbored. It is also understood," the owner noted, "that she has been (perhaps unknowingly,) employed by a white person as a washerwoman."[85]

Being harbored meant that the enslaved person had resources, a support system—people who could find her a job, feed her, provide shelter, or keep an eye and ear out for anyone inquiring about her. Harboring allowed enslaved people to stay away from owners for long periods of time. According to this owner, Tenah had run away to be with her free husband, and they had a support system that made it possible for the couple to remain together. The owner offered extra money for her capture with proof that a white person or a free person of color had harbored her.[86]

Of course, the vast majority of enslaved people did not run away even when faced with imminent separation. Escape was both physically and emotionally daunting. It meant taking more risks than most people could contemplate, and it required enormous resourcefulness to create and execute a plan. It was not easy to leave the small world you knew to venture into a world that you could not even imagine. Bethany Veney, who had been married by the itinerant peddler, recounted the process that she and her husband, Jerry, underwent as they considered escape to evade his imminent sale. Veney and Jerry had entered marriage with more than the knowledge that separation was always a possibility; Jerry's owner actually told them that he had plans to move to Missouri from Virginia, taking Jerry with him. As it happened, though, it was not the move that disrupted their marriage but Jerry's owner's debts. Veney recalled how she learned that she would lose her husband. Her brother-in-law came to see her, and as they talked, she suspected that something was wrong with Jerry. "Is Jerry dead? Is he sold?" she implored, immediately fearing the two worst things that could happen to a loved one.[87]

Jerry and his fellow slaves had been seized for payment of a debt and remained locked in a jail for months as their owner attempted to redeem them. In the end, they were put up for auction, and Frank White, a slave trader, purchased them. White offered to purchase Veney as well, but she realized that being sold to him would not guarantee that she and Jerry would be together in the long term, as the trader could sell them at any time. She made a significant calculation: "If separated," Veney reflected, "what would I do in a strange land? No: I would not go, it was far better for me to stay where, for miles and miles, I knew every one, and every one knew me." She was grounded by the familiar.

Before departing, White allowed Jerry to spend one last night with Veney, during which they tried to work out a plan to escape together; but as Veney recalled, "our utter helplessness overpowered us." They could not think of a way out of their dilemma. "We talked a long time, and tried to devise some plans for our mutual safety and possible escape from slavery altogether," Veney wrote, "but every way we looked, the path was beset with danger and exposure. We were both utterly disheartened." Jerry overstayed his permission and hid from his owner, but because he remained with Veney, he was soon captured. Veney described their parting: "I stifled my anger and grief, brought his little bundle, into which I tucked a testament and catechism some one had given me, and shook hands 'good-by' with him. So we parted *forever*, in this world."[88]

Suffocating grief. Veney stifled her grief and anger, suppressing her emotions in an environment that disallowed them. Instead of crying, she extended her hand in a formal gesture of farewell to the man she loved, the man on whose chest she had cried the night before. Other enslaved people also described repressing their emotions at times of loss. Moses Grandy said that at the sudden loss of his wife, his heart was so full that he could say very little. He could only seek permission from the man who held a gun on him to give her some coins and watch her move away in the trader's coffle. Henry Box Brown said that when he watched his wife and children being taken away, "words failed me, the gift of utterance had fled and I remained speechless. I was obliged," he said, "to turn away in silence."

Thomas H. Jones, who had already lost his family as a nine-year-old child, demonstrated at once the depths of the grief of separation and the limited expression some enslaved people were able to give to those feelings. Jones's wife, Lucilla, and their children were forced to move from Wilmington to Newbern, North Carolina, a distance of more than seventy miles. Jones despaired, and for the third time he contemplated suicide. He had considered it first when he was taken from his parents and siblings as a child; then years later when he realized that all of his family had been sold away and only his old, sick, defeated mother remained; and now, at the loss of his wife and children. "I was tempted to end my wretched life," Jones wrote. "I thought of my dear family by day and by night. A deep despair was in my heart." After a year and a half of separation, Jones saw his family once and only briefly, when Lucilla's owner returned to Wilmington on the way to her new home in Tuscaloosa, Alabama. The family spent one night together. According to

Jones, "Lucilla had pined away under the agony of our separation, even more than I had done. That night she wept on my bosom, and we mingled bitter tears together. The next morning Mrs. Moore embarked on board the packet. I followed my wife and children to the boat, and parted from them without a word of farewell. Our sobs and tears were our only adieu. Our hearts were too full of anguish for any other expression of our hopeless woe. I have never seen that dear family since, or have I heard from them since I parted from them there. God only knows the bitterness of my agony," he wrote, "experienced in the separation of my wife and children from me. The memory of that great woe will find a fresh impression on my heart while that heart shall beat."[89]

This stunned, even stoic silence contrasts with the descriptions of demonstrative mothers who wept and threw themselves on the mercy and compassion of buyers and traders in attempts to hold on to their children. Several interpretations are possible. It may be that this difference was a sign of gendered behavior; after all, the narrators who spoke of separation as children focused on the reactions of their mothers. It is conceivable that the cultures in which enslaved people lived permitted women to more openly express strong passionate feelings of loss and to demonstrate their anguish, while men were expected to hold back, or even to feel less in the first place. But Bethany Veney's experience challenges this gendered interpretation, because just like the men, she remained silent when she lost her spouse. It is possible that it made a difference who was being taken away—a child or a spouse. Perhaps people simply cared more deeply about their children than about their partners. Perhaps, though, they thought that their loud outcry over the loss of a child could have the power to halt the sale and separation. They knew that some owners were likely to sell a mother with her young children and may have believed that they had a chance of stirring compassion within the hearts of the men who purchased and sold them. Losing a husband or a wife, however, was a different story.

Bethany Veney, Moses Grandy, Henry Box Brown, and Thomas Jones were all silenced in their grief. It may be that these enslaved people, faced with separation from a spouse, knew that their pleas would not have been heard. There would be no sympathy for them. Perhaps they had learned the lessons of their vulnerability early in life and thought it would do no good to weep. Owners allowed marriage, even encouraged it, but they also made it clear that there was no permanence in the bond. It certainly was not legal, and owners and traders demonstrated through their actions that the emotional connection between a couple could not compete against monetary considerations. When these people faced slave traders or new purchasers, the possibility of evoking sympathy was even more remote.

The reality is that people expressed their sorrow and their anger and resentment in many different ways, and public expression, whether by a mother or a wife or a husband, was often constrained by the limits of what owners and other whites would tolerate. Even the mothers of infants were sometimes punished for grieving too long and too openly. Contemporary psychologists have come to call this social denial of the right to grieve disenfranchised grief. According to Kenneth J. Doka, who studies death, dying, and grief, "There are circumstances in which a person experiences a sense of loss but does not have a socially recognized right, role, or capacity to grieve. In these cases, the grief is disenfranchised. The person suffers a loss but has little opportunity to mourn publicly." Societies, Doka contends, construct norms, or grieving rules that specify who may grieve, for whom they may grieve, and for how long. Some grief is acknowledged, but other grief is denied or deemed illegitimate when a relationship or the griever is not recognized. In the case of marriage among enslaved people, for example, when Governor Charles J. McDonald instructed his sisters, "I have a negro preacher who marries them for the union to last as long as they live or until it is the pleasure of their owners to separate them," he transmitted his strategy for dampening any expectation of permanence by married slaves. And when Francis Terry Leak's carefully constructed wedding vows purposefully omitted the admonishment "let no man put asunder," he telegraphed to the couple that their marriage could indeed be destroyed at his whim. Both McDonald and Leak would have argued that enslaved couples had no right to weep or complain when the inevitable came to pass. Bethany Veney and the others who lost their spouses would have had to grieve alone or turn to the remaining members of their family and slave community to find empathy and solace.[90]

It is likely, too, that some people remained silent because the pain was unutterable, because they could not find words to give expression to their emotional devastation. As former slave Bayley Wyatt said in a speech he gave after slavery ended, "We would fold our arms and cry, 'O Lord, how long!' and that was all we could say." Some enslaved people experienced a grief so profound that it formed itself into "a hollow silence."[91] Finally, it is possible that some people remained silent because it was the only way they knew to honor the intimacy and significance of their relationships. When John Beck wrote his letter to Malinda, it may be that he had finally found a way to give voice to the feelings that he had stifled and denied for so long.

THREE

Bid 'em in

Get 'em in!
That sun is hot and plenty bright.
Let's get down to business and get home tonight.
Bid 'em in!

Auctioning slaves is a real high art.
Bring that young gal, Roy. She's good for a start.
Bid 'em in! Get 'em in!

Don't mind them tears, that's one of her tricks.
Five fifty's bid and who'll say six?
She's healthy and strong and well equipped.
Make a fine lady's maid when she's properly whipped.
Bid 'em in!

Six! Six fifty! Don't be slow.
Seven is the bid. Gonna let her go.
At seven she's going!
Going!
Gone!
Pull her down Roy, bring the next one on.
Bid 'em in! Get 'em in! Bid 'em in!

OSCAR BROWN JR.

They May See Their Children Again
White Attitudes toward Separation

Their griefs are transient. Those numberless afflictions, which render it
doubtful whether Heaven has given life to us in mercy or in wrath, are less felt,
and sooner forgotten with them. In general, their existence appears to
participate more of sensation than reflection.

THOMAS JEFFERSON, president and slaveowner

With regard to the negroes I possess, left together they promise prosperity:
but to seperate them, they would be trifling. Indeed, they are so related and
intermarried to and with each other, that a seperation is impracticable, without
the most inhuman violences. Among them are twenty working hands, mostly good,
and then about double that number of house and hired servants and children.

JUDGE GEORGE WALTON, signer of the
Declaration of Independence and slaveowner

African Americans described with poignant power the grief they felt at losing
their parents, children, sisters, brothers, husbands, and wives. Whether they
beseeched owners and traders to spare children from separation or stood in
stoic silence in the face of unspeakable grief, the pain was palpable. And in
the midst of these jarring separations there were almost always white people—masters, mistresses, traders, auctioneers, purchasers—participants in
the separations and witnesses to the pain. Into the routine of life in the slave
South came visitors from northern states who stood on the sidelines watching as separations occurred. Although not directly involved, northern men
were curious to see what this anachronistic slave trade was all about. It is
worthwhile to think about these white people, to consider how they perceived the emotional impact of separation on African Americans, and to
gauge their own feelings as they either caused or observed the separation of
enslaved families.

In January 1845 Thomas B. Chaplin began keeping a plantation journal. On January 12 he wrote, "Weather very windy and dry. Went to church. . . . Weather quite windy and chilly—but clear." For the next thirteen years, Chaplin made fairly regular entries, recording and commenting on the weather, his crops, his social activities, and his financial circumstances. In January 1845 Chaplin was twenty-three years old. He had been married for six years. He had four children. He owned 376 acres of land on St. Helena Island off the coast of South Carolina, and he owned between sixty and seventy slaves.[1]

Monday, January 13, brought more than the weather for Chaplin's commentary. He recorded an event that revealed some of his familial connections on St. Helena as well as the financial insecurity that characterized his life. A slave named January, who belonged to Chaplin's mother, brought a message from Chaplin's brother's 1,200-acre plantation, approximately fifty miles away. To satisfy a mortgage, "the sheriff had taken 27 Negroes" from one of the plantations Chaplin's mother owned. Thomas Chaplin firmly believed that this seizure of his mother's slaves was the result of interference from her fourth husband, Robert Baker. Isabella Chaplin Baker was an exceptionally wealthy woman who had inherited plantations and people from her father and her husbands, including her second husband, Saxby Chaplin, Thomas Chaplin's father. In 1845 she owned at least five plantations. At age seventeen Thomas had taken possession of Tombee, the plantation his father left for him, but his father had also left other properties for Thomas and his brother, Saxby, in Isabella's care, and their efforts to protect that property from Richard Baker embroiled Baker and the Chaplins in protracted court battles.[2] Baker, a bankrupt pharmacist, thought he would become wealthy upon marrying Isabella, but her marital contract, drawn up without his knowledge, deprived him of control over her wealth. By devising a marital contract prior to their marriage, Isabella Chaplin Baker undermined South Carolina law that would have handed her property to her new husband.[3] Baker had taken a mortgage on some of Isabella's property shortly after their marriage in June 1843. In January 1845 Thomas Chaplin believed that Baker had convinced the holders of the mortgage that they would have to seize some of her slaves in order to receive what was owed them.[4]

Entangled as Chaplin's wealth and financial well-being were with his mother's, this seizure of slaves was shocking and devastating. He blamed his "vengeful," "low," "vile," "pauper," "bankrupt," and "insect" of a stepfather for instigating "this mean transaction."[5] Competition between Chaplin and his brother with their stepfather for control over Isabella's property in land and slaves continued for years. Debt as well as squabbles between Baker and the

Chaplins resulted in financial losses for the white family, and it brought about disruption of African American lives. In this instance, twenty-seven people would be sold by the sheriff at auction to satisfy creditors. Chaplin did not contemplate in the journal what sale would mean to these people and their families.[6]

For the remainder of the winter and spring, Thomas Chaplin went about the business of running his plantation, fulfilling his civic duties, and socializing with family and friends. He noted that he "killed beef for market" and "killed the fifth hog for bacon this year," though his slaves likely did the actual killing. He noted the birth of a new slave and demonstrated his power as master to name the child: "Rose was confined last night and brought forth a boy. I named him David." He went deer hunting and fishing, and he served as the prosecutor in a trial of an enslaved man, "Old Curry, an old doctor and fortune teller" charged with assaulting another slave. He drilled with his militia company. His slaves packed bags of Sea Island cotton to take across the river to Beaufort, South Carolina, where it would be sold to merchants, likely for shipment to textile mills in Liverpool or New England. In February he noted "much sickness among the little Negroes." In March and April the slaves planted sugarcane, potatoes, and eighteen acres of cotton, and Chaplin had a long talk with his mother regarding disposal of her property. He depended on her to help keep him afloat.[7]

On May 3, Chaplin spent a lot of time worrying about the weather. St. Helena was experiencing a drought that affected his crops and livestock. "Everything is suffering for want of rain," he told his journal. "The little cotton that is up is dying. Potatoes and sugarcane also dying. The corn looks green in spots, but not growing. Water is getting scarce. My pump is almost dry—it sucks every evening. Nearly every pump & well in Beaufort has gone dry." Then he got to the matter that was causing him even more concern than the drought. Rain might come in time to save his crops, but this matter had ripened beyond intervention. "Trouble gathers thicker & thicker around me," he wrote. "I will be compelled to send about ten prime Negroes to town next Monday, to be sold. I do this rather than have them seized and sold in Beaufort by the sheriff—or rather sacrificed." Chaplin had decided to send ten enslaved people to a dealer in Charleston who would sell them on consignment. By so doing, he hoped to sidestep a levy of his assets by the sheriff. He could exercise a modicum of control by selling the people in Charleston.[8]

Seizure of slave property had now come directly to Chaplin's door, and he paused, as he had not done earlier, to reflect on his feelings about this development. He reflected, too, on the impact sale would have on the enslaved people. "I never thought that I would be driven to this very unpleasant extremity. Nothing can be more mortifying and grieving to a man than to select out some of his Negroes to be sold," he wrote. "You know not to whom, or how they will be treated by their new owners. And Negroes that you find no fault with—to separate families, mothers & daughters, brothers & sisters—all to pay for your own extravagances. People will laugh at your distress," he worried, "and say it serves you right, you lived beyond your means, though some of the same never refused to partake of that hospitality and generosity which caused me to live beyond my means. Those beings I shall find out and will then know how to treat them."[9]

In the space of a few lines Chaplin's thoughts raced from one priority to another. He moved from concern about the enslaved people to concern for his own social standing. He found his situation "mortifying and grieving." He was mortified by the humiliation that public knowledge of his fragile finances would bring. He grieved because of the pain the ten people and their families would feel, but there is a sense that he also grieved at having to "select out" some of his assets for liquidation. These were the same assets whose labor could enable him to produce crops and achieve some level of solvency. He thought about the feelings of the people whose worlds would become unmoored; through no fault of their own they would lose their loved ones. Then he considered his own responsibility for this financial and emotional disaster. His social extravagances, his spending on entertainment, had encumbered his property, and within a slave society that meant enslaved people would have to pay. Here is the debt that so many enslaved people blamed for their sale and separation. This is what Jim Allen from Alabama meant when he said, "Mars John Bussey drunk my mother up."[10] Finally, Chaplin contemplated how he would punish his social peers who would judge him harshly. They had enjoyed his extravagances, but he was certain they would relish his financial embarrassment and criticize his failure to maintain mastery over his finances. Borrowing and indebtedness were customary among antebellum planters, but this society that valued mastery and honor expected a man to meet his obligations. Community opinion carried great weight in this white southern concept of honor. Chaplin lived on a small island on which white family and social lines crossed and recrossed. Everyone would soon be aware of his predicament.[11]

The seventy or so people whom Chaplin owned would soon be affected by his troubles, too. The people in the slave quarters would learn of the impending sale that would disrupt their lives. They would begin to fret about whom Chaplin would send away. Would he sell Hannah, who had been sick frequently since January and who Chaplin thought was pretending? Would he sell Louisa, who had also been ill a great deal during the winter and early spring? If he was not benefiting from their labor due to illness or feigned illness, might he not decide to include them in the group to be sold? Peggy had also been sick since January, but by now Chaplin and everyone else on the plantation realized that she was pregnant, and big enough to have twins. Peggy may have felt fairly confident that Chaplin would not sell her and the children she carried, who would become his assets. But what of Rose and her new baby boy, whom Chaplin named David? He might see them as investments for the future, or he could see the baby as a drain on his resources for many years before he became productive. Or he might consider selling them together, as the infant would demonstrate Rose's fertility and therefore bring him a larger sum. Ben might feel confident that he would not be sold, because Chaplin trusted him enough to allow him to go duck hunting with a gun. Robert, Chaplin's slave driver, actually belonged to Isabella Chaplin Baker, so he would not be sold.[12] The truth was, though, no one within the slave quarters could feel much of a sense of security, because even if an individual were not sold, a close relative might be. Anyone selected would leave behind family and community on St. Helena.

The next day, May 4, Chaplin stayed home from church with a toothache. He may have already begun to hide from his judges, the family and friends who would mock his distress. Sunday brought no rest to his slaves, however. "The Negroes pulled up the floor to one of the outhouses & killed 56 rats— fine Sunday's work," he commented. "A few clouds flying about. Wind very fresh but no rain. Things look worse and worse. Rode over to J. L. Chaplin's to get him to take the Negroes up to Beaufort for me tomorrow." Chaplin planned to have his cousin and overseer, J. L. Chaplin, take the ten black people by boat to Beaufort and from there to Charleston. He hoped the timing would be such that the overseer would elude the sheriff who intended to seize the enslaved people and auction them off right there in Beaufort. Chaplin wanted to sell them in the larger Charleston market to get the best price. He would then be able to pay his debt and have funds remaining.[13]

That evening the overseer and an assistant arrived on the plantation. Chaplin had made his selection and sent the two men to carry out the separations. "After they had eaten dinner, they went to the Negro houses & took 10 Negroes, viz.—Prince, Sib, Moses, Louisa, Tom, Hannah, Paul, Titus, Marcus & Joe. Carried them over to the Riverside where Clark's boat was. Got them on board, but it was so rough the boat nearly swamped, so they had to come on shore & stop until the next day." The rough waters provided a brief reprieve for Hannah and Louisa, whose suspected malingering had caught up with them. They and the other eight people would have one more night on the island with their families.

"I cannot express my feelings on seeing so many faithful Negroes going away from me forever, not for any fault of their own but for my extravagance," Chaplin wrote in his journal that night. "It is a dearly bought lesson, and I hope I will benefit by it. The Negroes did not appear at all inclined to get off, but apparently quite willing and in good spirits, particularly Prince & Paul. I hope they will bring a good price in Charleston where I have sent them under the charge of Wm. B. Fickling, to be sold, and that I will not have to sell any more."[14] Here again, Chaplin reflected on his feelings as well as those of the enslaved people, and he invoked his own pecuniary interest. He knew that to the slaves, sale and separation were tantamount to punishment, but, he said, they had done nothing to deserve it. Again he blamed himself and hoped he had now learned the lesson of the price of excessive spending and would avoid future behavior that would incur debt and the resulting forced sale of slaves. He grieved their loss of family, and he grieved his own loss of self-control. But for now, he mostly hoped that their sale would enrich him.

Though acknowledging how sad he felt to see "so many faithful Negroes going away" forever, Chaplin also sought to underplay the emotional effect of separation on the people to be sold. To him they seemed to be in good spirits, willing to leave the island. This may indeed have been the case for some of the people. If Prince and Paul were young boys, for example, they may not have fully realized the permanence of their departure. Or as former slave Jacob Stroyer suggested, some people were simply happy to leave their owners even when they did not know what they would face in the market. Describing a scene of separation, Stroyer wrote, "While some were weeping, others were fiddling, picking banjo, and dancing as they used to do in their cabins on the plantations. Those who were so merry had very bad masters, and even though they stood a chance of being sold to one as bad or even worse yet they were glad to be rid of the one they knew."[15] So it was possible that some of the slaves were happy to leave.

But Chaplin's actions reveal that he did not quite believe that these particular people were at peace with their predicament. Just as he was afraid and ashamed to face his white peers on the island, Chaplin also hid from the black people. He sent the overseer, J. L. Chaplin, and an assistant into the slave quarters to take the people. He would not be the one to face them or their husbands or wives, their mothers and fathers, their sisters and brothers, or their children on a Sunday afternoon. He would not point to them or call the names of the people who would be abruptly taken away. He would not watch as they gathered their few belongings and said goodbye. Instead, the two hired men took the people onto the boat. It is difficult to even place Chaplin in the picture well enough to see where he stood to observe Prince's and Paul's reactions. The house at Tombee sat only yards from the water, so perhaps he peeked from behind the drapes.[16]

The next day, May 5, Chaplin followed the slaves to Beaufort but, once again, did not face them. "Went to Beaufort. Could not go down to the boat to see the negroes off, but am glad it is all over for it is the most unpleasant thing I have ever had to do, and truly hope it may never occur again." Chaplin does not explain why he "could not" go to the boat. He does not say whether he physically could not because he was busy somewhere else, or if his shame and guilt would not allow it. Perhaps it was both. Perhaps he busied himself to avoid the looks and pleas of his slaves. Perhaps he hid to avoid the humiliation.

Chaplin's expression of remorse over selling slaves was quite unusual but not unique among slaveholders. Among the few sources that express slaveowners' feelings about selling slaves, some show ambivalence, guilt, and a sense of having betrayed the people they owned. In a letter to her brother, one slaveowner disclosed, much as Chaplin did, her reluctance to sell her slaves. "My Dear Brother," Catherine Percy began her letter, "I never take up my pen to write to you but I have some obligation to thank you for." And she thanked him now for his "trouble in the sale of the negroes." She had wanted to sell them for years, she said, "but such was my concern for them that I never should have had resolution to have done it had I been on the spot for it requires more courage than I am mistress of to stand against their entreaties." In other words, she, like Chaplin, could not manage the sale herself because she knew that sale and the resulting separations would hurt the enslaved people, and she knew how difficult it would be to withstand their pleas to be kept together. Like Chaplin, she needed a middleman to manage the sale, to do the actual selling and separating, and her brother stepped in to do the job. In the long run, though, she concluded that her procrastination had paid off financially. "They have more than doubled the interest for I think they have sold most extravagantly high & I am so happy that it is over for though at this distance I felt senseably [sic] when the day arrived that they were sold."[17] Even though she had maintained her physical distance from the people being sold, Percy reported that she experienced intense feelings on the day they were sold. These feelings could have been of shame, guilt, pity, or sadness. Some whites boasted of never selling slaves or separating families precisely because they realized the horror and pain slaves felt at losing their families and because they wanted to be seen as loving and caring patriarchs and, in some cases, matriarchs. But compassionate self-image aside, money generally won out over sentiment. And again, like Chaplin, although Percy acknowledged that the slaves did not want to be sold, she relished the funds that their sale brought her. For both of these slaveowners, self-interest outweighed compassion.[18]

Both Percy and Chaplin expressed relief that their emotional turmoil had ended. "I am so happy it's over," Percy wrote her brother. "Am glad it is all over," Chaplin told his journal. They were sensitive to the feelings of the enslaved people, yet they focused on their own discomfort, which ended when the transactions were concluded. But it was not over for the enslaved people. Chaplin could convince himself that the people who left the plantation were content, but he could not avoid eventually facing the people at home whose relatives he had sent away. He could not completely ignore their expressions of grief, but here too, he began the process of distancing himself emotionally. He did not want to be reminded of their pain when he encountered them inside his house or in the yard or in the potato or cotton or sugarcane fields, and so in his mind and in his journal, he attempted to tamp down their pain, to abbreviate their suffering so as to ease his own guilt and discomfort and to dull his empathy. "The Negroes at home are quite disconsolate," he wrote on May 5, "but this will soon blow over. They may see their children again in time."[19]

To alleviate his feelings of guilt, Chaplin needed to believe it would blow over, that they would soon forget. In suggesting that the enslaved families' pain would be short-lived, Chaplin was in step with prominent white thinkers of the eighteenth and nineteenth centuries. By the time Chaplin inherited his father's land and slaves, he was already also heir to notions of white supremacy and black degradation that had been constructed over two centuries by some of the country's most prominent citizens. Thomas Jefferson, for example, wrote in his treatise *Notes on the State of Virginia* that black people felt less deeply than did whites. "Their griefs are transient," Jefferson wrote. "Those numberless afflictions, which render it doubtful whether Heaven has given life to us in mercy or in wrath, are less felt, and sooner forgotten with them. In general, their existence appears to participate more of sensation than reflection."[20] Jefferson suggested that whereas in the face of a tragic loss a white person would question why God had placed him on earth, this question would not arise for black people because they felt pain superficially and only briefly.

Part of the justification for enslaving Africans and their descendants lay in this assertion that blacks lacked the sensitivity and the capacity to feel emotional pain as white people did. Seventy years after Jefferson, Thomas R. R. Cobb, a prominent proslavery legal scholar from Georgia, expressed very similar sentiments regarding blacks. "His passions and affections are seldom very strong, and are never very lasting," Cobb claimed. "The dance will allay his most poignant grief, and a few days blot out the memory of his most bitter bereavement. His natural affection is not strong, and consequently he is cruel to his own offspring, and suffers little by separation from them."[21]

Chaplin's denial of long-term grief had much in common with Jefferson's and Cobb's sentiments; but Chaplin was also ambivalent, and his journal entry subtly betrayed the shallowness of the notion that the family members left behind on St. Helena would soon recover from their losses. When he hoped, just as they did, that they would see their children again, he implicitly acknowledged that their grief would likely last a long time. If he did not think his slaves felt long-lasting pain and longing, he would have had no reason to hope for reunification. This implicit acknowledgment of prolonged grief and depth of feeling among the enslaved people resembled the sentiments of Judge George Walton, a contemporary of Jefferson's, a signer of the Declaration Independence, and governor of Georgia. Like Chaplin, Walton was in deep debt when he wrote to a business colleague about the steps he had taken to meet the demands of his creditors. He was prepared to sell land, but he balked when it came to the possibility of separating and selling some of his slaves. "With regard to the negroes I possess," he wrote, "left together they promise prosperity: but to seperate them, they would be trifling. Indeed, they are so related and intermarried to and with each other, that a seperation is impracticable, without the most inhuman violences. Among them are twenty working hands, mostly good, and then about double that number of house and hired servants and children." Here, much like Chaplin, Walton acknowledged the significance of family relations among the people he owned, and he said he thought it would be inhuman to separate them. Still, when we read his letter carefully, it is clear that although he considered the slaves' emotional lives, he, like Chaplin, also resisted separation out of economic self-interest; selling the slaves would negatively affect his ability to raise a crop and improve his financial well-being.[22]

With only seventy slaves, Chaplin would have known each one individually. He had been face-to-face with these people when he walked through his cotton fields or gave out a clothing ration, or when they handed him his mail or served him a meal or swept his yard. He would have known family groupings, too. Although his journal does not fill in these details, he likely knew who would mourn most the loss of Toby or Sib, who would care about Moses or Prince. Before the families they left behind could even fully come to terms with their loss, though, he was eager to move on and detach himself from their pain and his guilt. But if the sixty people remaining on his plantation were like others who experienced separation, some of them would continue to feel the pain, to talk about it among themselves, to live in fear of when another sale would come, and to wonder where their family members had gone. Some would hope that they would indeed see each other again, and they would tell their children stories that kept memories of loved ones alive.

The Charleston slave market did brisk business in the spring of 1845 when Thomas Chaplin's slaves arrived to be sold. Several advertisements attesting to the condition of the trade appeared in Charleston's largest newspaper, the *Courier*, that week. On Saturday morning, May 10, Thomas Ryan, one of the largest traders in the city, offered a long list of people, including a boy 15 years old who was skilled as a tailor; a "young woman, seamstress and ladies' maid with her son, 6 years old"; a 17-year-old girl who was a house servant; two "single girls, 9 and 12 years old"; an elderly woman who was a "good cook, washer and ironer"; a single boy, 10 years old; and a 45-year-old man who was a "field hand and good axeman." The ad claimed "the above are all Carolina Negroes, accustomed to living in the low country." This meant they were used to the labor and climate of the low country and likely had experience working on rice or cotton plantations. St. Helena, where Chaplin's ten slaves had lived, was in the low country. Slave trader J. M. Gilchrist offered "Eighty Negroes at Private Sale," and he also sought to purchase even more slaves whom he would sell for a profit: "NEGROES WANTED," his ad read, "Persons wishing to dispose of SLAVE PROPERTY, may obtain the highest market price for their property by applying to John M. Gilchrist."[23]

In this vigorous market, sales were made in no time. On May 12, exactly one week after the ten people left St. Helena, Chaplin wrote in his journal, "Sent John to Beaufort, being very anxious to hear from Fickling." Chaplin need not have been anxious because he wrote later that day, "John returned after I had gone to bed, brought a note from Fickling stating 7 Negroes were sold to a man near Georgetown named Cowen. Marcus, Prince & Sib had not yet been sold." Hannah, Louisa, Tom, Moses, Paul, Titus, and Joe may have felt some comfort in having been sold together. Still, Cowen was from

Georgetown, a rice-producing area with a bustling seaport 110 miles north-east of St. Helena, approximately 60 miles north of Charleston—a world away from their families, for people who were not free to move about. The remaining slaves, Marcus, Prince, and Sib, may have been sold later to live near Charleston or to be taken to any of the places where people sold in Charleston ended up, including New Orleans or Shreveport, Louisiana; Georgia; Mississippi; Nashville, Tennessee; or Alabama.[24]

Chaplin's slaves joined hundreds of other enslaved people in the market. Some were local people being sold by owners; traders had purchased others in the Upper South states of Virginia, Maryland, and North Carolina, and they waited to be sold again. In 1845, slave auctions in Charleston still took place in the open in front of the Old Exchange or Customhouse building on East Bay near Broad Street. William Fickling, a lawyer and magistrate and Chaplin's agent, would have wanted to get the highest price possible for each one, because out of that sale price he would receive his commission. In keeping with customary practice, he or a trader would have had them washed and oiled and perhaps would have provided them with new clothing, all to make a good impression on potential purchasers. He might have questioned them to determine their skills and experiences and told them how they should present themselves to bidders—what they should disclose and what they should withhold. At the same time, some of the ten may have had their own ideas about how they wanted to be seen, and they may have attempted to intervene in their own sales, hoping to be purchased by someone who lived nearby or who appeared to be or had a reputation for being a decent human being. Purchase by a trader, they knew, meant there was no telling where they might end up; it could be in the low country or on a rice or cotton or sugarcane plantation in Alabama, Mississippi, Louisiana, or Georgia. Perhaps Prince, Sib, and Marcus, Chaplin's as-yet-unsold slaves, had behaved in a way that made them unappealing to buyers; perhaps they had impressed potential buyers as troublesome property. Or perhaps they were too old or too young.[25]

The people from St. Helena entered a public spectacle in the slave market that drew many white observers and inspired some to leave a record of their responses to the sale of slaves at auction. Auctions forever changed the lives of the enslaved people, determining where they lived and worked and whether they would ever see their families again. White observers usually did not know the individuals or their stories, yet they were attracted to the scenes of separation that transpired regularly in cities such as Charleston, Richmond, Columbia, New Orleans, and Washington, D.C.

In small towns and cities, local white men and women went to town on court days, the days on which owners hired out or sold slaves, to conduct business and to socialize. In large cities such as Charleston, the site of the slave auction also served as a meeting place for local people to hear news, see friends, and mingle with people they aspired to know.[26] And slave markets were busy places with reputations that extended beyond the slave states. These places where traders and owners put black people's bodies on public display appealed to outsiders, both those who opposed slavery and those who were simply curious. The auction was the most public aspect of slavery and the domestic slave trade; not everyone had access to a plantation or a farm to see slaves at work or to witness the enormous number of private sales that took place on owners' property or the division of property among heirs following the death of an owner. However, anyone could have easy access to these public displays of commodification and objectification.[27]

In the slave market, whether on a street corner, on the courthouse steps, or indoors in a dedicated space, traders, purchasers, and slaves regularly acted out painful and dramatic scenes. The market was a site where husbands and wives said final goodbyes. It was where many black people parted from place, from family, and from the lives they had known. And whether they opposed slavery, defended it, or remained unmoved by it, white people converged in the slave market to participate or to observe. Some appeared apathetic, some were repelled by what they saw, and others kept looking, riveted by the specter of fellow human beings sold as merchandise.

If we pay close attention to the perceptions white individuals included in their letters, books, news reports, and journal entries, it is possible to get a sense of what they saw, what they were unable or unwilling to see, and what they allowed themselves to feel. Those who were nonchalant or unsympathetic offer insight into just how it was possible for this trade in humans to continue for so long, despite the disruption that it produced in African Americans' lives. Those who were appalled by the spectacle demonstrate that although most white Americans accepted slavery, some in the nineteenth century were able to see it as wrong and to attempt to do something to end it.

Slavery and the slave market amounted to a tourist attraction for some visitors, who became excited at the prospect of seeing slaves when they ventured south. Nehemiah Adams described his unabated titillation at the prospect of seeing slaves for the first time when he traveled from Boston to Georgia in

1854. Even before leaving home he began to imagine what slaves would look like, and he pictured the black waiters he encountered in Boston as slaves. If they could be free and look so sad, how must the slaves look? he wondered. After three days on a southbound steamer he could hardly contain himself: "The sight was yet in reserve. Curiosity, sympathy, pity, the whole assemblage of northern fancies and feelings which gather together at the mention of a slave" were all there as the ship entered the Savannah River. He expected at any moment to hear the groans of slaves and the clanging of chains. "I felt afraid to trust myself in scenes such as I had heard described; yet, as we came near Savannah, there was a natural impatience to see and feel the direful object of so much anticipation." Finally, when he boarded a tugboat in Savannah, Adams got his chance. "On board this tug I looked for the first time in my life upon a slave. All hands on board were slaves. As the boat labored up the stream, I had leisure to indulge my eyes and thoughts in looking at them. Two, with unquestionable marks of servitude in their whole appearance, were talking together in the stern of the boat, the broad brims of their old black hats flapping in the wind over their faces, hiding partly the glances which they gave me as they noticed my interested looks at them." Adams stared at these men intently, eager to fit them into the descriptions and categories that he had formulated long before he ever encountered them. Seeing his first slaves, he said, was like a southerner seeing a snowstorm for the first time. It was something to marvel at and to remember.[28]

After 1852 northern and foreign visitors often had read about the slave trade in Harriet Beecher Stowe's hugely successful novel, *Uncle Tom's Cabin*, which demonized slave traders and the "slave warehouses" where they conducted business and offered people for sale. The novel was first serialized in the *National Era*, an abolitionist newspaper based in Washington, D.C. Stowe published the work as a book in 1852, and it sold 300,000 copies in the United States in its first year. Only the Bible had ever sold so many copies in such a short time.[29] At the heart of Stowe's critique of slavery lay her condemnation of the separation of families through sale. The novel spawned a host of spin-offs, including stage plays, figurines, tableware, candlesticks, vases, and the "Uncle Tom and Little Eva" card game in which the goal was family reunification.[30]

Some travelers wanted to see for themselves the scenes that Stowe described in the novel, and they likened the people they saw to her characters. "I don't tell half the truth," a writer who witnessed an auction in Richmond wrote. "I have said nothing of the brutality of the audiences I saw at four of these auctions. I tell you for a truth that I saw full one hundred Legrees, and even worse than he."[31] A writer whose article appeared in a black abolitionist newspaper wanted readers to know of the link between his observations in New Orleans and the novel. "NOTA BENE," he wrote at the end of his article, "the place I have above described, I should have before mentioned, is the scene of 'Uncle Tom's' sale after the death of St. Clair. Mrs. Stowe has painted it well and faithfully."[32]

White writers for the abolitionist press had an antislavery audience in mind, and they expressed outrage at how a civilized country could allow such an inhuman trade. They could travel a few states down from New York and witness sales taking place in a trader's room in Richmond or on a street corner in Washington, D.C. What they saw at these auctions held political power for them in the fight against slavery, and they sent their observations to antislavery newspapers that could publicize a critical view of the slave trade. Many of them reported that they turned their eyes away from the spectacle of the market and felt the shame of the country.

Attraction and repulsion coexisted in the space of the market and often within one individual observer. After seeing an auction in Richmond, Virginia, a reporter from an abolitionist newspaper wrote, "I have never in my life witnessed a sight with such mingled feelings of horror, amusement and ridicule."[33] Another wrote from Columbia, South Carolina, "Being acquainted with men and women auctions only from reading, I determined however painful it might be to the feelings or revolting to the moral sense, to be a witness at this one."[34] A contributor to the *National Era* was drawn to the market and wanted to comment on the inconsistency of such a sale of humans taking place in the nation's capital but said he could not bring himself to watch the actual transaction. "At the corner of Seventh street and Pennsylvania Avenue, the great thoroughfare of Washington," he scolded, "is a vacant spot, overlooking the principal market, in the very centre of our city-life, conspicuous, commanding, at which public auction is held on certain days of the week. A short time since," he said, "a slave woman, in the open day, while a throng of men and women was passing along the avenue, was put up for sale. The owner said that he had bought her as sound, had been deceived and now would have her sold for what she would bring! The attendants on the sale were called upon to examine her. We did not see the transaction—scarcely any inducement could persuade us to witness such an exhibition." This observer was outraged that human beings could be sold in public on a major street in the nation's capital. He had not lived in Washington, D.C., for long and had a suggestion for the citizens of the city. "If they could only appreciate the feelings excited in strangers from States where no slavery exists by such exhibitions, and understand how effectually the immigration of persons from a large portion of the Union is thereby repelled, such spectacles would certainly cease."[35] The slave states, this observer believed, were out of step with the rest of the nation, and their insistence on retaining slavery was holding them back.

These articles that expressed repulsion at the sale of people in the nation's capital were meant to indict and shame the nation that could speak of liberty and perpetuate its opposite. One abolitionist writer said that he had "never witnessed a sale of human beings; it is so abhorrent to all our feelings that we involuntarily recoil from it." But he had seen advertisements for auctions to be held at the corner of Ninth and Pennsylvania, where the Department of Justice and the Federal Bureau of Investigation stand today, and he found them offensive. "Nobody is revolted when a horse is 'put up' in the marketplace," he wrote, "but a human being on the block!—good God! Is he not our brother? Is a man fit subject for merchandise?" Half of the states of the Union, he said, did not recognize slavery, and their representatives in Washington should not have to see advertisements for the sale of slaves. "Our city, too, is thronged with strangers from all parts of the Union," he argued, "and here reside the representatives of foreign nations, whom we seek to impress with the beneficent workings of Democratic Institutions. And yet, in open day, where the world may look on and wonder, we sell men in the marketplace."[36]

While abolitionist writers pursued a political agenda when they attended and wrote about slave auctions, other, more casual visitors tended to say that they had simply stumbled onto an auction. However, after reading several such accounts, one suspects that seeing an auction was part of their unofficial itineraries. It certainly was not difficult to find an auction. Indeed, with the domestic slave trade in full force in the mid-nineteenth century, the public sale of slaves was so commonplace that even someone unfamiliar with Richmond or Charleston or New Orleans could easily find the slave market or see coffles of people being marched to the market or out of town to be sold again. Slaves and the evidence of the slave trade constituted part of the landscape of the southern city. "I little dreamed two hours ago, of attending a 'Negro auction' as I did of taking a trip to the moon," one journalist wrote from New Orleans in 1855. "Let me tell you how it came about." He then recounted his experience. "I was sauntering along St. Louis St., (in the 'French part,') when I observed a crowd of Negroes composed of men, women and children, marching under the escort of a white man towards the St. Louis Hotel. A moment afterwards, I observed another gang going in the same direction, and soon after a third. I had the curiosity to follow them, and as I entered the Rotunda of the Hotel, observed, I should presume, no less than one hundred and fifty Negroes ranged in front of the different auctioneers' stands. Operations had not yet commenced," he said; "fresh 'lots' of Negroes were constantly coming in and the various 'dealers' were making examinations of the different 'articles' on exhibition."[37] If he did not search the newspapers for advertisements or if he missed the flyers posted around the city announcing auctions, a visitor needed only follow the stream of black people or walk toward the rhythmic shouts of the auctioneer. Once at the site of the auction, the visitor became part of the crowd gathered to watch and participate in the spectacle.

C. Abner from New York easily folded a visit to the slave market into a business trip when he stopped in Richmond on his way to Charleston. Abner wrote back to his business partner in New York to tell what he had seen. "At Richmond," he wrote, "I visited the slave pens & auction sales & I have never looked upon a more disgusting sight, young girls are put on the stand, & undergo the most indecent examination & questioning, they are made to march up & down the room with their clothes above their knees, so that a gang of slave traders can see the motion of their limbs, dirty fingers are put into their mouths to see if their teeth are good, and if they are pronounced 'sound & kind' the bidding commences, & the girl is sold to the highest bidder, I saw several sold," he said, "to go to the cotton fields of the far south, at these sales, the slaves are treated more like brutes than human beings made in the image of God—about 200 slaves left Richmond the time we did, to go to their new homes at the south." Abner expressed disapproval of the sale of people, but he was intent on describing his brief exposure to this unique southern experience. Having done that, he urged his partner to attend to their business: "I have nothing more to write about to day," he closed; "take good care of our finances & I hope that you will leave as much cash on hand as I did when I left town."[38]

Charles Barrow's fleeting contact with slavery took place in Charleston. The young man wrote to his parents in Maine, seeking permission to quit his job on a ship. He had been ill, he said, and did not like associating with the sailors, who were so corrupt that they smoked and played cards on Sunday. Barrow wanted to get off in Charleston, where the ship was docked, and work in a store. Apparently many of his fellow employees also hated work on the ship, as several crew members had run away and the captain had locked up essential workers in the city jail to keep them from also abandoning their jobs. Barrow himself had only left the ship two times. "I see plenty of slaves here," he told his parents. "I never saw any before. . . . The Blacks appear to live easy. I saw four slaves to day going to market they were in a boat rowing." In a second letter to his father two weeks later, Barrow was more contented with his situation and happy to have heard from his family. He reported that he had now been into town several times and had had encounters with the slave market. "I was up to the jail 3 times to carry up some things to the cook and steward. There was fifty two stewards and cooks in there and some blacks for sale," he reported to his father. "I have seen 14 slaves sold since I have been here 2 families they were sold at auction. One family was sold all together. They did not appear to mind it. The others were sold just as any one wanted, one woman a cook was sold for 800 Dollars cash." Barrow had decided to continue working on the ship. He and the newly hired crew would leave Charleston in the morning.[39]

The slave market appeared new and exotic to these northern visitors. It was akin to traveling to a foreign country and observing unfamiliar cultural practices. By the 1850s slavery and the slave trade had been gone from most northern states for decades, but northern whites held a wide range of views toward the institution of slavery and enslaved people themselves. Not all were opposed to slavery, and not all had any particular sympathy toward slaves. However, all who wrote wanted to record for others and for their own memory what this aspect of American life looked like, and they aimed to convey the excitement and the tone of the auction to people who were hungry to hear of their adventures in the South. Letter writers therefore eagerly recounted the details of precisely what the auctioneer said, incorporating newly acquired vocabulary associated with the auction—a slave was "a likely negro," or the person was "knocked down" for a particular price. Sometimes they passed on their perceptions of the black people's feelings. Other times, perhaps distracted by the activity of the market, they paid little attention to the slaves' expressions.

In March 1851 Edwin T. Evans wrote from Charleston to his sister, updating her on his travels. "Dear Sister, As I have not changed my location since I wrote you last I have no new place to describe to you but will try to give you some idea of the town a little more extended than my last. Monday morning after I closed your letter I started for the Post Office and when I was pretty close I heard a great noise and on looking round saw a lot of auctioneers selling darkies, horses, mules land etc. all huddled into a little space by the P.O." Evans was intrigued. "This was something new to me," he wrote, "and of course attracted my attention especially the slave auction." He described the auction to his sister, providing vivid details of the bidding as he attempted to reenact the scene. "There are always two criers to each nigger. The head one calls out the name of the slave he wishes to sell who steps upon the platform as nimbly as possible," he said. "The Auct then reads the conditions for instance 'One half in cash the rest in one year secured by bond and mortgage on the slave.' He then begins 'What's bid for Moses? Start him gentlemen a real prime nigger, (here states what kind of work he can do) sold for no fault warranted perfectly sound and kind is $1000 bid is 800 is 500. Going at 500 quick or I'll knock him off at 500. 55 is bid 550, 550, 550, 555, 555, 560, 65, worth twice the money look at him gentlemen ask him questions, going or I knock him off at 565.'" Here, he said, potential buyers stepped up to examine the arms, the legs, and the mouth of the person being auctioned. Finally, someone purchased him. "The niggers don't mind it at all," Evans observed, "but try their best to show off to the best advantage. They never chain them as you probably have heard nor secure them in any way but the blacks who are for sale sit about on the ground anywhere till they are called on the stand. I did not see a tear in any of their eyes but they everyone seemed in fine spirits laughing and joking and I have seen a good many sold since I came into Charleston (never before) they *never* take the little niggers from the mother but sell them all together and they very seldom divide families." Then Evans moved on to report on the other tourist attractions in Charleston: "In the upper part of the city," he wrote, "is the Citadel which is now used as a Military school."[40]

Reminiscent of Thomas Chaplin's claim that Prince, Paul, and the other eight people he was sending away seemed "quite willing and in good spirits," several of these white observers of auctions thought they detected indifference or even contentment on the part of enslaved people in the market. "The niggers don't mind it at all but try their best to show off to the best advantage. . . . I did not see a tear in any of their eyes but they everyone seemed in fine spirits laughing and joking," Evans wrote to his sister from Charleston. "One family was sold all together. They did not appear to mind it. The others were sold just as any one wanted," Charles Barrow wrote to his parents. A writer who observed an auction in Williston, North Carolina, contradicted himself when he commented, "None seemed to care about it as each bid was made they would turn quickly to see who it was—I saw tears from one woman with a child about a year old & two others 4 to 8 around her." Even a writer whose letter appeared in the *National Era* who vowed never to vote for another proslavery candidate and pledged that he was "bound for the [abolitionist] fight" read a lack of concern in the majority of the enslaved people he saw in the marketplace. "I must say," he remarked, "that the slaves did not display as much feeling as I had expected, as a general thing—but there was *one* noble exception." He went on to describe the "noble exception," a woman who, when asked by a trader why she was crying, replied, "Because I have left my man behind, and his master won't let him come along." The trader said he would supply her with a better husband, but the woman insisted that she would never marry again, nor would she have any more children. Even whites who apparently opposed slavery could sometimes think most enslaved people were without emotion.[41]

There was certainly no monolithic white response to family separation. Certainly white abolitionists abhorred slavery, and many agreed with Harriet Beecher Stowe that family separation was one of its most repulsive features; but even some of them questioned African Americans' ability to feel deeply. It is fair to say that most white people had been so acculturated to view black people as different from them that they did not perceive the existence of slavery in America as a problem, and when exposed to slaves, they barely noticed the pain that they experienced. These whites compartmentalized their lives and experiences, putting themselves and other whites into one sphere and enslaved people or even free black people into another. It did not even occur to them that emotions experienced in the white sphere could also be experienced by the enslaved people.

Sarah Brownrigg Sparkman, for example, could listen to the ninety-one enslaved people she took to Mississippi express their concerns about leaving their loved ones behind yet speak of them as being cheerful, childlike, and without a care. She did not layer their concern and anxiety over their curiosity and awe; instead she saw only one dimension. When she wrote of the enslaved people singing into the night even though they had to walk for miles the next day, she did not consider whether, as Frederick Douglass believed, "the songs of the slave represent the sorrows of his heart and is relieved by them, only as an aching heart is relieved by its tears." She could not see that the slaves who sang together at night may have done so in part to soothe themselves and to hold their community together. She also did not seem to notice if some people were too sad to participate in the singing, or whether Rose had wandered off alone to grieve for her husband whom she had left behind in North Carolina. These details eluded Sparkman even as she wrote about missing her own relatives; she was able to see only simpleminded people who were able to walk all day and stay up all night enjoying themselves. Most other white slaveowners, traders, and casual observers of the domestic slave trade would likewise have had only a very limited sense of what enslaved people felt, and they did not pause to ponder the morality of an institution that deprived humans of their liberty and wantonly destroyed their families.[42]

Without even thinking about it, white Americans created compartments and erected boundaries that walled off their emotions from the emotions of enslaved people. Some, such as Thomas Jefferson and Thomas Cobb, postulated about the relative capacity of blacks and whites to experience emotion, but others operated on the unexamined, and perhaps only semiconscious, assumption that they were more sensitive souls than were enslaved people, and likely all black people. This sensibility was evident in Sarah Sparkman's letter, and it was clear in the letter that a slave trader sent to his wife while he was on the road with a coffle of slaves.

Obadiah Fields lived in Rockingham, North Carolina, but spent much of his time on the road purchasing people in Virginia, North Carolina, and South Carolina for sale in South Carolina. He corresponded with his wife, Jane, during these trips, informing her of the progress of business and expressing his love for her and their four children. No lines or boxes divide the page of the letter Fields wrote to his wife on November 29, 1822, from Greenville, South Carolina, but even as he flowed from one topic to the next, it is evident that intellectually and emotionally he kept the slaves he sold and the family he loved in very separate spaces. "Loveing wife," he wrote, "this will inform you of whare I am at this time. . . . I am well I have sold all but four negroes. . . . I shall leave this [place] also to hunt a market for the balance of the negroes I have on hand this is my sales of what I have sold." Here Fields listed people and items he had sold thus far: Rachel $400, Steven $525, Henry $525, Carry and children $675, Amy $300, Eaton $150. "The cost of the twelve negroes and the bay mare is $2939 I think I will clear nine hundred dollars on this trip," he reported. Then came the transition to his family. "You may look for me between this and crismas [sic] as it is out of my power to say in a day or two of the time but my dear you may rest assured that it will be as soon as possiable Kiss my dear little children and tell them their Pap will soon come home and give my compliments to mother and B. Johnson. I send you twenty dollars use it as you think proper I will be with you as soon as my business will admit. . . . I hope you will rest satisfied until we meat I am yours with all the affection in my breast till death. Kiss our dear baby Jane Emilyne and Robert." He signed himself "Obadiah Fields husband of Jane M. Fields till time shall be no more."[43]

Fields was evidently a loving husband and father, and he was a man who broke up other people's families. He was caring and romantic, and he purchased people apart from their husbands and wives and sold them several states away. He was attentive to his wife's needs, and he seemed to be oblivious to any loneliness or sadness that the people on his coffle felt about being sold. He longed to see his wife and children and was impatient about the three remaining weeks of their separation, yet he probably did not give a thought to the fact that the people he was selling on the road would likely never find their way back home again. The people he sold had names that he knew and listed, but more significant for him was the figure attached to the name. To him they were not individuals or members of families; they were goods that brought a price and a profit. News of the enslaved people fit onto the same page yet never connected with his love for the people who were real to him, those who held value that had nothing to do with a marketplace or an account book.

This is how slavery was able to flourish for more than 250 years in a country where white people avowed a love of liberty and equality of human beings. These daily encounters in which whites ignored or denied the feelings of enslaved people but counted their own feelings as special and significant derived from and shored up a society in which sharp lines could be drawn between blacks and whites. The conscious machinations of statesmen and intellectuals blended with the passive acceptance of the status quo by ordinary whites to extend and prolong the institution they had created and from which most benefited directly or indirectly.

The apparent indifference, contentment, and even enjoyment that some whites perceived in enslaved people as they faced sale and family separation contrasts starkly with the descriptions of former slaves who saw wrenching scenes of separation in the slave market. How are we to understand the differences? It is possible that even when they felt pain, some enslaved people did not reveal it and that some whites were eager to believe in the appearance of contentment as the only reality. It took a particularly discerning white person to realize that African Americans were not transparent, that they sometimes held their true ideas and sentiments closely. In 1835 when white abolitionist Ethan Allen Andrews toured the southern states, including the Franklin and Armfield slave pens in Richmond, Virginia, he remarked on the emotional and intellectual barriers that he thought rendered blacks unknowable to whites. "The real sentiments and feelings of the negroes, in respect to their situation," he wrote, "it is very difficult for any white person to ascertain, and for a stranger, it is nearly impossible. They regard the white man as of a different race from themselves, and as having views, feelings and interests which prevent his sympathizing fully with theirs. Distrust," he theorized, "even of their real friends, is no unnatural consequence of the relation which they and their ancestors have so long borne to the whites. When therefore a white man approaches them with inquiries concerning their condition, they are at once put upon their guard, and either make indefinite vague replies, or directly contradict their real sentiments." It may have been an exaggeration to say that black people thought of whites as being a different race, but Andrews was perceptive in his assessment of some people's dissemblance and inscrutability. He had quite likely been subjected to this distrust as he moved about the slave pen and slave market attempting to gather information.[44]

Like Andrews, another white observer was able to get a glimpse of the possibility that something more lay beneath the surface of the black faces he observed. As he watched an auction in St. Louis, Missouri, this writer paid close attention to the bidding on a young woman named Caroline who, it seems, had a preference for one bidder over another.[45] An astute observer, the writer noted subtle changes in her expressions to which he attributed emotions. Significantly, he also hinted at his realization that what he was able to see and interpret could not reveal everything Caroline felt. First he saw anxiety on Caroline's face as the bidding got under way. Then he thought he saw "a hopeful meaning smile gradually spread over her dusky, good natured face." He suggested she was pleased that her price had gone so high compared with the boy who had been purchased before her. In his estimation, she had internalized a connection between her monetary value and her sense of self-worth. He thought she developed a preference between her would-be purchasers and watched in suspense as the two placed their bids. When the one she preferred hesitated, the writer noted, "the hopeful look had gone from her features, and was replaced by something akin to a feverish dread—still she looked in his face, wishing she might dare to urge him on." The bidding slowed, Caroline's preferred purchaser offered $505, and according to the writer, "From this moment she seemed to have cast aside all hope it was a matter of perfect indifference to her, which might buy her; at least all outward signs had fled, and she glanced round calmly at the crowd of heads looking on her, as on some jack in the box, shown publicly and gratuitously." At this point, the writer "grew sick of the scene" and turned to leave. The auctioneer proclaimed $510 as the sale price; it seems the preferred purchaser had been outbid.[46]

In recounting this episode, the writer made a link between Caroline's seeming loss of hope and the look of "perfect indifference" he read in her expression. This expression of indifference may have masked the fear or pain that had displaced her hope of being sold to a purchaser she thought might be less cruel, or who might live closer to her family, or who may have already owned some of her family members. This observer lacked the details of Caroline's concerns, fears, or commitments but was discerning enough to realize that what he saw as indifference was only an outward sign, an expression that blocked him from having further access to her feelings. It may have been such outward signs that some less insightful observers read as contentment. Most could not have perceived that some enslaved people willed inscrutable facial expressions to camouflage their pain and to maintain a dignity that even powerful whites could not strip from them. Those who took the time to look or who were willing to imagine a range of feelings within an enslaved person knew, as South Carolina slaveholder and wife of a Confederate general Mary Chesnut did, that a great deal was hidden behind the facades that enslaved people daily presented to their owners and to the audiences who observed their public encounters with humiliation and pain in the marketplace.[47]

Even the most astute and compassionate person who had never been enslaved could not truly know how an enslaved person felt on that auction block. It took someone who had experienced it to describe her own fear and anxiety as she approached the auction block and to disclose the method she used to soothe herself as she was put on display and faced the prospect of being sold away from her family forever. Bethany Veney offers such a description. Some time after Veney's husband Jerry was sold away, Veney's owner placed her in the custody of jailer John O'Neile to be sold without her young daughter. Veney first attempted to get a white person from her church to purchase her; but that effort failed, so on the order of the jailer's wife she put on her best calico dress to make the journey to Richmond, where she was to be auctioned. At the jail in Richmond, Veney prepared to be sold. "I had never in my life felt so sad and so completely forsaken," she recalled. "I thought my heart was really breaking. Mr. O'Neile called me; and as I passed out of the door, I heard Jackoline, the jailer's daughter, singing in a loud, clear voice,"

When through the deep waters I call thee to go,
The rivers of woe shall not thee overflow;

For I will be with thee, and cause thee to stand,
Upheld by my righteous, omnipotent hand.

Veney was familiar with this hymn that appeared in both Baptist and Methodist hymnals in the mid-nineteenth century under the subjects of Trial, Suffering, Submission, Christian Courage, and Cheer.[48] She had likely sung it many times at Sunday services and at the Methodist camp meetings she regularly attended. It constituted part of the reservoir of hymns from which church members drew to sustain themselves between services. As Veney moved through the jailer's office, Jackoline's song reminded her that no matter how bad the situation appeared, no matter how hopeless life seemed, her faith would take her through.

How firm a foundation, ye saints of the Lord,
Is laid for your faith in his excellent word;
What more can he say than to you he had said,
You who unto Jesus for refuge have fled.

The song insistently promised Veney that although she had lost her husband and now her child, she would never be alone.

The soul that on Jesus hath lean'd for repose,
I will not, I will not, desert to his foes;
That soul, though all hell should endeavor to shake
I'll never, no never, no never forsake.

Years later Veney recalled her feelings on that day. "I can never forget the impression these words and the music and the tones of Jackoline's voice made upon me," she wrote. "It seemed to me as if they all came directly out of heaven. It was my Saviour speaking directly to me. Was not I passing the deep waters? What rivers of woe could be sorer than these through which I was passing? Would not this righteous, omnipotent hand uphold me and help me? Yes, there was His word for it. I would trust it; and I was comforted."[49] Much as other Christian enslaved people did, Veney took the promises of the song personally and believed that she had help in her struggle.[50]

Veney relied on her faith in God, and she also called on her belief in other powers. Before going to Richmond, she met with "an old negro woman" who gave her tricks to help impede her sale. As a result, according to Veney, "when the doctor, who was employed to examine the slaves on such occasions, told me to let him see my tongue, he found it coated and feverish, and, turning from me with a shiver of disgust, said he was obliged to admit that at that moment I was in a very bilious condition." Veney's apparent physical condition stopped her sale. However, observers viewing her on the auction block could not have imagined the strategies she deployed to hold herself together. They would have had little intimation of her anxiety, fear, and grief. And they would not have imagined the courage that the hymn and her "tricks" provided her.[51]

When Thomas Chaplin's ten slaves entered the market in Charleston, they, like other enslaved people, carried with them a range of mechanisms for coping with their circumstances and the anguish that derived from their inability to control their lives. Some people held their tongues. Some plastered their faces with the grins that traders demanded. Many were silenced by their pain and their outrage, and they stifled their grief. Some people, though, would not be quieted and could not be comforted. And once in a while, their wrenching wails pierced the walls that white people constructed between themselves and the pain of black people.

Austin Bearse, a white man from Massachusetts, was present when a black woman disturbed the peace and broke down the walls. Bearse worked on a Massachusetts-based ship that transported enslaved people from Charleston to New Orleans. "These slaves were generally collected by slave-traders in Charleston," he wrote, "brought there by various causes, such as the death of owners and the division of estates, which threw them into the market. Some were sent as punishment for insubordination, or because the domestic establishment was too large; or because persons moving to the North and West preferred selling their slaves to the trouble of carrying them." The ship sometimes transported as many as eighty people to plantations in New Orleans. Before setting out, Bearse said, "we used to allow the relatives and friends of the slaves to come on board and stay all night with their friends before the vessel sailed. In the morning it used to be my business to pull off the hatches and warn them that it was time to separate, and the shrieks and cries at these times were enough to make anybody's heart ache." After twelve years of hearing these cries, Bearse had become inured to them, but one woman managed to get through.

In 1828, "while mate of the brig 'Milton,' of Boston, bound from Charleston, S.C., to New Orleans," Bearse wrote, "the following incident occurred, which I shall never forget. The traders brought on board four quadroon men in handcuffs. An old negro woman more than eighty years of age, came screaming after them, 'My son! O, my son!' She seemed almost frantic." Bearse recalled that when they left the port and were more than a mile out on the harbor, he could still hear this mother's piercing screams. The four men swore that they would never live to be slaves in New Orleans, and according to Bearse, within forty-eight hours of their arrival, each man had killed himself. Bearse continued in the business for a few years after this incident but eventually stopped participating in the slave trade. "In my past days," he concluded, "the system of slavery was not much discussed. I saw these things as others did, without interference. Because I no longer think it right to see these things in silence, I trade no more south of Mason and Dixon's line."[52]

Slaveowners such as Thomas Chaplin and Catherine Percy knew that black people had feelings. They knew that they grieved, so they hid from them and their grief and anger while attempting to diminish the profundity of the people's pain because they did not want to see it or face it or feel it. If they did, they might not be able to continue to hold people as slaves or to sell them away from their families. If they acknowledged that these black people were people just like them, who hurt as they did when they lost their loved ones, and if they faced them in their grief, then they might not be able to live with themselves. Others who participated in the slave trade demonstrated even less concern than did Chaplin and Percy. Sometimes it took the desperate screams of a disconsolate mother to penetrate their consciousness, trigger their empathy, and break their silence. White people had the capacity but not always the will to care.

It took insight and courage for a white individual to challenge the privileges and seeming naturalness of white superiority. It took strength of character and risk of ostracism and violence to reject the notion that blacks had lesser feelings and were intended for white exploitation. It took commitment to empathize. As in most societies in most times, it was easy in the mid-nineteenth century to avoid examining accepted ideas that held currency in the society and had been passed down from one generation to the next. Indeed, most whites in the North and certainly in the South did not even question their assumptions of black inferiority and suitability for slavery. For those who did think about the assumptions and who allowed the reality of other people's pain to enter their awareness, it took courage to turn their backs on slavery, as Angelina and Sarah Grimké, daughters of a South Carolina slave trader, did when they renounced slavery, moved out of the South, and became activists in the abolition movement.[53] It took courage and a moral commitment to quit the slave trade and wage a struggle for the eradication of slavery, as Austin Bearse did, or to release slaves and move out of the South, as many Quakers did in the eighteenth and nineteenth centuries. It took courage, but it was nonetheless possible for white people to see and hear and acknowledge the grief of enslaved people as they lost their families. It was always possible to choose to walk away from slavery and the destruction that it wrought.

PART TWO
The Search

Love

Courage

Faith is being sure

FOUR

Without a word of warning, and for no fault of
their own, parents and children, husbands and wives,
brothers and sisters, were separated to meet no more
on earth. A slave sale of this sort is always as solemn as
a funeral, and partakes of its nature in one important
particular,—the meeting no more in the flesh.

WILLIAM PARKER, former slave

Blue Glass Beads Tied in a Rag of Cotton Cloth
The Search for Family during Slavery

I wish to [k]now what has Ever become of my Presus little girl. I left her in
Goldsborough with Mr. Walker and I have not herd from her Since.

VILET LESTER, enslaved woman

—————————————

"They may see their children again in time," Thomas Chaplin wrote as he ru-
minated over his decision to sell ten people. Indeed, seeing each other again
was the hope and the intention of African Americans who lost their families.
Their search began in slavery even as they reeled from losing relatives at an
auction, in a private sale, or in a caravan that accompanied a white, slaveowning family into new territory. As the runaway ads in newspapers attest, some
people set out on the roads to get back to relatives from whom they had been
separated. Others relied on word of mouth, sent messages in owners' letters,
and wrote their own letters in efforts to locate or communicate with their
family members. Sometimes they knew exactly where loved ones were and
wanted to make contact or to arrange for reunification. More often they had
no idea what had become of their family, and they wrestled with competing
emotions of hope and despair. In these circumstances many enslaved people
likened separation to death: an ending here on earth, with the possibility of
reunion in heaven. At the same time, without knowing where their family
members had gone or, for that matter, whether they were alive or dead, some
people searched, hoping that word would circulate enough to bring about a
reunion.

"O, fare ye well, O, fare ye well! God bless you until we meet again; Hope to
meet you in heaven, to part no more," Peter Randolph heard other slaves sing
at moments of sale and separation.[1] Jacob Stroyer recalled slaves singing a
similar song when his sisters were sold to a trader who planned to take them
and others from Columbia, South Carolina, to Louisiana. "The victims were
to take the cars from a station called Clarkson turnout which was about four

miles from master's place," Stroyer recalled. "The excitement was so great that the overseer and driver could not control the relatives and friends of those that were going away, as a large crowd of both old and young went down to the depot to see them off." According to Stroyer, Louisiana "was considered by the slaves as a place of slaughter, so those who were going did not expect to see their friends again." As the friends and relatives walked to the train station to say goodbye, Stroyer said, "many of the negroes left their masters' field and joined us as we marched to the cars, some were yelling and wringing their hands while others were singing little hymns that they were accustomed to for the consolation of those that were going away, such as,"

When we all meet in heaven
There is no parting there
When we all meet in heaven
There is no parting no more.²

In Randolph's and Stroyer's accounts, separation through sale was so familiar that slave communities created songs and rituals tailored for these mass departures. It was customary to think of heaven as a meeting place after death, but for these enslaved people, separation was like unto death, so the songs contemplated a reunion in heaven.

The forced partings, former slave William Parker said, resembled funerals. As a young boy in Anne Arundel County, Maryland, Parker experienced the fear and chaos in the slave quarter that accompanied an impending sale of people. "Men, women, and children, all were crying," he said, "and general confusion prevailed. For years they had associated together in their rude way,—the old counseling the young, recounting their experience and sympathizing in their trials; and now, without a word of warning, and for no fault of their own, parents and children, husbands and wives, brothers and sisters, were separated to meet no more on earth. A slave sale of this sort," he observed, "is always as solemn as a funeral, and partakes of its nature in one important particular,—the meeting no more in the flesh."³

Some owners knew that enslaved people regarded separation as death and used it to their own advantage. Thomas Jefferson, for example, acknowledged the potential finality of separation, and demonstrated that owners sometimes *intended* sale to simulate death. When Cary, one of the people he owned, assaulted another enslaved man named Brown, Jefferson pondered the punishment he would inflict if Cary were not convicted and imprisoned. On June 8, 1803, in a letter from Washington, D.C., the president of the United States sent his directions for punishment to Thomas Mann Randolph. "Should Brown recover so that the law shall inflict no punishment on Cary, it will be necessary for me to make an example of him *in terrorem* to others, in order to maintain the police so rigorously necessary among the nail boys." Jefferson wanted to punish Cary to issue a warning or threat to the other men and boys who worked in his nail-making "factory" in Monticello, Virginia. "There are generally negro purchasers from Georgia passing about the state," he wrote, "to one of whom I would rather he should be sold than to any other person. If none such offers, if he could be sold to any other quarter so distant as never more to be heard of among us, it would to the others be as if he were put out of the way by death. I should regard price but little in comparison with so distant an exile of him as to cut him off completely from ever again being heard of."[4]

It was no wonder that some enslaved people and their owners perceived in separation the same finality as death. Even a distance of a few miles could be insurmountable if they did not know where they were or if traveling was too dangerous or would trigger physical punishment or sale. Separation of hundreds of miles, into unknown parts of the country, was even more permanent, more final. When Bethany Veney's husband or Thomas Jones's wife and children were led off on a coffle, they disappeared into the vastness of the slave states. Traders could sell them at any point on the trek from Richmond or Wilmington to Charleston or New Orleans or Natchez.

Psychologists call this sort of separation ambiguous loss, a loss that is uncertain, a disappearance in which those left behind or those taken away remain unaware of the whereabouts or status of loved ones. Family therapist Pauline Boss suggests that ambiguous loss, such as an accident in which a body is never recovered, may even be worse than certainty of death. "Of all the losses experienced in personal relationships, ambiguous loss is the most devastating because it remains unclear, indeterminate," she says. "One cannot tell for sure if the loved one is dead or alive. Not only is there a lack of information regarding the person's whereabouts, there is no official or community verification that anything is lost—no death certificate, no wake or sitting shiva, no funeral, no body, nothing to bury."[5] This is the type of loss that thousands of African Americans experienced during slavery. Often when an owner sold family members, those who remained behind had no knowledge of where the loved ones had gone and had no means of making contact. And the vast majority of those who were sold would not have had any way to retrace the steps of their journey on a coffle or on a ship.

Many African Americans juggled this sense of permanent loss with a stubborn hope that they would find their family members. They may have had faith that they would see each other in heaven, but the ambiguity of the loss also led them to hope they would meet again right here on earth. Hope was more than a simple wish; it was an active desire and a belief that life could be better, combined with a perceived capacity to help to bring about the change.[6] It is interesting to ponder whether this hope was a help or a hindrance. Would it have been easier to simply accept the permanence of separation and go about the business of living without clinging to the thought that you would find your relative again? Humans have contemplated this question of the value of hope for centuries. The ancient Greeks questioned whether hope was an evil in the myth of Pandora, and in the nineteenth century, German philosopher Friedrich Nietzsche argued that hope was the worst of all evils because it prolongs the agony of loss. It is certainly true that had the grief of these enslaved people been transient, had they not held out hope for reunification, they would have felt the absence and the longing less deeply and they may have had more peace. But for many African Americans the losses had been so consequential and the emotional connections so significant that although the odds were against them, they held on to hope, and they actively sought to find their loved ones.[7]

It is not possible to even begin to estimate how many people acted on their hope and searched for family members or sent messages or received news through the grapevines that stretched from Canada to Texas, from Boston to California, and frayed under the strain of the distance and the silence. Some people, unable to cope with the dissonance of caring for someone who might already be dead and, in any event, would not likely return, surely erased loved ones from their memories. But others carried the memories with them as they went about the labor of slavery, passed through the hands of one owner to another, and created new families. They were slaves with few material resources and severely constricted mobility, yet some made efforts to search for their families. They had to be opportunistic, willing to seize any chance to make contact with a lost relative. And they had to be strategic, devising targeted appeals for help. When they were able, they sent out missives and messengers who might bring back the dead.

Sella Martin's mother sent such a messenger to find her son. Martin, along with his mother, Winnie, and his older sister, had been sold to break up the relationship between Winnie and the white man who was the father of her two children. The three were taken to Georgia and sold to a man whom Martin referred to only as Dr. C. After some time, Dr. C's gambling debts led to the seizure of his slaves, and Martin, still a young boy, was taken away from his mother and sister and became the property of a man who owned a hotel in Columbus, Georgia, frequented by gamblers. The young boys in the neighborhood adopted gambling as a pastime, and Martin traded his skills as a proficient marble player for reading lessons from a white boy. As he accumulated the money he won at marbles and funds he earned by reading to other enslaved people, Martin made a plan. "I was laying up my money," he said, "to pay my traveling expenses in going to see my mother, and to purchase something to carry to her as proof of my love." The problem was that he had no idea where his mother was.[8]

One day Martin encountered a "coloured man from the country who had brought in a load of cotton." The man was looking for Winnie's son. "I trembled all over," Martin recounted, "as I asked her son's name, for I was sure he knew where my mother was. I stopped, and sat down on a stump to collect myself, and when I got the strength I told him who I was." The man replied, "'Winnie told me to give you dis 'ere'; and he handed me a rag of cotton cloth, tied all about with a string. I opened it, and found some blue glass beads—beads given to my mother by her mother as a keepsake when she died. I knew," Martin said, "by that token that he was a messenger from my mother, though of course my mother and myself had had no time to agree to any such thing before we were parted. But I had often heard her say that nothing would make her part from these beads."

Sella Martin's mother sent material objects loaded with history, sentiment, and significance to ensure that her son would recognize and respond to her messenger. The blue beads that she wrapped in cloth and tied all about with a string were much like the blue glass beads that enslaved people in New York City; Newton Cemetery, Barbados; Montpelier Plantation in Jamaica; and Parris Island, South Carolina, wore, carried, and sometimes buried in the graves of their loved ones. These particular beads held meaning to Winnie because they were keepsakes, a possession that her mother had prized enough to pass on to her. Now the daughter risked sending the treasured beads on the road with a man she hoped would use them to find her son.[9] As they went about doing the work of slavery, some enslaved men experienced a degree of mobility. Taking messages for owners, picking up the mail at the post office, making deliveries, fetching the doctor, and transporting goods to market or to a storehouse, these men moved about the landscape and became couriers of information able to deliver news and messages from enslaved people to friends and relatives, thereby establishing a physical connection between them. Winnie knew that this man who was a part of her community would travel within miles of the place where she had last seen her son, and she enlisted his help.[10]

Martin spent more than a year gathering the courage to run away to find his mother, but eventually, as many other African Americans did, he took to the roads. All who did so assumed great risks; they might be caught by patrollers and beaten and sold by their owners, or they might be caught and sold by strangers. Their experiences constitute the backstories of the ads that owners placed in newspapers offering rewards for escaped slaves. They had no road maps, few were familiar with areas beyond a few miles of their homes, and they moved about amidst the presumption that every black person belonged to someone and had to account for his or her movements. Martin was more prepared than others. He now had a good sense of where his mother lived, and he was literate. He wrote a pass for himself, took pen and ink with him in case he could convince his mother to run away too, and set out to walk the sixty miles to her plantation. It took three nights to reach her.

His mother said that in the year since she had found out where he lived, she had run away three times, intending to make her way to him in Columbus. Each time she had been captured and beaten, leaving "terrible furrows made by the cow-hide" on her back. Martin could not convince her to try escaping one more time. She had lost her nerve. "I have borne a great deal in my life," she told her son, "so much that my spirit is crushed and all courage is gone from me, and my body is worn out with labour and the lash." She believed it would not be long before she died, and as she despaired of ever living with her children again on earth, she welcomed the prospect of death. "There is no hope of our ever being together on earth," Martin recalled his mother saying, "and therefore, the sooner I start on my journey to heaven the sooner will my misery from our separation and from slavery cease." Their reunion was short-lived; mother and son were still slaves, after all. Winnie's owner caught Martin and returned him to his owner, who soon sold him. For a long time both Sella Martin and his mother had held on to hope that they would see each other again. Martin made plans, but his mother acted, first sending her messenger, then attempting to run away. But now her hope had been transformed into despair. The beads had served as a code between mother and son, representing their ties to each other and to a family history, but all they had remaining was his mother's faith that they would meet again in heaven.[11]

Although he received no messages, signs, or signals, Moses Roper also longed for his mother and hoped he could find her. Roper had been separated from his family in Caswell County, North Carolina, when he was about six years old. During a division of property after their owner died, one heir drew Roper's name and another his mother's. He experienced several subsequent sales, finally ending up in Kershaw County, South Carolina. Following severe beatings as a teenager, Roper decided to escape and make his way to "the Free States," planning to visit his mother on his way north. Because he had very light skin, he was able to pass himself off as a white child who had been bound out to a cruel master, trying to find his way home. He made his way back to Caswell County and found his mother, who only recognized him after he described in detail the scene of their separation. According to Roper, his mother finally recognized "her own son before her, for whom she had so often wept; and, in an instant, we were clasped in each other's arms, amidst the ardent interchange of caresses and tears. Ten years had elapsed since I had seen my dear mother." For a week Roper hid in the woods during the day and slept with his family at night. But, as with Sella Martin and his mother, the reunion did not last. Roper was captured and taken to the jail at the Caswell County Courthouse. He never saw his mother, stepfather, or siblings again. His grandmother, however, visited him at the jail several times. She was the last relative he ever saw, and it would be several years before he finally made it to freedom.[12]

Sella Martin and Moses Roper set out on foot to find their relatives. Some enslaved people instead used the written word to attempt to contact family members and to express their desire to see them again. The people who belonged to the Brownriggs sent messages back to their relatives in owners' letters as they walked from North Carolina to Mississippi. John Beck sent a letter with hopes that his former wife, Malinda, would hear his message. James Tate wrote to his wife expressing his emotional ambivalence and his desire to have her and their children return to him.[13] These people relied on white owners and former owners to get their messages through, so in addition to the conventional platitudes of nineteenth-century letter writing, they also knew that success in reaching family members depended on their expressions of caring and concern for white owners. They couched their letters in a language that may in some cases have been sincere but in all cases was necessary to gain access to their loved ones.

In July 1825, an enslaved man in Alabama named Charles wrote to his former owner, William Greenhill in Nottaway County, Virginia. It had been a long time since he had communicated with his relatives or his former owner, but a new piece of information spurred him to get a letter to them. "Tho I may ere this be obliterated from your memory, you and family and connexions are yet remembered by me with grateful feelings," he wrote. But it did not take him long to get to the true purpose of his letter: his desire to make contact with his brother. "It has been a long time since I heard from you all, my Brother Jacob, if he is yet alive perhaps may suppose that I am no more but thanks be to all superintending power I am yet numbered with the living and in the enjoyment of health and strength superior to most of my age." Charles acknowledged that neither he nor his brother knew if the other was still alive. "I belong to Mr. David Callahan to whom I have belonged for 25 years or upwards—it would be extremely consoling to me to hear from my Brother, and his welfare would exhilerate and strengthen me in my declining years." Word had reached Charles that led him to believe he might see his brother again. "I have been told that you design moving to the state of Alabama," he informed his former owner. "If so you will pass near where I live as I live in a mile of the road you must travel if you come thro Campbell. Should you come this road if you will name me at Master Thomas Williams's he will contrive me word and I may yet have the satisfaction of seeing you all and my Brother Jacob whom I suppose will go with you—at any event will you my dear Master write to me." He wanted another favor. "Please inform my Brother of the receipt of this and convey him my best wishes for his health and happiness and accept dear Master for yourself and family the unfeigned regard of an old family servant." He signed himself "Charles, formerly Joseph Greenhill."[14]

Charles had not seen his brother Jacob in a very long time, perhaps as long as twenty-five years, yet he had not forgotten him. He probably did not think about him all the time—did not always feel the urgency of seeing him. Perhaps, though, sometimes a sound, a taste, or a scent brought him to mind, and hearing of Jacob's owner's intention to move to Alabama provoked old hopes. Charles was getting older, reaching a time in life when he wanted to finally satisfy long-held yearnings. Still, even if he never saw him again, Charles wanted his brother to know that he was alive and that he still cared about him. The success of his endeavor depended completely on the owner, who could choose to deliver the message to Jacob and to stop on the way to Alabama. Charles understood this imbalance of power, and he tellingly assured his former owner of his "unfeigned regard" for him. He was humble and solicitous, but at the same time he seemed to invoke an obligation due to him as "an old family servant."

In an 1857 letter to her former mistress, Vilet Lester also appealed for help. Lester wrote from Bullock County, Georgia, to her former owners who lived in Randolph County, North Carolina. Like Charles, she began by paying her respects to the white people who had owned her, and she brought them up to date on her circumstances. Perhaps she also intended to stir some guilt in them for having sold her. "My loving, Miss Patsy," Lester wrote, "I have long bin wishing to imbrace this presant and pleasant opertunity of infolding my Seans and fealings Since I was constrained to leav my Long Loved home and friends which I cannot never gave my Self the Least promis of returning to." Then she listed numerous sales she had experienced, providing the details that might someday be folded into genealogies of separation within her family. "When I left Randolf [North Carolina] I went to Rockingham and Stad there five weaks and then I left there and went to Richmon virgina to be Sold and I Stade there three days and was bought by a man by the name of Groover and braught to Georgia and he kept me about Nine months and he being a trader Sold me to a man by the name of Rimes and he Sold me to a man by the name of Lester and he has owned me four years and Says that he will keep me til death Siperates us without Some of my old north Caroliner friends wants to buy me again."[15] Lester had changed hands in the marketplace several times. Her life had been chaotic, but she now held on to her owner's promise of stability and reached back to North Carolina to see if she could put her family back together.

Lester had been away from North Carolina for about five years. Although she wrote that she had never nurtured any hope of returning there, it is apparent that she wanted to explore all the possibilities. She wanted her former owners to know that her current owner would be willing to sell her back to someone in the state. And to urge them to consider purchasing her, she immediately expressed her desire to be with them again. "My Dear Mistress," she wrote, "I cannot tell my fealings nor how bad I wish to See you and old Boss and Miss Rahol and mother I do not [k]now which I want to see the worst Miss Rahol or mother I have though[t] that I wanted to see mother but never befour did I [k]no[w] what it was to want to see a parent and could not I wish you to gave my love to old Boss Miss Rahol and bailum an give my manafold love to mother brothers and sister and pleas to tell them Right to me So I may here from them if I cannot see them and also I wish you to right to me and Rigth me all the nuse." Lester did not hint at why she had been sold away, but she made clear that she had left behind many close family members, including her mother and siblings.

But she left for last the one person about whom she was most concerned. "I wish to [k]now what has Ever become of my Presus little girl," she wrote. "I left her in Goldsborough with Mr. Walker and I have not herd from her Since and Walker Said that he was going to Carry her to Rockingham and gave her

from them if I cannot See them and also I wish
you to right to me and Right me all the nuse I do
want to now whether old Boss is Still living or
now and all the rest of them and I want to now
whether builum is married or no I wish to now what that
Ever become of my Presus little girl I left her in
goldsborough with Mr Walker and I hair not heard
from her Since and Walker Said that he was going
to Carry her to Rockingham and gave her to his
Sister and I want to no whether he did or no as
I do wish to See her very mutch and Boss Says
he wishes to now whether he will Sell her or now
and the least that can buy her and that he wishes
a answer as Soon as he can get one as I wis him to
buy her and my Boss being a man of Reason and
fealing wishes to grant my trubled breast that
mutch gratifycation and wishes to now whether he
will Sell her or now So I must come to a close
by Escribing my Self yours long loved and well
wishing filly mate as a Survant until death vilet Lester
                    of Georgia
                Io Miss Patsey Padison
                of North Caroliner

My Bosses Name is James B Lester and if you Should
think a nuff of me to right me which I do beg the
faver of you as a Servant direct your leter to Millray,
Bullock County Georgia Pleas to right me So
                Fare fare you well in love

Letter from Vilet Lester to her former mistress, August 29, 1857
(Duke University Special Collections Library, Durham, N.C.)

to his Sister and I want to [k]no[w] whether he did or now as I do wish to See her very Mutch and Boss Says he wishes to [k]now whether he will Sell her or now and the least that can buy her and that he wishes a answer as Soon as he can get one as I wish him to buy her and my Boss being a man of Reason and fealing wishes to grant my trubled breast that mutch gratification and wishes to [know] whether he will sell her now."[16]

Any possibility of reunification between Lester and her daughter depended on so many other people. Her correspondence starkly laid out her vulnerability. Mr. Walker said he might give her daughter to his sister, but five years later, Lester had no idea what had become of her child. She was now depending on Miss Patsy to send information, first about whether they would buy Lester, something she sincerely doubted, and then about who currently owned her daughter. Finally, Lester had to rely on her current "Boss" or owner to make the purchase. It is not clear what the full nature of their relationship was or why he expressed willingness to help Lester. He said he would keep her until death separated them, language that was often included in the bill of sale for slaves, yet he also said he was willing to sell her back to North Carolina. She was counting on his being "a man of reason and feeling" who would help her, one way or the other, to see her daughter again.

Vilet Lester ended her letter by appealing to a personal relationship with her former mistress. "So I must come to a close by Escribing my Self your long loved and well wishing play mate as a Servant until death," she wrote. The assertion seemed to be that Lester was not just an ordinary slave. She was like Charles in this. He called himself an "old family servant," one who had served the family for a long time. Lester described herself as a former playmate of her mistress; they had been children together and likely played in the yard of Miss Patsy's parents. Both Lester and Charles hoped that calling on an old personal relationship would help give them access to their loved ones. Still, she did not want to cross the lines that divided owners and slaves, so Lester, like Charles, impressed upon her former mistress that she knew her place as a servant. In addition to being a former childhood friend, she emphasized that she was also a loyal servant. Her postscript read, "My Bosses Name is James B. Lester and if you Should think a nuff of me to right me which I do beg the faver of you as a Servant direct your letter to Millray Bullock County Georgia. Pleas to right me So fare you well in love."

Charles and Lester carefully straddled the line between deference and assertiveness. Both were keenly aware of the delicate balance they had to strike in their communications with former owners. They acknowledged their subordinate positions while they appealed to old loyalties, even perhaps old debts. They dared not assert any hint of equality but suspected that an appeal to the humanity of their former owners might pressure them to act in accordance with their self-image as caring members of the slaveowning class. After twenty-five years for Charles and five for Lester, each grasped the opportunity to reach out to former owners. Although both stubbornly attempted to initiate contact, however, there was no assurance then that they would connect with their family members, or any confirmation now that they ever did. The sources do not reveal whether the intended recipients, Charles's brother and Lester's daughter, ever heard the messages contained in the letters. Nor do they reveal if there was any further correspondence, or whether they saw their relatives again. It was a painful situation for these two enslaved people, frustrating for those who come now to read their letters.

It was worthwhile, though, for an enslaved person to take action, because the possibility always existed that the message could get through. This likely did not happen often, but an article in the *Voice of the Fugitive* provides a reminder that although powerful, slaveowners could not control everything. The article, titled "Another Family Are Free," told this story. William Murdock was enslaved in Arkansas; his wife and children belonged to a different owner, who sold them away. On the way to Kentucky with their new owner, Murdock's wife and the children escaped, hiding themselves on a boat that carried cotton freight. They then took another boat to Cincinnati, where they found people who helped them get to Canada. Once free, "she wrote back to her former master and family in Arkansas, dating her letter in Canada, but not in any particular place. She wrote that she was well, and free, and happy, and if she should never see her husband again on earth, she hoped to meet him in heaven." She may indeed have looked forward to seeing her husband in heaven, but this woman was not one to wait—she was shrewd and actively took the step of getting word to her husband, indirect as the method had to be.[17]

Her sub-rosa message got through. Back in Arkansas, her husband learned from the five-year-old daughter of his wife's former owner "that they had been talking about his wife—that she was in Canada, and that the child's father had a letter from her." According to the article, "The bereft husband's anxiety was great, and his curiosity excited to the highest pitch. It was strange news to him, and he knew not what to make of it. At length, he cautiously inquired of an older sister of the little girl, about 16 years old, who managed to get the letter and privately read it to him," warning him not to reveal her involvement. Murdock's family was back from the dead. His wife and children had been lost to him, but this message sent by his wife brought the possibility that they would see each other again. Murdock went after them. He eventually made it to Canada and, after traveling through several cities, found them in Hamilton, Ontario.[18]

The written word, then, could play a significant part in the search for family members even during slavery. In 1844 a group of free African Americans in Columbus, Ohio, launched the state's first black newspaper, the *Palladium of Liberty*, and a few people took the opportunity to place Information Wanted ads that aimed to get the word out about missing relatives. These ads were the precursors to the hundreds of ads that people used at the end of the Civil War to search for their relatives. In the first, T. Fisher of Oberlin, Ohio, searched for his father, who had escaped from slavery.

INFORMATION WANTED

Oberlin, Ohio, May 20, 1844

Mr. Editor—Nature prompts me to action. Some eighteen or twenty years ago, my father assumed the privilege of wringing [freedom] from the hard hands of tyrants, and his unfortunate son has done the same thing; and it is my desire to find him if it is possible. Thomas Fisher was his name, from Nashville Tennessee. He left a wife and two children. Mary Stump was his wife's name, and his son T. Fisher is now in Oberlin, Ohio. I suppose these lines will be sufficient. He lived four miles north of Nashville. The man's name that he lived with was Rice. I think that if this letter should reach him, or any person that is acquainted with him, I would be very much gratified if they would write to me.

"Nature prompts me to action," Fisher wrote, asserting that his feelings of loss and grief were only natural. His father's escape, not sale, had brought about the separation of their family. The author of the ad had since also escaped and had made it to Oberlin, Ohio, in 1844, an important site of abolitionist activity where in 1835 Oberlin College admitted the first African American college students in the country.[19] The son, T. Fisher, had likely been named after his father, Thomas. He may have grown up hearing stories about his father and, depending on his age when Thomas Fisher left, may have been old enough to form his own living memories of him. Now the son took action to see if his father had also made it to freedom in Ohio or some other place to which the newspaper might circulate. This son had likely dreamed of seeing his father again for some twenty years, and the existence of a newspaper offered a new possibility that he could not squander. T. Fisher provided the information he had about his father that he thought would be helpful in finding him: His wife's name was Mary Stump, and he had lived with a man named Rice; in other words, he had belonged to a man named Rice, four miles north of Nashville. He hoped this information would be enough to lead him to his father.[20]

In a second ad, titled "Lost Brother," John Johnston of Columbus, Ohio, searched for his brother, Major, who had been sold thirty-five years earlier at age five. Johnston's search intimates that some enslaved people and, later, former slaves who searched for family members may have been motivated not only by a sense of personal loss and grief, but also by a need to set things right. One wonders how attached John could have been to his five-year-old brother to sustain a desire to see him after thirty-five years. It may be that John Johnston searched for his brother out of a desire to re-create a family. Perhaps beyond the sadness or grief there was something else, some sense that families belonged together—a sense that if you had a brother out there in the world, you ought to know where he was.[21]

No one engaged in a more prolonged and persistent search than Henry Bibb, and no one learned more profoundly than he that finding your loved one could also open a new world of pain. What had begun as a tale of romantic love that overpowered his ambivalence about getting married while a slave ended up costing Bibb and his family a great deal of pain. Indeed, the story of his separation from Malinda and their daughter, Mary Frances, became a mainstay of Bibb's antislavery lectures in Ohio and Michigan, so much so that an antislavery group reported on it in the *Palladium of Liberty* in August 1844. "On last Monday evening, at the Baptist church, Mr. Bibb, a fugitive from slavery lectured on the subject of slavery," the article read. "The house was crowded to overflowing." According to the writers, Bibb presented himself as simple and unassuming, which inspired confidence in his audience. He told of his many attempts to escape slavery and of his most cruel owner, a deacon in the Baptist Church. The most compelling portion of the speech, however, concerned his separation from his family. "The separation of him from his wife, is certainly beyond all circumstances of the kind we have heard of in the whole course of our life. It is of no use to labor in words to describe only what can be conceived, by the poor unhappy creature who has endured its aching pangs." Then the men described the parting scene between Malinda and Henry Bibb, much the same as Bibb would later recount it in his published narrative. "She clung to his neck until she seemed as tho' her heart would break, then both him and his wife fell on their knees, and prayed that he would keep or sell them both together, but his master refused, and tore her from his bosom, and bid her go to her work; but like all women, as the speaker remarked, she clung to her husband's neck, until her master dragged her from him, and applied the cowhide at the same time. Mr. Bibb states that until he was out of hearing, his wife was still screaming." Bibb, the article said, ended his speech with the words, "I never expect to see my dear wife again in this life." The audience was overcome by the emotional power of these words of despair, the authors reported. "As he pronounced these words, the coldest hearts were warm, and every eye gave a tear." The men were certain that Bibb's story would attract many to the abolitionist cause.[22]

Members of the antislavery society in Michigan were so affected by Bibb's story that they devised a plan both to keep him on the abolitionist lecture circuit and to find his family. In 1845, according to Bibb, "the anti-slavery friends of Michigan employed me to take the field as an anti-slavery Lecturer, in that state, pledging themselves to restore to me my wife and child, if they were living, and could be reached by human agency." It had been four years since Bibb last saw Malinda and Mary Frances, and neither he nor his supporters knew if they were still alive. The organization designed a plan in which individuals in different parts of the state would collect "contributions for the freedom of Mrs. Bibb and the child." The funds would also be used to help support Bibb as an antislavery lecturer.[23] In his narrative, Bibb said he had every reason to believe the men of the society had acted faithfully but without success. They wrote letters, he said, attempting to find her, but to no avail. With this failure to find Malinda and Mary Frances, Bibb said, "the small spark of hope which had still lingered about my heart had almost become extinct."[24]

But the hope was not completely gone. Although his friends urged him to consider Malinda dead and to remarry, Bibb found it impossible to give up. He wanted to know for certain what had become of her. He could not live with the ambiguity of not knowing whether she was alive or dead, and so once more, he left his tenuous freedom in Michigan and set out toward the slave state of Kentucky to see if he could get any news of his family. He made it as far as Indiana, ten miles from his former home in Kentucky, and there received the news that would change his life forever. According to Bibb, "I learned, on inquiry, and from good authority, that my wife was living in a state of adultery with her master, and had been for the last three years."

Malinda had reportedly sent a message to her mother and friends in which she described her last separation from Bibb. She said she did not know where he had been taken and had finally given up on him. In her mind, he may as well have been dead. Malinda was sold to a man at a high price to become his mistress, and according to her, she "was better used than ordinary slaves." It certainly was not unusual for an enslaved woman to be purchased for such purposes.[25] Despite being married, this woman to whom Bibb had been so attracted was now her owner's concubine. "This was a death blow to all my hopes and pleasant plans," Bibb later recalled.

Bibb waffled between an attempt to understand Malinda's powerlessness and his own feelings of anger and betrayal. He said that he did not blame her, but his words belied the fact that he held her responsible. Bibb was angry and hurt that Malinda had capitulated to the immorality of slavery, and this sincere grief was likely compounded by the fact that as a member of the abolitionist movement, he addressed an audience of religious people who he thought would judge him morally deficient for leaving his wife. He wanted them to know that *he* had honored his marriage even though it had not been legally sanctioned, and in the end it was Malinda, not he, who had broken their vows. "From that time I gave her up into the hands of an all-wise Providence," Bibb wrote. "As she was then living with another man, I could no longer regard her as my wife. After all the sacrifices, sufferings, and risks which I had run, striving to rescue her from the grasp of slavery; every prospect and hope was cut off. She has ever since been regarded as theoretically and practically dead to me as a wife for she was living in a state of adultery, according to the law of God and man."[26]

But even as he condemned Malinda, Bibb also criticized the immorality that the institution of slavery made possible. "Poor unfortunate woman," he wrote, "I bring no charge of guilt against her, for I know not all the circumstances connected with the case. It is consistent with slavery, however, to suppose that she became reconciled to it, from the fact of her sending word back to her friends and relatives that she was much better treated than she had ever been before, and that she had also given me up." He attempted to soften what he saw as Malinda's moral breach. "It is also reasonable to suppose that there might have been some kind of attachment formed by living together in this way for years; and it is quite probably that they have other children according to the law of nature, which would have a tendency to unite them stronger together." He was back to thinking that her feelings had changed and that she now wanted to be in the relationship with her owner. For Bibb,

Malinda's intimate relationship with her owner was more emotionally devastating than any physical separation had ever been.[27]

He stood in Indiana just across the river from where she lived, but her relationship with her owner created an uncrossable chasm between them. The river and his fear of capture had not stopped him before. What whippings and sale and threats had failed to accomplish, Bibb's belief that Malinda now cared for someone else brought about. He seems to have been stunned by the news. He had kept going back to get her out of slavery but this situation in which she found herself froze him. Malinda had turned away from him and made her peace with slavery in a way that they had both vowed never to do.

Bibb stopped searching for Malinda, but she remained on his mind and probably in his heart as well. A few years after deciding not to see her, Bibb met a new woman, Mary Milles of Boston. He married her in June 1848 and wrote of her, "My beloved wife is a bosom friend, a help-meet, a loving companion in all the social, moral and religious relations of life. She is to me what a poor slave's wife can never be to her husband while in the condition of a slave for she can not be true to her husband contrary to the will of her master. She can neither be pure nor virtuous, contrary to the will of her master. She dare not refuse to be reduced to a state of adultery at the will of her master; from the fact that the slaveholding law, customs and teachings are all against the poor slave." He clearly compared his new wife to Malinda.[28]

Five years after he pronounced Malinda dead and three years after he remarried, Bibb published the lyrics of a song in *Voice of the Fugitive*, the newspaper he published in Canada. To help people make good on their vows to become free, this abolitionist paper printed train schedules, described the best points for crossing into Canada, and warned about the deepest parts of the Ohio River that lay between slavery and freedom. Bibb regularly reported on individuals and families who had made it to Canada and bemoaned the failure of those captured attempting to escape. Yet his mind seemed to remain on Malinda and the loss that he had suffered. In *Away to Canada*, sung to the tune of *Oh, Susannah*, Bibb celebrated his decision to seek freedom in Canada even as he grieved the loss of his wife. The song's first stanza reflected Bibb's own thoughts about choosing not to die a slave:

I'm on my way to Canada,
That cold and dreary land
The dire effects of Slavery
I can no longer stand.

My soul is vexed within me so,
To think that I'm a slave,
I've now resolved to strike the blow,
For freedom or the grave.
O! Righteous Father,
Wilt thou not pity me,
And aid me on to Canada,
Where colored men are free?

In two of the song's eight stanzas the songwriter addressed his sorrow at leaving his wife behind and lamented the choice he felt compelled to make between love and freedom. Remaining in slavery, he asserted, would hurt her more than his leaving, as neither of them had the power to ensure they would remain together.

Grieve not, my wife—grieve not for me;
O! do not break my heart; For nought but cruel slavery
Would cause me to depart
If I should stay to quell your grief,
Your grief I would augment; For no one knows the day that we
Asunder may be rent.
O! Susanna!
Don't you cry for me—
I'm going up to Canada,
Where colored men are free.

I'm landed safe upon the shore,
Both soul and body free;
My blood, and brain, and tears no more
Will drench old Tennessee;
But I behold the scalding tear
Now stealing from my eye,
To think my wife—my only dear,
A slave must live and die.
O, Susannah!
Don't grieve after me;
For ever at the Throne of Grace
I will remember thee.

The wife of the song could have been the wife of any man who had escaped to freedom, but she was also Malinda. Bibb sanitized their specific situation, elided the fact of concubinage, and instead presented himself as a man who had chosen freedom over slavery, despite the attendant loss.

For Sella Martin, Vilet Lester, Henry Bibb, and so many other enslaved people, the losses were profound, the memories persistent, and the search frustrating. It took a war to end slavery and the forced separations, and as African Americans entered freedom, many continued to hope that they would see their loved ones again. While still enslaved, they had latched on to rare opportunities to search for their loved ones; with newly attained freedom, they poured new energies into finding lost family members.

FIVE

"I bet the Lord done forgot who I am by now."

"Go see Reverend Pike, Ma'am. He'll reacquaint you."

"I won't need him for that. I can make my own acquaintance. What I need him for is to reacquaint me with my children. He can read and write, I recon?"

"Sure."

"Good, 'cause I got a lot of digging up to do." But the news they dug up was so pitiful she quit. After two years of messages written by the preacher's hand, two years of washing, sewing, canning, cobbling, gardening, and sitting in churches, all she found out was that the Whitlow place was gone and that you couldn't write to "a man named Dunn" if all you knew was that he went West.

Beloved, TONI MORRISON

Information Wanted

The Search for Family after Emancipation

> After the war closed all the Negroes was looking around for their
> own folks. Husbands looking for their wives, and wives looking for their
> husbands, children looking for parents, parents looking for children,
> everything sure was scrambled up in them days.
>
> SARAH FITZPATRICK, former slave

In 1864 Thomas Chaplin scribbled notes in the margins of his journal updating some of the entries from 1845. On May 4, 1845, he had written regarding the sale of ten slaves: "I cannot express my feelings on seeing so many faithful Negroes going away from me forever, not for any fault of their own but for my extravagance. It is a dearly bought lesson, and I hope I will benefit by it." On May 5, 1845, he wrote of how unpleasant it was to watch the people leaving. "The Negroes at home are quite disconsolate but this will soon blow over. They may see their children again in time." In these two entries Chaplin had expressed remorse over selling some of his slaves, but in 1864, having lost everything during the Civil War, including the people he once owned, Chaplin now took a very different tack. In his updated entry for May 4 and 5 he noted, "It was a trying time then. But could I or anyone forseen [*sic*] how things would be 19 years after, when every Negro was set free by 'force of war' I & everyone else would have gladly put them all in their pockets. Besides, I would not have felt bad about it, for in truth, the Negroes did not care as much about us as we did for them."[1]

This note suggests a few things. First, Chaplin had been sincere in his earlier expression of regret at selling the ten people. He now regretted his regret. Second, he, as many other slaveholders, had been so removed from the inner lives of their slaves as to believe that the slaves cared so much about owners that they would choose to remain even when the law said they could go. Chaplin and others had convinced themselves that black people would choose former owners over freedom. Whites had lived close to, yet worlds apart from, these people. Chaplin had likely observed with shock the elation of the enslaved people right before he and the rest of St. Helena's whites fled the island as Union forces took over in late 1861. Perhaps he had sensed that his words fell on deaf ears when, before leaving the island, he told three of his slaves to take care of his plantation until normalcy could be restored. He was bitter that he had not sold them all, "put them in his pocket," when he had the chance. When Chaplin wrote this addendum, his mother was dead, he and his brother were engaged in a heated court battle with her husband over her will, he had lost his plantation to the U.S. government for failure to pay tax, and the people he owned at the start of the war were free.[2]

The world that Chaplin and his former slaves had known was in complete turmoil. Slavery had been put into place haphazardly, colony by colony, North and South, starting in the early 1600s. It expanded over time, and black people became more locked into perpetual bondage as individual colonies and, later, states imposed legislation that restricted blacks' rights and movement. Slavery in the South unraveled haphazardly as well between the spring of 1861, when the Civil War began, and the spring of 1865, when it ended. When Confederate leaders voted to secede from the Union in late 1861 and early 1862, they made it clear that their actions had much to do with a desire to maintain and expand slavery. On the other side, President Abraham Lincoln did not always see the Civil War as a means to end slavery. Elected to the presidency by an antislavery Republican Party, Lincoln nonetheless only reluctantly made the abolition of slavery a war aim in 1862.[3]

Still, the war marked a period of profound transition as African Americans began the journey from slavery into freedom, and some people began to use the disruptions of the conflict to actualize long-hoped-for reconnections with family members. Missionary Charles Day watched as escaped slaves crowded into Union-occupied Camp Hamilton, near Richmond, Virginia, in search of freedom and family. "The numbers of 'contrabands' is still increasing," Day noted. "Mothers are having restored to them children whom they never expected to see again this side of eternity. Wives are brought upon their knees in praise to God at the appearance of husbands long ago torn from them and sold to the dreaded South and the meeting between these husbands and wives, parents and children no pen can describe. They do not usually exhibit their joy in loud salutations," he noticed, "but the convulsive grasp of the hand and the tears of joy silently coursing down their cheeks tell of happiness too deep for utterance."[4]

The scenes of family reunification Day described took place in 1862 in the midst of war, as thousands of enslaved people in Virginia and elsewhere fled to find freedom at Union army camps. The freedom they received was tenuous. Dubbed by the Union government contrabands of war—the seized property of the enemy—they straddled a status that lay between slavery and freedom. As they escaped from plantations and farms and congregated in these camps, where they dug ditches, built fortifications, cooked, or washed for northern white soldiers, they also searched for family members. The reunions at Camp Hamilton likely took place among people who had remained in Virginia or perhaps in neighboring North Carolina, not those who had been sold or taken to distant states such as Georgia, Alabama, or Mississippi. People in the Deep South would not have made their way back north this early. At great physical risk, these local people took the opportunity opened up by the presence of Union soldiers and the disarray of war to escape, and when they did, some found family members who had also journeyed to the camps.

The times were marked by conflict, chaos, movement, and danger, and once again, even as some found family members, other black families experienced disruption and loss as men went off to fight, some of them to die in battle or in Confederate massacres. Between 1863, when the Emancipation Proclamation permitted them to enlist, and 1865, when the war ended, more than 140,000 black men from slave states enlisted. The vast majority of them escaped from owners to do so. Thousands of women and children followed these soldiers to camp to escape slavery as well as to maintain connections with husbands, fathers, and sons. Back on plantations and farms, some slaveholders abused or sold relatives of black Union volunteers, while others threatened to do so. Freedom did not come easily.[5]

With Confederate surrender, the end of the war, and full-scale emancipation in April 1865, the vast majority of African Americans stood poised to move into freedom with nothing of material significance. They had no land and few belongings. They and their ancestors had labored for generations without enrichment or benefits, and as the Union had not entered the war with the intention of emancipating slaves, the government had no strategic plan in place for their future. After generations of exploitation it seemed that freedpeople would have to create new lives for themselves essentially on their own.

Even in this unsettled climate, thousands of African Americans sought out people they had lost in slavery. Some searched for relatives whom they had lost recently during the war. Others searched for family members they had not seen in many years. Some parents searched with mental images of young children, though those children were by now adults, and search-ers used names that may have long since changed. Husbands searched for wives. Children searched for parents. And one man simply searched for any friends he could find from the plantation on which he had lived.[6] They re-lied on word of mouth and on written words in letters and newspapers, and they traveled long distances to find their loved ones. The task was daunting. As William Robinson, who searched for his mother and siblings, recalled, "There was great difficulty in finding our people because they were sold so often, and had to take the name of each master." As so many others did, Rob-inson wrote letters to churches, and he got on the road, traveling to towns where he had promising reports that his mother might be. The search had begun during slavery. It continued throughout the war, and with the close of the war and the arrival of freedom, the African American search for family took on even greater urgency.[7]

From his post as assistant commissioner of the Freedmen's Bureau in charge of Washington, D.C., Maryland, and Virginia, General John Eaton Jr. had a broad view of the effects of emancipation on African Americans and whites alike as he regularly received reports from subordinates in the bureau concerning life on the ground after the war. In December 1865, eight months after the close of the war, Eaton sent a report to his superior, General O. O. Howard, commissioner of the Freedmen's Bureau. Many freedpeople, Eaton said, had gathered in Washington, D.C., "as at a city of refuge, for safety from their bitter foes." It was the bureau's job to move some of those people out of the crowded city into outlying areas. "Many women and children had no adult male support; the men had been run off by the enemy, or gone into our military service," Eaton observed. In this environment of uncertainty and hostility, "families torn asunder by the various forms of violence that had be-come an essential part of slavery, came with their tears and sighs for reunion. Husbands and wives," John Eaton observed, "fathers and mothers, sons and daughters, brothers and sisters, limited by no shade of color or grade of intel-ligence, sought each other with an ardor and faithfulness sufficient to vindi-cate the fidelity and affection of any race—the excited joys of the regathering being equaled only by the previous sorrows and pains of separation."[8]

African Americans now had both more freedom to move about and more reason to believe they could begin to live the lives they had previously only imagined. For many, this meant reuniting with family, so they urgently at-tempted to get to the places where they thought their loved ones might be. Sometimes they found them there; other times the people were gone. If any of the ten people Thomas Chaplin sold in 1845 made it back to St. Helena after the war, for instance, they would have been sorely disappointed, as one year after their sale forty of the remaining enslaved people had been seized to pay more of Chaplin's debts. There was never any guarantee that the family you left behind would have remained in place, but people kept looking. Nettie Henry recalled the long journey that her father took to find his family. When she was just an infant, Henry, her two sisters, and their mother had been given to the newly married daughter of their owner, who took them from Livingston, Alabama, to Meridian, Mississippi. "My pappy didn't go with us to Meridian," Henry told her interviewer. "He belonged to one set of white people, you see, and my mammy belong to another." From time to time, her father traveled from his home in Alabama to theirs in Mississippi to see his wife and children. When the war began, however, his owners took him to Texas, and his family did not see him for several years. "But after the war," Nettie Henry proudly told an interviewer, "he come back to us, walked most all the way from Texas." He rented land, and "my pappy built us a shack on that land."[9]

A man who had undertaken a journey even longer than that of Nettie Henry's father in search of his family made an impression on John Dennett, a white northern writer who traveled through the South as a special correspondent to the *Nation*, the New York–based weekly journal. Dennett sent the following report from Concord, North Carolina, in mid-September 1865: "Just before reaching Concord, where I passed the night, I met a middle-aged negro plodding along, staff in hand, and apparently very footsore and tired. He had walked more than six hundred miles, he said, having set out from a plantation in Georgia, near the Alabama line, and had consumed almost two months in making the journey." The man had been sold south four years earlier, and as soon as he learned he was free, he made up his mind to return to North Carolina to find his wife and children. In Georgia, he said, African Americans were doing very well, but in South Carolina many did not even dare to acknowledge that they were free. His "own color was friendly to him all the way," the man told Dennett. "He had no fear but that he would find work to do in Salisbury." He was now only about thirty miles away; he had almost made it back home.[10]

They had been on these roads before, these black people, carrying messages for owners, delivering loads of cotton, walking to the towns where they hired themselves out, and taking goods to be sold in markets. They had been on the roads as members of the coffles that dotted the landscape between the Upper and Lower South as slave traders first purchased and then took them as goods to markets in Richmond, Columbia, Charleston, New Orleans, and

Natchez. They had been on the roads accompanying white families such as the Brownriggs as they moved farther south to establish new plantations. And they had been on the roads as runaways, moving toward the free states and Canada, or back to the families from which they had been sold. In freedom they took to the roads once more, usually in the reverse direction of their forced migrations to the Deep South, embarking on personal missions of reunification. They set out with their own priorities in mind, carrying their own memories and messages for loved ones.

Often these freedpeople turned to the government through the offices of the Freedmen's Bureau for help with transportation. Freedom found most of them destitute, and they sought help to pay train fare or passage on a boat so that they would not have to walk as Nettie Henry's father and the man Dennett met had. Sometimes help was forthcoming and sometimes not. Congress had established the Bureau of Refugees, Freedmen, and Abandoned Lands, commonly known as the Freedmen's Bureau, in March 1865 with a mandate to supervise and manage all land abandoned by Confederates who had fled during the war, and to be in charge of matters related to freedmen and freedwomen. Congress imagined the Freedmen's Bureau intervening to mitigate the difficulties this group of people would now encounter as they set out to establish new lives in freedom away from domination by former owners who, accustomed to being in control, sought to return to the prewar status quo.

As the bureau was largely concerned with establishing systems of labor that would keep black people working to produce the cotton, rice, sugarcane, and other crops that had helped to drive the economies of both the South and the North, many agents focused on creating and enforcing labor contracts that sought to keep African Americans tied to the land.[11] But bureau officials performed numerous other duties as well. They adjudicated conflicts between blacks and whites and among blacks. They helped fund the building of schools, administered hospitals, supported orphanages, paid transportation for northern teachers, and issued rations of clothing and food to freedpeople who had nothing. Most bureau agents were former soldiers and officers, and their level of experience and efficiency varied greatly.[12] So did their commitment to helping freedpeople. Some brought a condescending arrogance as well as racism to the job; others brought a determination to set things right for the former slaves and truly advocated on their behalf. There were, however, never enough agents to carry out all the work that needed to be accomplished. The bureau also lacked adequate funds, particularly in its first year, when Congress failed to appropriate funding for the new organization and the bureau relied on rents collected from lands abandoned by southern whites during the war.[13]

The bureau feared encouraging dependency on the government and so was wary of providing financial support to former slaves. Guidelines issued in 1867 made the restrictions clear: "Transportation is to be given only to relieve the Government of the support of the indigent, and to enable those in extreme want to reach places where they can provide for themselves." The memorandum required that every application "must set forth clearly the fact of extreme destitution, which must be certified by the Assistant Commissioner in person." The qualification of "extreme destitution" seemed likely to apply to large numbers of former slaves, so some Freedmen's Bureau agents took very seriously the rigid conditions laid out in bureau policies to eliminate most people who appealed for assistance.[14]

John William De Forest worked for the Freedmen's Bureau in South Carolina, where he only grudgingly and infrequently approved payment of transportation expenses. Son of a Connecticut cotton manufacturer, De Forest served as captain of a New Haven volunteer company during the war. While many southern whites expressed frustration and even rage about the movement of African Americans away from plantations and from the control of former owners, De Forest exhibited a keen understanding of what motivated their restlessness. "They had a passion," he said, "not so much for wandering, as for getting together; and every mother's son among them seemed to be in search of his mother; every mother in search of her children. In their eyes the work of emancipation was incomplete until the families that had been dispersed by slavery were reunited. One woman wanted to rejoin her husband in Memphis," he recalled, "and another to be forwarded to hers in Baltimore." De Forest understood but did not respect freedpeople's deep-seated longing to return to the places they considered home and the people they considered family. A disdain for African Americans was evident throughout his account. "The Negroes who had been brought to the up-country during the war by white families were crazy to get back to their native flats of ague and country fever. Highland darkeys who had drifted down to the seashore were sending urgent requests to be 'fotched home again,'" he wrote. Whether DeForest and other whites liked it or not, these people had spent years in slavery holding on to the hope of finding their families, and at the first opportunity they wanted to transform hope into reality.[15]

This lack of regard for the people he was supposed to help played itself out in De Forest's interactions with freedpeople. "In short, transportation was a nuisance," he recalled of the time. "It seemed to me that if the Negroes wanted to travel they should not insist on doing it at the expense of the nation, but should earn money and pay their own fare like white people." He did not mention why black people were apart from their families in the first place, or why they did not have the funds to provide their own transportation. "I learned to be discouragingly surly with applicants for transportation papers and to give them out as charity as if the cost came from my own pocket. I claim that in so doing I acted the part of a wise and faithful public servant." With a slight shift in perspective he might have seen how transportation could help to reunite families and thereby encourage self-sufficiency; instead, he was quick to accuse people who had worked all of their lives and had been forced away from their families of being pariahs attempting to draw from the public coffers.[16]

Freedpeople had to navigate these obstacles as they attempted first to locate relatives and then to put their families back together. Jane Harris, a freedwoman, experienced directly how the rules of the Freedmen's Bureau could impede the search for family as she became entangled in the bureaucracy. In the fall of 1866 Bvt. Major Sherwood, a Freedmen's Bureau agent in Wytheville, Virginia, requested transportation for Harris, her mother, her daughter, and her sister. "The facts of the case are these," Sherwood informed his superior: "Jane Harris was sold before the war and taken to Little Rock, Ark., and there remained until very recently. She came to this place in search of her daughter Mother and sister and have found them." Harris told the agent that when she left Arkansas, she had $120 but "was cheated out of most of it buying rail road tickets she not being able to read or write or even count paper money." When she met with Sherwood, she had only $10 remaining and, therefore, requested transportation for herself and her relatives to Memphis, Tennessee, where her husband had acquaintances who would help her get home to Arkansas. The agent expressed his assessment that Harris was a "very worthy woman and deserves great credit for what she has done. She says," he reported, "that she and her husband are very comfortably situated at home and that he is doing well and making money."[17]

Despite this endorsement, Harris's situation did not move higher-ups in the bureau to underwrite her return home. Sherwood's superiors wanted clarification that Harris's circumstances fell under the rules governing dispensation of transportation funds. The agent persisted in his advocacy for the family, replying that the four fell within the guidelines "for the reason that they are without a home here and can have a good one on arriving at Little Rock, Ark." It seemed to make sense. But the response was "Cannot the parties themselves or the Bureau officer obtain a home for them where they now are without cost to the government?" When Sherwood's immediate superior stepped in again to inquire whether the situation met the bureau's requirements, Sherwood sent a terse response: "Respectfully returned to Bvt. Maj. J. H. Remington, Supt. with the statement that Jane and Sophia Harris have found means to leave this place with their children."[18]

Although she had lost most of her money, Jane Harris evidently did not fall within the definition of destitution, and a desire to have her family all in one place did not convince officials that she should receive funds from the bureau's limited resources. Despite a bureau employee's advocacy, the agent in charge wanted to know why she did not simply remain in Virginia, ignoring the fact that she had a home and other relatives in Arkansas and would be able to support herself there. It was logical to Sherwood, though not to his superiors, that Harris would want to return to Arkansas. As her advocate, he also expressed his moral judgment that Jane Harris was a "very worthy woman" who deserved great credit for having made her way from Arkansas to Virginia to find her family. Agents' moral judgments often determined that freedpeople were not worthy of support; in this instance a positive judgment was not enough to help Harris. As the government employees read and reread rules and drafted memoranda, Jane Harris and her relatives found a way to pay for their own transportation to Arkansas.

Marie Johnson had better luck. In September 1866 the Freedmen's Bureau agent in Raleigh requested transportation from there to Edgecombe County, North Carolina, for her. According to the agent, "This woman states that about fifteen years before the War she was living with her husband at Tarboro NC. Each were the property of a different slaveholder. The one that she belonged to moved to Miss. She states that her husband is living in Tarboro that she has walked, worked and scuffled from West Point, Miss to this city and has now neither strength nor means to go further."[19] She had made it all the way from Mississippi to Raleigh, and as Johnson only had to travel across two more counties to get to Tarboro, the cost was low and the agents granted her request for transportation. Johnson was close to home when she gave out from exhaustion, but now she would have help in making the last leg of her journey. People like her were stranded all over the South in places they did not consider home, taken there by owners and traders, miles away from their relatives. Others such as Jane Harris had made a home where owners took them and wanted to have all of their family together again.[20]

Freedpeople could not rely on help from the federal government, but they still tried. Some wrote letters to Freedmen's Bureau offices asking for information, believing that agents of the federal government would be linked into networks that could provide some word of their relatives. Hawkins Wilson wrote such a letter to the bureau in Richmond, Virginia, in May 1867. He was in Galveston, Texas, and he sought information about the relatives whom he had left in Virginia when he was sold. In the letter, addressed to the chief of the Freedmen's Bureau, Wilson got directly to his purpose in writing. "I am anxious to learn about my sisters, from whom I have been separated many years—I have never heard from them since I left Virginia twenty four years ago—I am in hopes that they are still living and I am anxious to hear how they are getting on." After many years of separation and a few years of freedom, Wilson turned to the government for help. "I have no other one to apply to but you and am persuaded that you will help one who stands in need of your services as I do," he wrote. "I shall be very grateful to you, if you oblige me in this matter—one of my sisters belonged to Peter Coleman in Caroline County and her name was Jane—her husband's name was Charles and he belonged to Buck Haskin and lived near John Wright's store in the same county—they had three children, Robert, Charles and Julia, when I left—Sister Martha belonged to Dr Jefferson, who lived two miles above Wright's store—sister Matilda belonged to Mrs. Botts in the same county." Wilson also wanted information regarding his extended family, including his "dear uncle Jim" and Jim's wife and son. "These are all my dearest relatives," he wrote, "and I wish to correspond with them with a view to visit them as soon as I can hear from them—my name is Hawkins Wilson and I am their brother, who was sold at Sheriff's sale and used to belong to Jackson Talley and was bought by M. Wright. You will please send the enclosed letter to my sister Jane, or some of her family, if she is dead." He included a letter to Jane in which he reminisced about their childhood and updated her on his life as an adult, particularly his involvement in the church.[21]

Wilson provided information he thought would help the bureau identify his relatives: He gave their names, where they lived, and who had owned them. During slavery, letters such as these had been sent to former owners who already knew the details. Miss Patsy, for example, needed no introduction to Vilet Lester, and Charles had known his owner well. After the war, though, many freedpeople called on strangers for assistance. By identifying the members of his family group, Wilson hoped the bureau would tap into its sources of information to reconnect him to his sisters after more than two decades of separation. Beyond the identifying information, Wilson also transmitted the emotional urgency of his request: "These are all my dearest relatives," he said. He had been sold at a sheriff's sale, meaning that perhaps, like Thomas Chaplin's slaves, he had been sold to pay the debts of his owner.

When he left, all his family members were in Caroline County, and since he'd had no contact with them over the decades, he hoped they were all still there. It did occur to him that some might not be alive, but short of death, his memory held them in place in Caroline County with the possibility of reunification. People such as Hawkins Wilson had not forgotten those they left behind when they were taken into the domestic slave trade. They built new lives in the places where they lived but remained concerned that the people connected to them were still missing. His letter remains in the Freedmen's Bureau files, so his sister Jane may not have ever heard its contents.

Numerous people wrote to the Freedmen's Bureau office in New Orleans searching for family members. This had been a hub of the domestic slave trade, the site of a major market in which people from the Upper South had been bought and sold. In 1868, bureau agent L. Tolisaint did not simply file the letters; he actually went out into the city to make inquiries regarding lost family members. In January he responded to an inquiry from the West Virginia field office on behalf of Henry Johnson, who searched for his two sons and two daughters and thought they might be living in New Orleans. The agent turned to "ministers of colored churches in the city, requesting them to forward to this office any information they might have regarding Samuel, Henry, Sarah and Annie Johnson." One month later Tolisaint reported, "No tidings of such people have reached this office." He later sent notices to local black churches for information regarding Martha Ann Wood, the daughter of Robert and Sophia Wood of Falmouth, Virginia. According to her family, "She had been taken to New Orleans, La. By Henry Atchison, a trader, when she was 16 years of age—she is now about 28. She was at last accounts bought by Dr. J. Green." Again the churches had no knowledge of Martha Ann, and the agent was unable to locate her former owner.[22]

In February, Tolisaint worked on a similar request from the Baltimore, Maryland, office to look for Charles Counsey, a freedman who had been sold by William H. Adams of Baltimore to Wilson and Hines slave traders. The inquiry stated that the Wilson of the slave-trading firm now lived in New Orleans. Tolisaint went out looking for Wilson and located him, but he could give no account of Counsey. He had sold so many people that this particular man did not stand out in his memory. He thought, however, that his former clerk might have some information, but the clerk was out of town for two weeks. Three weeks later, when Tolisaint received a request from Baltimore for an update, he visited Wilson again, then sent a reply to Baltimore. Wilson, he said, could offer "no additional information respecting the whereabouts of Charles Counsey, freedman. The said Wilson suggests that information would most likely be obtained by consulting 'Bills of sales' in possession of Wilson and Hines, Baltimore."[23]

Wilson's response served as a reminder that the slave trade had been a business enterprise. Jonathan M. Wilson, the trader who purchased Charles Counsey, was one of several traders who had been active in the slave trade from Baltimore to New Orleans between 1848 and 1859. Relatives in Baltimore searching for Counsey knew this information, and they had come close; but as a trader, Wilson did not know Counsey and had not cared about where he was sold or who purchased him. He now referred the searchers to the defunct firm's business records. Bills of sale, part of the business transactions, might indicate who had purchased Counsey, but there was no reason for Wilson or his clerk to have remembered such information.[24]

Freedpeople had to piece together fragments of information to generate leads about their family members. They believed that a trader or an owner—a white person with a civic presence—would be identifiable, and they hoped he would be able to recall what he had done with the slaves he had purchased or sold. But many freedpeople learned that it was difficult for owners and traders to dig back into slavery to identify people who had been mere sales items; such people may have only been known to these owners and traders as "likely" or "prime" or an experienced cook, a good seamstress, or a field hand. Thomas Chaplin sent ten people with first names only to be sold in Charleston; in his letter to his wife, Obadiah Fields listed only the first names of the people he sold and did not say who had purchased them. Searchers needed some sort of organized mechanism, but there was no logbook into which enslaved people's names and owners had been systematically entered and through which their movements could be traced. Their movements, when recorded at all, were scattered in individual owners' journals, in traders' letters home, in the financial ledgers of slaveowners and slave traders, and in wills and bills of sale.

A few efforts attempted to bring some coherence to the search for family members. In one case a private organization tried; in another, it was the federal government that devised a system for providing information. In June 1867 a group of white men in Washington, D.C., including James Harlan, a U.S. senator from Iowa, founded an organization to offer help. The Freedmans Association for the Restoration of Lost Friends laid out the reasons for its founding. First, it asserted, "prior to the war, and during the existence of slavery, thousands of families in the slave holding States, were separated and scattered by the system of slave trading." Second, "during the same period, thousands of slaves escaped and sought refuge in the Northern States or Canada, and as their security depended upon secrecy, they have never informed their friends and relatives of the location of their new homes, or even of their existence." Third, "during the war, the march of armies, the breaking up of plantations and the voluntary flight of men and women there held as slaves, have also separated thousands who would gladly gain information of their friends and relatives, and if possible be reunited with them." The organization aimed to systematize the efforts of those who searched. They proposed to set up books in which the names of freedpeople from all over the United States and Canada would appear alphabetically by state of residence. Along with the registered names would be a brief history of the individual, "showing the present and former residence, former owner, and such other main facts as will lead to identification." If someone looked for an individual whose name did not appear in the books, the organization would initiate a search, calling on the support of other organizations such as the Freedmen's Bureau, the Union League, and African American churches and schools. The organization would charge anyone searching for a lost friend a fee of twenty-five cents to help defray expenses.

The association's circular remained silent as to the practicalities of the registration, including where in each state the books would be located. It relied on the Freedmen's Bureau to publicize the registration and "earnestly urged upon all freedmen and women in the States and Canada to register their names with brief statements of facts pertaining to their history. If no advantage to the individual is at first suggested to the mind," the association coaxed would-be registrants, "it should be remembered that *others* may be seeking information about *them*."[25] Despite the obvious obstacles, the need for such a clearinghouse was quite evident, as the association outlined so well. In this regard, an article in the *Boston Daily Advertiser* noted, "The reunion of families which have been separated by slavery in times past and during the war was supposed to have been provided for by the Freedman's Bureau; but this resource having failed to answer the purpose fully, this new organization has been established. It is sanctioned by prominent public men and is in the charge of men of respectability." It is not clear, however, whether the organization's plans ever got off the ground or if any former slaves ever registered.[26]

In April 1865, as the war ended, the federal government also attempted to minimize the confusion of family separation by instituting a system intended to assist enlisted men who wanted to know the whereabouts of family and friends whom they had left on plantations. The sense of loss and displacement, the army realized, affected the soldiers as much as it did the women and children who had been left behind when the men enlisted. This system covered the Department of the Gulf. The *Black Republican*, one of the newspapers that began publishing immediately after the war, printed an announcement captioned, "Important Information for Colored Troops and their friends in the Department of the Gulf." The notice said, "As large numbers of colored troops have been hastily enlisted and separated from their families, with no means of ascertaining anything about them afterwards, this information will be of value." The Freedmen's Bureau had created a registry containing the names and locations of all African Americans on the plantations in the area. A soldier searching for his family members could give the superintendent the "familiar name" of the person, and the bureau would search the registry and "respond without delay." This more localized initiative likely worked more efficiently than the one proposed by the Freedmans Association for the Restoration of Lost Friends.[27] It was one more effort inspired by the unmistakable longing that former slaves expressed for finding their families, whether they had been separated for decades during slavery or more recently by the chaos of war.

Some African Americans shaped their memories into brief messages that they published in newspapers, hoping that word would come back to them about their lost relatives. Decades of separation had scattered African Americans all over the South, and manumission and escape had taken some as far north as Canada. A few had also made it to California. Following the war, African Americans used the new black and Republican newspapers to help carry out their search. Although newspapers were a written medium, illiteracy likely did not present an impenetrable barrier, as some people would have dictated their notices directly to the editor, and others would have received help from a literate person in their community. Further, as they and their children began to attend freedpeople's schools, more and more would have been able to write their own advertisements.

Among the newspapers were relatively short-lived ones such as the *Black Republican*, published in 1865 in New Orleans; the *Colored Tennessean*, published in Nashville from 1865 to 1866; the *South Carolina Leader*, published in Charleston from 1865 to 1868; the *Free Man's Press*, published from 1868 to 1869 in Galveston, Texas; the *Colored American*, also known as the *Loyal Georgian*, published in Augusta from 1865 to 1868; and the *Colored Citizen*, published in Cincinnati, Ohio, from 1863 to 1869. Only a few issues of these newspapers have been preserved. People also used several church-sponsored newspapers. These included the *Christian Recorder*, published in Philadelphia by the African Methodist Episcopal Church (A.M.E.); the *Southwestern Christian Advocate*, published in New Orleans by the Methodist Episcopal Church South from 1873 to 1929; and the *Star of Zion*, published in Charlotte, North Carolina, by the African Methodist Episcopal Zion Church. The *Christian Recorder*, which predated the Civil War but became much more accessible in southern states following the war, and the *Southwestern Christian Advocate* carried many more ads than all of the others.

Placing an ad required an expenditure of time, effort, and hope by people who had already invested emotionally by continuing to care about the relatives they had lost. For some publications the ads also cost money for people who had so little. In the spring of 1866 the *South Carolina Leader* invited advertisements with the following notice: "Persons wishing information of their relatives, can have them advertised one month for two dollars and a half." The *Southwestern Christian Advocate* included the following notice: "We make no charge for publishing these letters from yearly subscribers. Others will be charged 50 cents." An annual subscription cost $1.25. Even at 50 cents, placing an ad required a significant monetary investment, as a recently freed person in the South could expect to earn between $5 and $25 per month as a field hand working six days per week. African Americans, whether in the North or the South, who had been free before the war did not fare much better. There were exceptions, of course, but most of the black population lived in poverty on the margins of the economy.[28] But newspapers provided a public airing of freedpeople's memories and hopes and offered the best possibility that many people would read or hear their appeals for information.

Advertisements appeared most often with the captions INFORMATION WANTED or, in the *Southwestern Christian Advocate*, LOST FRIENDS. Newspaper ads for runaways during slavery had carried an icon of a figure with a bag slung over his or her shoulder. The Information Wanted ads often featured an icon of a horizontal hand with the index finger pointing, making these ads easy to spot on large pages of newsprint among the formal notices of marriages, deaths, and rooms for rent as well as the more ornate, illustrated advertisements for hoopskirts, hair straighteners, artificial eyes, and medicines that promised to cure all manner of ailments. Ads generally ran for one month of weekly issues, but some ran much longer. In fact, some ran for several months, suggesting several possibilities: the person had not been found, the searcher was persistent and had the resources to continue paying for publication, or perhaps merely that the newspaper had space to fill. In a few instances the same person placed ads in more than one newspaper.

Thornton Copeland's
Information Wanted
ad, *Colored Tennessean*,
October 7, 1865

Ads came from people living all over the United States. They wrote from New York, New Jersey, Ohio, Massachusetts, Connecticut, Rhode Island, Pennsylvania, Illinois, Indiana, Iowa, Michigan, Delaware, Washington, D.C., Maryland, Virginia, North Carolina, South Carolina, Kansas, Missouri, Alabama, Louisiana, Kentucky, Mississippi, Tennessee, Georgia, Florida, California, and the newly established Idaho Territory. They wrote from cities such as Harlem, Detroit, Philadelphia, Richmond, New Orleans, Charleston, and Savannah, and they wrote from obscure, small towns. People wrote from Canada too: from Hamilton, Ontario, and Newberry Post Office, Chatham, and Buxton, all in the region of Canada West that was bounded by New York, Michigan, and Ohio. Enslaved Americans had gone to Canada as early as the Revolutionary war period and continued to escape to freedom there throughout the nineteenth century, particularly after passage of the federal Fugitive Slave Act of 1850 that mandated the capture and return of escaped slaves within the United States.[29]

African Americans had developed mechanisms in slavery that helped them to survive: faith, hope, music, community, and literacy. Many had buried their grief, suppressed their anger, smiled, danced, and denied abuse at the command of owners and traders. They had sung as they wept and had sung to keep from weeping. Some had spent time at the crossroads trying to figure out how they would go on. Through all of it, many had held memories of their children, spouses, parents, siblings, and friends. The newspaper ads that they crafted often consisted of just a few lines of text, yet they offer rich suggestions about the people who placed them as well as those for whom they searched. Thornton Copeland, for instance, whose ad appears in the Introduction, searched for his mother twenty-one years after he had last seen her. He knew that her name had been Betty, and he knew that Colonel Briggs sold her to James French. He also knew that Robert Rogers had sold him to Samuel Copeland. He and his mother had been separated in Fauquier County, Virginia, and he now lived hundreds of miles away in Tennessee. Even after such a long time apart, he hoped that somehow his Information Wanted advertisement in the *Colored Tennessean* would lead him to his mother.

It is perhaps reasonable for those who now read these ads to wonder if former slaves such as Copeland acted out of hope or out of a final desperation bordering on despair. Did he and the others who paid for these ads truly believe that word would reach their loved ones? How rationally did they act when they invested their hard-earned funds? It is only barely conceivable that people who had experienced so much loss could continue to care about their family members, and more baffling still that they would believe they could find their relatives who had been lost across so much time and space. Perhaps, like Kate Drumgoold, the young girl who kept sight of a clear place in the sky after her mother's departure, people who placed these ads participated in a bit of magical thinking, believing that *their* loved ones would also return.

In fact, they had centuries of collective experience developing resources out of what seemed like nothing. And they had had a great deal of practice hoping and believing that their worlds would change. As they transitioned into freedom, they continued to use well-exercised coping mechanisms. To prepare for the search, they scraped together fragments of memory and made judgments about the salience of the information they possessed. They provided names, ages, and physical descriptions of skin color, blemishes, and limps. They enumerated relationships, locations of plantations, points of separation, details about the men and women who had owned them, and names of the men who had traded them—whatever they thought would trigger recognition among readers and listeners. They called out from the newspaper pages to the people who they thought would care and would be able to help. To encounter the ads as they appeared in the newspapers is to begin to grasp the power and poignancy of these brief, compelling, and urgent dispatches that former slaves put into circulation to seek out their loved ones.

Colored Tennessean (Nashville)   March 24, 1866

Information Wanted of our five children, whom we have not seen for four years. Their names are as follows, viz: Josephine, aged 20 years; Celia, aged 14 years; Caroline, aged 13 years; Ellen, aged 10 years, and Augusta, aged 8 years. They were in Charlotte, N.C., or at Rock Hill when we last heard from them. Any information concerning these children will be thankfully received by their mother. Our address is, Augusta, Ga.

AUGUSTUS BRYANT, LUTITIA BRYANT.

N.B.—These persons were formerly owned by John L. and Virginia Moon, of Augusta, Ga.

Christian Recorder   April 7, 1866

INFORMATION WANTED of the children of Hagar Outlaw, who went from Wake Forest. Three of them, (their names being Cherry, Viny, and Mills Outlaw) were bought by Abram Hester. Noah Outlaw was taken to Alabama by Joseph Turner Hillsborough. John Outlaw was sold to George Vaughn. Eli Outlaw was sold by Joseph Outlaw. He acted as watchman for old David Outlaw. Thomas Rembry Outlaw was sold in New Orleans by Dr. Outlaw. I live in Raleigh, and I hope they will think enough of their mother to come and look for her, as she is growing old and needs help. She will be glad to see them again at her side. The place is healthy, and they can all do well here. As the hand of time steals over me now so rapidly, I wish to see my dear ones once more clasped to their mother's heart as in days of yore. Come to the capital of North Carolina, and you will find your mother there, eagerly awaiting her loved ones.

Hugh Outlaw, if you should find any or all of my children, you will do me an incalculable favor by immediately informing them that their mother still lives.

Christian Recorder   June 18, 1870

INFORMATION WANTED of my sister, Mrs. Martha Holeman, who lived in Lebanon, Wilson county Tenn. My mother and I lived in Somelia county, Tenn. Our mother's name is Sophia Hosley. My sister's husband's name is Robert Holeman; they were both sold from Lebanon jail to Huntsville, Alabama, to a man named Branum. Any information of their whereabouts will be thankfully received, by their sister, Mary Hosley. They were sold some twenty odd years ago. Address, Mrs. Mary Anthony, Lafayette, Ind., in care of box 397.

Lafayette, Ind. June 8th, 1870.

Those who searched well knew that churches provided the spaces in which black people gathered to worship, to learn, and to hold political meetings. African American churches and ministers therefore proved to be critical resources to whom many turned for help, as L. Tolisaint, the Freedmen's Bureau agent in New Orleans, did. It made sense to enlist the help of ministers and churches, as one newspaper read at a service or a meeting had the potential to reach hundreds of listeners. Ministers served congregations full of potential informants and were also likely to have contacts in congregations throughout the community. The *Southwestern Christian Advocate* included the following message: "Pastors will please read the requests published below from their pulpits, and report any cases where friends are brought together by means of letters in the SOUTHWESTERN."[30] Freedpeople were not entirely without resources, and they put what they had to work, as the following ads from Eliza Silas and Kansas Lee illustrate.

Christian Recorder   May 11, 1867

INFORMATION WANTED

Information wanted of my parents, Joseph and Julia Ann Silas, my brothers, George, David and Wolbert Silas, and my sister Henrietta Silas, of Prince George County, Maryland. I was owned by Luke Hutchins. The rest of the family were owned by his mother, Caroline Hutchins. ELIZA SILAS.

Information addressed to South Orchard St., New Bedford, Mass., Will be thankfully received. Ministers in the States of Maryland and Virginia, and the District of Columbia, will please read the above to their congregations.

Christian Recorder   August 25, 1866

INFORMATION WANTED

Kansas Lee wishes to learn the whereabouts of her children, four girls and one boy, who were, when last heard from, living in Baltimore, Md. Their names are as follows: Annie, Selia, Sarah, Elizabeth, and Adam Lee. My children were owned by the mother of Benjamin Keene. Address KANSAS LEE Box 507, St. Joseph, Mo.

N.B. Ministers South, who take this paper, will please read the above in their congregations.

Eliza Silas had made it to New Bedford, Massachusetts, where Frederick Douglass and other escaped slaves had also found refuge.[31] She does not appear in the census in New Bedford, nor does she indicate when or under what circumstances she left Virginia. However, hoping that her children were still in the vicinity where she had left them, she specifically asked ministers in Maryland, Virginia, and Washington, D.C., to take note of her search. Kansas Lee, on the other hand, was prepared to have to search more broadly, so she asked all ministers in the South to read the ad to their congregations.

Some who searched also relied on ministers in their hometowns to serve as contacts and likely to help them to write the advertisements.

Christian Recorder   November 21, 1868

INFORMATION WANTED

Of my father, Joshua Clarke, my mother Polly Clarke, my brother, Joshua and sister Kate. In our family there were four daughters and one son. I am the oldest daughter. I was sold about thirteen years ago, to Alabama. My father, mother, brother and sisters were then living in Richmond, VA. ALICE MITCHELL, (Care of Rev. Levi Walker) Glenville, Barbour Co., Ala.

Ministers will please read in their congregations.

Christian Recorder   January 21, 1871

INFORMATION WANTED

Information is Wanted of my daughter Lauriah Smith. She belonged before the war to J. R. Thomson, in Louisville, Ky., about 1859, and was sold South to traders. She was about fifteen years old when sold. Her mother was named Emily Holms, who lives in Indianapolis. Any information of her whereabouts will be directed to Rev. Wm. C. Trevan, of Bethel A.M.E. church, Indianapolis, Ind.

The tenuous nature of enslaved people's public identities did not augur well for the possibility of finding family members. Their births had not been routinely noted and registered. Their sales had not been consistently recorded and archived. Even their names, such an essential signifier of identity, had been unstable. Many functioned with only a first name, and as Thornton Copeland suggested about his mother, even that name was not always permanent. An enslaved person's name could have changed at the whim of an owner, or due to sale, or to provide cover while escaping, or because a woman had married, or because people took new names once they became free. People who searched sometimes acknowledged these changes, and some acknowledged that they could not be certain of the current name of even the closest relatives.[32]

Christian Recorder December 16, 1865

Fanny Frazer wishes to ascertain the whereabouts of her six children, who were owned by a family of the name of Bailey, who lived in Clarksville, Va. Some years ago the children assumed the name of their owners, and are known by the following names: Nelson Bailey, Hannah Bailey, Maria Bailey, Charlotte Bailey, Norah Bailey and Amie Bailey. Any information respecting them will be thankfully received by Fanny Frazer, Buston, Canada West.

Southwestern Christian Advocate April 26, 1877

LOST FRIENDS

I desire information concerning my kindred. Our family belonged to Mr. John C. Paine, in Louisiana. My father's name was Randall and my mother's Celia. I had four brothers, Levi, William, Leonard and Warren; one sister named Elvira, but usually called Puss, and one named Hannah. The family had the name of Paine but since they were free may have changed it. I was separated from the family in 1857, when I was five years old, being brought to Texas by my young mistress whose name was Florida and who married a Mr. John Bailey. Address, care of Rev. Paul Douglass, Galveston, Texas, Sarah Williams (formerly Bailey).

Southwestern Christian Advocate July 17, 1879

Dear Editor: I want to enquire for my father. He went from Franklin Co., Miss. about 1850 to Alabama with a man by the name of Doctor Baker, who was said to be his young master. My father's name was Milzes Young. I learned that after he left here he went by the name of Milzes Arbet. I now go by the name of Dock Young and am his youngest son. Address me in care of George Torrey, Union Church, Jefferson Co. Miss. Dock Young.

To counter the impermanence of their own public identities, searchers frequently offered the more stable names of the men and women who had owned or traded them. These were people with public profiles who may have owned businesses or held public office or may have been connected to wealthy and powerful people. Their names would be much more recognizable to a broader range of people than the name of an individual slave. Amidst the turmoil and grief of sale and separation, some enslaved people, like the Counseys, had also managed to learn the names of the traders who purchased their family members, and they had some sense of where those traders were headed. Knowledge of a trader's destination may have only been rumored, or it might have been confirmed by the enslaved men who worked for traders and routinely followed a particular circuit of purchases and sales.[33] Some people may have received news through letters from loved ones, or they may have overheard the conversations of whites discussing the movements of traders. When slavery ended, they called the names of former owners and traders to help with the search, much as Charles Counsey's family attempted to find him through the trader they thought had taken him to New Orleans. The possession of these small bits of information is precisely what had kept enslaved people hoping and perhaps even believing that they could find their relatives someday.

Black Republican (New Orleans)   Saturday, April 22, 1865
INFORMATION WANTED

EVANS GREEN desires to find his mother, Mrs. PHILLIS GREEN, whom he left in Virginia some years ago. She belonged to old Squire Cook, of Winchester, whose son was an attorney-at-law. Any information respecting her will be thankfully received. Address this paper. Winchester paper please copy.

South Carolina Leader (Charleston)   May 12, 1866

Information Wanted OF NANCY YOUNG, who was living in Summerville in 1861, and belonged to Mrs. Edward Lowndes, but was afterwards sold to Mr. Colder, and carried up the country, perhaps to Spartenburg or Columbia. Any information respecting her whereabouts will be thankfully received by her son, Thomas S. P. Miller, at Charleston, S.C.

Colored Tennessean   March 24, 1866

Information Wanted of my two sons, Sidney and Harrison who belonged to Clem. Cannon, who formerly lived in Shelbyville, Bedford county Tenn., and were sold to Goodbar, a trader and when last heard from were in Montgomery, Ala. The oldest one is about 26 years of age. My name is Sidney. When they left I belonged to a man by the name of Elliott. Information of them will be thankfully received by myself or their mother, whose name is Eliza Cannon. Please Address *Colored Tennessean*, Box 1150.
SYDNEY ELLIOTT

Christian Recorder   September 11, 1869

Information Wanted of Ann Roscoe, formerly lived near Gallatin, Tenn. Belonged to a Mr. Patton, but was purchased by Thos. Roscoe, was left with a trader named John Taylor, who is said to have sold her to South Carolina.

Please address her daughter, Amanda Allison, formerly Amanda Shaw, No. 35 North High St, Nashville, care of Daniel F. Carter.

Southwestern Christian Advocate   July 26, 1877

I will be most thankful for information concerning my two sisters, Phillis and Letitia (called Tishia). Our mother is named Itty, and formerly belonged to Billy Carter, at Big Springs, Wilson Co., Tenn. My sisters were sold to a slave trader named Pat. Anderson, and we afterwards heard that he sold Phillis fifteen miles below New Orleans; this was the last word we had concerning them. Address, Mrs. Martha Smith, care Rev. Jos. Smith, Lebanon, Tenn.

In addition to former owners and slave traders, searchers named the places where they had parted from loved ones. They identified the location of plantations or courthouse steps or traders' yards in which white men had poked, examined, and purchased them. These moments had been etched into their memories, and some carried with them for years the names of the places of separation.

Colored Tennessean (Nashville)   October 14, 1865

INFORMATION WANTED of Caroline Dodson, who was sold from Nashville Nov. 1st 1862 by James Lumsden to Warwick, (a trader then in human beings), who carried her to Atlanta, Georgia, and she was last heard of in the sale pen of Robert Clarke, (human trader in that place), from which she was sold. Any information of her whereabouts will be thankfully received and rewarded by her mother,

LUCINDA LOWERY,

Box 1121, Nashville, Tenn.

Christian Recorder   November 18, 1865

INFORMATION WANTED

Of my mother and father, Caroline and Isaac Denna; also, my sisters, Fanny, Jane and Betsy Denna, and my brothers, Robert R., Hugh Henry, and Philander Denna. We were born in Fauquier Co, Va. In 1849 they were taken from the plantation of Josiah Lidbaugh, in said county, and carried to Winchester to be sold. About the same time I left my home in Clark Co., and have not heard from them since. The different ministers of Christian churches will do a favor by announcing the above, and any information will be gladly received by

GEO HENRY DENNA,

Galva, Henry Co., Illinois.

Christian Recorder August 29, 1868

INFORMATION WANTED of my mother, Virginia Shepherd, also of my sisters, Mary, Louisa, Mandy and Caroline Shepherd; of my brother, William H. Shepherd; my uncle Paten Shepherd, and my aunt Dibsy Madison, all of whom belonged to Ben Shepherd. Also of my Aunt Martha Young, who belonged to Henry Young. All lived in Prince Edward Co., Virginia. My mother and her four children were sold, at Prince Edward County Court House, to a slave trader named Sam Jenkins. Any information of the above named persons will be thankfully received by Martha Shepherd.

Address   MARTHA PARIS, Lebanon, St. Clair Co., Ill.

Ministers will please read this notice to their congregations.

Christian Recorder May 19, 1866

INFORMATION WANTED

Of John Humphrey; also of my mother, Milly Humphrey and my sister Sarah Ann Humphrey. I left them at Fairfax County Court House, Va., in 1851.—They were owned by Cook Fitzhugh. Any information concerning them please send to HENRY HUMPHREY,

Williamsville, Mich.

Rev. Wm. J. Anderson

Niles, Michigan.

Ministers please notice for them and govern yourselves accordingly.

Despite the dispersal of their relatives, some people had doggedly kept track of sales and movements for some time. Rachel Davis, for example, knew of her daughter Abbie's owners and movements over decades, even including time spent in Cuba. However, she had lost track of her during the Civil War. Eliza Ann Ratlif knew of her young sons' movements in Virginia even after she was sold to Tennessee. And Martha McDermit had received bits of information about her brother over the years. It must have been painful and frustrating when they lost even a hint of where a child or parent or spouse might be as the sources of information evaporated.

Christian Recorder August 5, 1865

INFORMATION WANTED

Of Abbie Davis, daughter of Rachel Davis, who was born at Wilmington, Delaware. She was carried to Cuba, by Mr. Guelle, for Mr. Peter Bodway, over thirty-five years ago.

Since then she has been with Mr. Martin, of Texas, and latterly with Mr. A. Bell of New Orleans. She kept a wash house in New Orleans, about 1862. Her husband died about 7 years ago.

Any information will be most thankfully received by her distressed mother.

RACHEL DAVIS,

Care *Christian Recorder*

Box 2975, Philadelphia, Pennsylvania.

Colored Tennessean (Nashville)   March 24, 1866

Of my sons, George William, and Bearty Lewis. George was born in 1848; Bearty was born in 1853, in Culpepper county, Va. In 1858, they went to the Eastern Shore of Virginia with Mrs. Nottingham. In 1860, they went to Petersburgh, Va. In 1855, I came to Tennessee with Mrs. Hemps, and now reside in Williamson county, Tenn.

ELIZA ANN RATLIF.

Colored Tennessean (Nashville)   Saturday, August 12, 1865

OF A MAN BY THE NAME OF ELIAS LOWERY MCDERMIT, who used to belong to Thomas Lyons of Knoxville, East Tennessee. He was sold to a man by the name of Sherman about ten years ago, and I learned some six years ago that he was on a steamboat running between Memphis and New Orleans, and more recently I heard that he was somewhere on the Cumberland river in the Federal army. Any information concerning him will be thankfully received. Address Colored Tennessean, Nashville, Tenn. From his sister who is now living in Knoxville, East Tennessee. MARTHA MCDERMIT

With slavery behind them, a few people who advertised in the *Christian Recorder* launched rhetorical challenges to the legitimacy of the institution and to those who had thought it justifiable to own and sell other human beings. Their relatives, they said, had "belonged" to, had been the "property" of, or were "claimed" or had been "stolen" by slaveholders. They may have had to keep those critical views to themselves during slavery, but with emancipation, they felt free to publicly sneer at the institution of slavery and those who had claimed ownership of them and their relatives. Doing so would not help in the search, but it likely provided some degree of satisfaction to be able to lash out against those who had brought about their losses.

Christian Recorder   August 25, 1866

INFORMATION WANTED of our children. Titus and Ellen Shropshire wish to be informed of the whereabouts of Josephine and Thomas B. Shropshire, their two children, who were stolen from them by Brown and Rodgers, in 1860, from Schuyler County, Missouri. Any person or persons knowing any thing of importance concerning the missing parties will confer a favor on the parents by dropping a few lines to them at Keokuk, Iowa. Very respectfully TITUS AND ELLEN SHROPSHIRE

Christian Recorder   April 7, 1866

INFORMATION WANTED of my children, Lewis, Lizzie, and Kate Mason, whom I last saw in Owensboro, Ky. They were then "owned" by David and John Hart, that is the girls were—but the boy was rather the "property" of Thomas Pointer. Any information will be gladly received by their sorrowing mother, Catherine Mason, at 1818 Hancock St., between Master and Thompson, Phila.

Christian Recorder   June 16, 1866

INFORMATION WANTED

Of my father and mother, David and Rebecca Tennerson. When I last saw them they were at Parisville, Va. My father was claimed to be owned by a man named Benjamin Adams and my mother by a woman named Nancy Green. I have not seen nor heard from them for seven years. I earnestly request the different pastors, especially those presiding over Southern Churches, to read this notice in their charges. DAVID TENNERSON 103 Meeting Street, Providence, R.I.

Christian Recorder   September 14, 1867

INFORMATION WANTED

Information is wanted of my two sons—Jeremiah and William Rhodes. I left them at Ellicott's Mills, Md. They "belonged" to Caleb Dorsey. This was before the war. Any information of their whereabouts will be thankfully received by their aged mother, Catherine Rhodes, at No. 631 Pine St. Philadelphia, Pa.

    N.B. Ministers, please notice.

The duration of some separations was staggering. Some people lost relatives to sale as late as 1864 as slaveholders held on to the belief that slavery would survive the Civil War. Some lost husbands and fathers when they went off to fight in the war. Others had been gone for several years, and still others were missing for decades. It is likely that those who searched after a long time had created other significant relationships in their lives; they may have remarried or had other children, but the memories and the caring lingered.

Loyal Georgian (Augusta, Ga.)   October 13, 1866

Of Richard, Martin, Lucy and Frances Nagles, who were carried from the trader's office, in Hamburg, S.C. to Twiggs County, Ga., Mary Nagles who formerly belonged to Mr. Samuel Gilchrist of Florida, and Harriet Nagles who was carried to New Orleans, by Mr. Edward Holaway about 20 years ago. Any information of the above parties will be gladly received by their mother who is now living in Augusta, Ga.

Christian Recorder   July 2, 1870

INFORMATION WANTED of my sisters, Jennette, Eliza, Caroline, America, and of my brother Harry. Also of our mother, whose name was Dinah Hickson. They were sold from Liberty, Mo. Over 30 years ago, and the last time I heard of them they were on Red River. They belonged to Andy Hickson, and were sold to a man named Francis Benware. Any information of these parties will be gladly received by MOSES HICKSON NOW MOSES SISSENEY, St. Joseph, Mo., Box 507.

N.B. Pastors of churches will please read this.

Christian Recorder   January 28, 1871

INFORMATION WANTED

Information wanted of my sister Rosanna. We parted in Richmond, Va., thirty-five years ago. Learned that she was carried to Alabama by a man named Templeman. She is now about 58 years old. My name then was Anthony Terrill. Also information wanted of Harriet Chapman, mother of Sidney Oliver. When last heard from she was at Chapman's Mill, Monroe county, Ga., upward of 40 years ago. Any information address,

ANTHONY FLEMING,

Plaquemine, La.

Christian Recorder   July 2, 1870

INFORMATION WANTED

Of my father, Jerry Hodges, of Norfolk county, Va. I was sold from him when a small girl, about 30 years ago. My mother's name was Phoebe, and she belonged to a man named Ashcroth. Should any of the family be living in the vicinity of Norfolk, they will please address EMELINE HODGE Leavenworth, Kan.

NB. Ministers please read in church.

Even now the immensity of their loss, the persistence of their longing, and the depth of their grief are evident in the ads. One can almost feel them expectantly reaching out for any shred of information to hold on to.

Christian Recorder   March 17, 1866

INFORMATION WANTED

I had two children sold from me about ten years ago by a man by the name of Pate, then living with James Evans. My boy's name was Monroe Early, and my daughter's name Mary Early. Any information of their whereabouts may be sent to the care of Rev. Wm. D. Hains, pastor of 3rd st A.M.E. Church, Richmond, Va.

Francis Early

Christian Recorder   June 24, 1865

INFORMATION WANTED

Can anyone inform me of the whereabouts of John Person, the son of Hannah Person, of Alexandria, Va., who belonged to Alexander Sancter. I have not seen him for ten years. I was sold to Joseph Bruin, who took me to New Orleans. My name was then Hannah Person, it is now Hannah Cole. This is the only child I have and I desire to find him much. Any information of his whereabouts can be directed to HANNAH COLE, Cedar St., New Bedford, Massachusetts

Southwestern Christian Advocate   September 13, 1877

I enquire for my long lost sister. She once belonged to Graves, in Middletown, Missouri, but was sold to Malby. Our mother was named Phebe Graves, and we had a sister Mary. Address Martin Scott, Hempstead, Texas.

Christian Recorder   April 2, 1870

INFORMATION WANTED

Information wanted of Sarah Williams, who I left at Halifax Court House, Va., about 25 years ago. She belonged to a man whose name was William Early, who kept a dry-goods store. Any information of her will be thankfully received by her sister, Martha Ann Good, who was taken away from Nathan Dexter, who kept a hotel in Halifax, at 12 o'clock at night, when quite small, and sold in Alabama, but now lives at 225 Currant Alley, Philadelphia, Pa.

NB. Ministers in the South, please read in our churches.

Loyal Georgian (Augusta, Ga.)   October 13, 1866

OF ESTHER who formerly belonged to Mr. Thomas Singleton, who formerly lived in North Carolina. Her husband was named Thos Simmons. She had two sisters by the names of DARKUS and VIOLET. Her daughter's name is RACHEL, but was called SIDNEY, is living in Augusta, Georgia, and is very anxious to hear of the whereabouts of her mother ESTHER, if living. She was sold from her when ten or twelve years of age, about twelve or thirteen years ago. Any person having any knowledge of her will please write to HENRY ROUNDFIELD, care of Wyman and May, Augusta, Ga.

The ads are laden with pathos and expectancy, and they speak of hope and memory. But even people with the strongest sense of hope and who deployed all their scraps of information and resources must have sometimes despaired that the geographical and temporal distances, the instability of names, and the paucity of registries made success impossible. They must have wondered at times if it was worth their investment of money and emotion. But, it seems, the intensity of their loss and the strength of their desires propelled them to make one more effort. And every once in a while it worked. The *Southwestern Christian Advocate* published this update in March 1877.

A FAMILY RE-UNITED

In the SOUTHWESTERN of March 1st, we published in this column a letter from Charity Thompson, of Hawkins, Texas, making inquiry about her family. She last heard of them in Alabama years ago. The letter, as printed in the paper was read in the First church Houston, and as the reading proceeded a well-known member of the Church—Mrs. Dibble—burst into tears and cried out "That is my sister and I have not seen her for thirty three years." The mother is still living and in a few days the happy family will be once more re-united.

The desires of former slaves to find family members were rarely fulfilled; but the possibility kept them hoping, and intermittent stories of success kept them encouraged.

PART THREE
Reunification

Love

Courage

...and certain...

...what we...

...Faith is being sure of...

SIX

When we met neither of us spoke for some moments—
speech is not for such occasions, but silence rather, and
the rush of thoughts. When the first flash of feeling had
passed I spoke, calling him by name, and he
addressed me as brother.

LOUIS HUGHES, former slave

Happiness Too Deep for Utterance

Reunification of Families

Christian Recorder   July 20, 1867

INFORMATION WANTED

Information wanted of Mary Buckner, George Buckner, and Robert R. Wilford Buckner. I found Rueben Buckner in Chilicothe, Ohio. I left them in Rappahannock County, Va. Any information of them will be thankfully received by their father, ROBERT BUCKNER, (Care of Rev. W. J. Davis,) Box 317, Logansport, Indiana.

Most people never found their relatives. Too many miles and too many years lay between them. As Tines Kendricks, a former slave from Georgia told an interviewer, "They was heaps of families that I know what was separated in the time of bondage that tried to find they folks what was gone. But the most of them never get together again even after they set free because they don't know where one or the other is."[1]

The rare accounts of reunification that survive help us to begin to get a sense of the intensity of the feelings people experienced. Stories of reunification also present some of the difficulties that surfaced when people had not seen each other for many years. How would they know each other? What would spark the recognition? How would they fit into each other's lives after so many years apart? A child had become an adult; a parent was now aged; a husband or wife had a new relationship. How would freedpeople reconcile these challenges?

Two works of fiction offer dramatic and useful frameworks for examining the complexities of encountering lost family members. Elements of the stories—divergent paths, changed circumstances, recognition, memory, and incorporation of a newly found family member into a life—resonate with the lived experiences of former slaves. In abolitionist literature, including *Uncle Tom's Cabin*, separation of families served as a trope that signified the horrors of slavery. Likewise, in the aftermath of slavery, the challenges and the poignancy of searching for family members, as well as the difficulties inherent in reunification, became so much a part of the African American cultural landscape that they found their way into the works of two eminent writers of the nineteenth century, Mark Twain and Charles Chesnutt. As African American essayist G. M. McClellan wrote in an encyclopedia entry on black literature in 1902, "Who has not sat at some time in a Negro church and heard read the pitiful inquiry for a mother, or a child, or a father, husband or wife, all lost in the sales and separations of slavery times—loved ones as completely swallowed up in the past (yet in this life they still live) as if the grave had received them. At such a reading, though it was given with unconcern, one heard the faithful cry of faithful love coming out of the dark on its sorrowful mission." Even at the turn of the century, stories of separation and loss still circulated.[2]

White author Mark Twain wrote an account that he claimed was a true story, and African American author Charles Chesnutt wrote a fictional account. Though from different backgrounds, both writers perceptively and dramatically conveyed the complexities of family separation and reunification. Twain, born in Missouri in 1835, grew up in a family in which his father owned at least one slave and his uncle owned several.[3] Chesnutt was born in Cleveland, Ohio, in 1858, a few years after his free parents fled North Carolina in the wake of legislation that further restricted the rights of free blacks. His parents met during the wagon trip to the Midwest and married in Ohio. They returned to Fayetteville after the war when Chesnutt was eight years old, and he came of age in postemancipation North Carolina. Stories of separation, loss, longing, searching, and the occasional reunification circulated around the two men. Mark Twain, in fact, claimed that "A True Story" came directly from the lips of Mary Ann McCord, who had been a slave before she worked as his housekeeper in Hartford, Connecticut, after emancipation. Both Twain and Chesnutt demonstrate in their stories that former slaves spent many years searching for loved ones, but those who found them had to face the challenges that time and space and pain and resilience created.[4]

In "The Wife of His Youth," first published in the *Atlantic Monthly* in 1898, Chesnutt explores the complications of finding a loved one when the circumstances have changed dramatically. The story opens with Mr. Ryder reflecting on the social gathering he will host later that Friday evening for members of his upwardly mobile African American blue vein society in the northern city in which he lives. The organization aims to "establish and maintain correct social standards among its members," and Mr. Ryder, as the "dean of the society," polices observance of the standards and traditions. He has gained some authority within the group because of his leadership qualities as well as his looks, for "while he was not as white as some of the Blue Veins, his appearance was such as to confer distinction upon them. His features were of a refined type, his hair was almost straight; he was always neatly dressed;

his manners were irreproachable, and his morals above suspicion." Although lacking in formal education, Ryder is solidly middle class; he recites poetry, saves money, and owns his home. At this ball he will propose to Mrs. Molly Dixon, a widow half his age and new to town who is "whiter than he, and better educated." Chesnutt, himself light enough to have "passed" as white, makes Ryder an active participant in a color- and class-conscious social world.[5]

As Mr. Ryder sits on his porch reading Tennyson and preparing the toast that he will offer at the ball, an elderly woman appears at his gate. Her face is "crossed and re-crossed with a hundred wrinkles," and tufts of gray hair are visible beneath her bonnet. "She was very black,—so black that her tooth-less gums, revealed when she opened her mouth, were not red, but blue." To Ryder she "looked like a bit of the old plantation life, summoned up from the past by the wave of a magician's wand." She speaks in a shrill voice and in dialect: "Scuse me, suh, I's lookin for my husban'. I heerd you wuz a big man an' had libbed heah a long time, an' I 'lowed you wouldn't min' ef I'd come roun' an ax you ef you'd ever heerd of a merlatter man by de name er Sam Taylor 'quirin' roun' in de chu'ches ermongs' de people feer his wife Liza Jane?" There used to be many such cases after the war of people searching in the churches for family, Ryder replies, but a lot of time has passed and he has forgotten them. "But tell me your story," he encourages, "and it may refresh my memory." He listens as Liza Jane recounts a story of love and marriage and the sudden, stunning sale of her husband, Sam. She has been searching for him ever since. She has traveled to New Orleans, Atlanta, Charleston, and Richmond and has finally come to the North. She is confident that Sam is also searching for her because he would have to be sick, physically or mentally, not to remember his promise to her. She believes they will find each other and be as happy in freedom as they had been for a short time in slavery.[6]

Ryder responds to Liza Jane's story with questions that could have been posed to anyone who searched for loved ones after slavery—any of the people who placed an Information Wanted or Lost Friends ad or wrote to the Freedmen's Bureau or walked miles in search of family members. Does Liza Jane really expect to find her husband? He might have died years ago. What if he has married another woman? Their slave marriage was not legally binding, so he could have married again. Perhaps he has outgrown her. What if he has moved up in the world and does not want to be found? What if she has passed him on the street a hundred times without recognizing him? Twenty-five years is a long time. People change. But Liza Jane's confidence cannot be shaken. Sam would never have remarried because he loved her. He had promised to return for her and he was a man of his word. He would not have outgrown her, and she is certain that she would recognize him.[7]

Chesnutt could not have drawn a more vivid contrast between these two people. He employs skin color, literacy, dialect, age, and social class to construct very clear lines between Ryder and Liza Jane. Ryder is of light complexion, self-educated but educated just the same, and a member of the "colored" elite. Liza Jane is a toothless, dark-skinned, old woman who believes in the signs and dreams that say her husband is alive and that she will find him. Their class positions could hardly be farther apart: He is Mr. Ryder; she is Liza Jane. He patrols the borders of an elite society of people of color; her body and demeanor evoke memories of the old plantations on which she has labored. He memorizes the English poets; she speaks in a dialect of broken English. He belongs to a new contingent of upwardly mobile people of color who hope to eventually become absorbed into whiteness; she is so out of place in this modern, urban space that people who pass her on the street "turn and look back at her with a smile of kindly amusement." Ryder and Liza Jane belong to separate worlds. It would have been highly unusual for such vast differences to exist between two former slaves, but Chesnutt uses the chasms of color and social class to demonstrate how profoundly people and situations could change over many years of separation.

Chesnutt takes us to the ball later that evening, where a black servant greets and ushers guests who enjoy a literary program, popular airs played by a string band, and a lavish supper. Finally it is time for Mr. Ryder to give his toast. He begins by speaking of the fidelity and devotion of women and says none was more so than one who had come to see him earlier in the day. He repeats Liza Jane's story, then says he had attempted to imagine Sam's story. Suppose that Sam had moved to the North and improved himself.

> Suppose, too, that, as the years went by, this man's memory of the past grew more and more indistinct, until at last it was rarely, except in his dreams, that any image of this bygone period rose before his mind. And then suppose that accident should bring to his knowledge the fact that the wife of his youth, the wife he had left behind him.—not one who had walked by his side and kept pace with him in his upward struggle, but one upon whom advancing years and a laborious life had set their mark,—was alive and seeking him, but that he was absolutely safe from recognition or discovery, unless he chose to reveal himself.

"My friends," Ryder asks the silenced crowd, "what would the man do?"[8]

Mrs. Dixon is the first to speak: "He should have acknowledged her," she says. At this, Mr. Ryder leaves the room and returns with Liza Jane, "who stood startled and trembling at the sudden plunge into this scene of brilliant gayety. She was neatly dressed in gray, and wore the white cap of an elderly woman." Mr. Ryder breaks the silence: "Ladies and gentlemen, this is the woman, and I am the man, whose story I have told you. Permit me to introduce to you the wife of my youth." So ends the story with all its ambiguity. Ryder "acknowledges" Liza Jane, but readers are left to wonder if he takes this dark-skinned, elderly, illiterate woman as his wife. The contrast between the two persists to the end. No miraculous transformation has taken place; Liza Jane appears at the ball in the clothing of an elderly woman and is jolted at being introduced into a social scene for which she has no reference.

Prominent in Chesnutt's story is the element of recognition. Although Liza Jane carries a daguerreotype of Sam wrapped in layers of paper, tied to a string around her neck, and tucked inside her bosom, she does not recognize him in the person of Mr. Ryder. For his part, Ryder stares at the image "long and intently" but does not betray any knowledge of the man. When Liza Jane leaves that afternoon, Ryder enters his bedroom, his private space, and stares at his reflection in the mirror for a long time as though trying to find something there. It takes him time to recognize the person for whom Liza Jane is searching, but peering beyond his image, into his memory and his soul, Ryder comes face to face with both the old self and the new. For Chesnutt, this is a story of recognition and self-recognition; it is also a meditation on whether it is possible to reconcile the past with the present and with the future. Chesnutt ends the story with Ryder having disclosed his past relationship with Liza Jane but with their future relationship open to speculation.

Recognition is an essential element in Mark Twain's 1874 "A True Story" as well.[9] Aunt Rachel, an old woman, tells the narrator about her husband and their seven children being sold by their owner. She thinks often of her little son Henry, who said he would escape and find her. During the Civil War she and Henry, now a soldier in the Union army, are reunited after he recognizes an expression she uses. Aunt Rachel, in turn, identifies Henry by scars on his wrist and on his forehead. Here Twain tells of a mother who held a memory of a child thirteen years after their separation and a son who was young at separation and did not remember what his mother looked like. They meet again completely by chance and recognize each other only through their words and physical markings. Where Chesnutt uses class and color, Twain employs age as the dramatic divide; a mother looks for her eight-year-old child and finds, instead, an adult, a soldier in the Union army.

This problem of recognition held great significance for people who hoped to find loved ones. Doubtless, like Aunt Rachel, many parents who published Information Wanted or Lost Friends ads carried in their memories images of the small children they had lost, with no updated sense of what they might look like many years later. And many sons and daughters had only the most vague recollections of their parents. People told stories of having to relearn who their mother was. Anna Barker, whose mother demanded custody of her children from their former owner following the war, described the children's first interactions with their mother: "She came out of the house to get us and at first I was scared of her cause I didn't know who she was. But she put me up in her lap and loved me and I knowed then I love her too."[10] Mingo White was sold from South Carolina to Alabama when he was four or five years old. In Alabama, his father's friend John White and a woman named Selina White took care of him. "The next time that I saw my mammy," he told an interviewer, "I was a great big boy. There was a woman on the place that everybody called mammy, Selina White. One day mammy called me and said, Mingo, your mammy is coming. I said that I thought you was my mammy. She said, 'no I ain't your mammy, your mammy is way way from here.' I couldn't believe that I had another mammy," White told the interviewer "and I never thought about it any more." Some time later, "I was setting down at the barn when a wagon come up the lane. I stood round like a child will. When the wagon got to the house, my mammy got out and broke and run to me and throwed her arms round my neck and hug and kiss me. I never even put my arms round her or nothing of the sort. I just stood there looking at her." His mother said, "Son ain't you glad to see your mammy?" White just stared at her then walked away. It was all so confusing, but Selina, who had been a mother to him, explained that he had hurt his mother. "I went off and studied and I begins to remember things," White said. "After I had talked with my real mammy," he recalled, "she told me of how the family had been broke up and that she hadn't seed my pappy since he was sold. My mammy never would have seen me no more if de Lawd hadn't a been in the plan." Although White had been separated from his mother for a relatively short time of about four years, he had been so young when he left her that he did not even know to miss her and would never have recognized her without prodding.[11]

For Louis Hughes, who lost his family when he was eleven, the clue to recognition was a missing finger. A coworker on a boat that ran between Wisconsin and Michigan thought he had seen a man in Cleveland who bore a striking resemblance to Hughes and asked if he had a brother. "Yes, but I don't know anything about him," Hughes replied. "We were sold from each other when boys." Hughes recalled that he had accidentally cut off his brother's forefinger when they were children. His coworker had not noticed this detail, and so Hughes put the matter out of his mind. Sometime later while working in the coatroom of the Plankinton House Hotel in Milwaukee, Wisconsin, a guest again asked Hughes if he had a brother. Hughes recounted the conversation: "'Say, Hughes, have you a brother?' I answered, 'Yes, I had two, but I think they are dead. I was sold from them when a mere lad.' 'Well,' said he, 'if you have a brother he is in Cleveland. There is a fellow there who is chief cook at the Forest City Hotel who looks just like you.'" Hughes now grew eager. This man had not noticed a missing finger either, but he promised to check the next time he was in Cleveland. "Now that the second person had called my attention to the fact that there was a man in Cleveland who looked very much like me," Hughes recalled, "I became deeply interested—in fact, I was so excited I could hardly do my work. I awaited the agent's return with what of patience I could command; and at last, one day, when I was least expecting him, I was greeted with these words: 'Hello Hughes! I have good news for you.'" The man in Cleveland was indeed missing a forefinger and corroborated Hughes's story about their separation as children in Virginia. He even recalled the name of their former owner. "Words failed me to express my feelings at this news," Hughes wrote in his narrative. "The prospect of seeing my brother, lost so many years before, made me almost wild with joy. I thanked the agent for the interest he had taken in me, and for the invaluable and comprehensive information he had brought. He could hardly have done me a greater favor, or bound me to him by a more lasting obligation." Hughes had never dared to imagine that he would see one of his brothers again; in fact, he assumed they were dead, but this news awakened a longing in him.[12]

He took a leave of absence from his job and traveled by express train to Cleveland, becoming more excited by the moment. Hughes described the reunion at the hotel where his brother worked: "When we met neither of us spoke for some moments—speech is not for such occasions, but silence rather, and the rush of thoughts. When the first flash of feeling had passed I spoke, calling him by name, and he addressed me as brother. There seemed to be no doubt on either side as to our true relationship, though the features of each had long since faded forever from the memory of the other."[13] This, then, was the other side of ambiguous loss. Hughes had assumed his brother was dead. His brother may have believed the same of him. Their separation as children had seemed so permanent, and time had all but erased their memories of each other; but here they stood, each looking into a face that resembled his own enough to prompt two strangers to take notice. Several factors had converged to bring about this reunification: a strong physical resemblance, the fact that both brothers worked in public accommodations where they had contact with the traveling public, and finally, the physical marker of the missing forefinger. Hughes would likely have continued to ignore the reports about a man who resembled him without confirmation of this physical mark.

For some, recognition came only through a feeling, a sense of familiarity. As a young boy, Robert Glenn had been sold away despite his father's efforts to purchase him. After being taken from North Carolina, Glenn spent his childhood and early adolescence working in Kentucky. At the end of the Civil War, he worked hard to adjust to his new state of freedom. He took his freedom by degrees, he explained, trying to internalize the fact that he no longer had to respond to his employer as though he were still his owner, and began dreaming about what he would do with his life. After a few years he decided to search for his mother. "One cold morning in early December," he told an interviewer, "I made a vow that I was going to North Carolina and see my mother if she was still living. I had plenty of money for the trip. I wrote the postmaster of Roxboro, North Carolina, asking him to inform my mother I was still living and telling him the circumstances, mailing a letter at the same time telling her I was still alive but saying nothing of my intended visit to her." Glenn left Illinois, where he then lived, and in a few days reached his mother's home. For some reason, he at first tried to fool his mother. "There were two men with me and they called me by a fictitious name," he said; "but when I shook my mother's hand I held it a little too long and she suspicioned something, still she held herself until she was more sure." Glenn had been eight years old when she last saw him, and now he was a young man of about twenty. She did not recognize him physically, but she sensed something. "When she got a chance," Glenn recounted, "she came to me and said ain't you my child? Tell me ain't you my child whom I left on the road near Mr. Moore's before the war?" At this, Glenn was done with games. "I broke down and began to cry," he said. "Mother nor father did not know me, but mother suspicioned I was her child. Father had a few days previously remarked that he did not want to die without seeing his son once more. I could not find language to express my feelings," he recalled. "I did not know before I came home whether my parents were dead or alive. This Christmas I spent in the county and state of my birth and childhood; with mother, father and freedom was the happiest period of my entire life, because those who were torn apart in bondage and sorrow several years previous were now united in freedom and happiness."[14]

"Ain't you my child?" Robert Glenn's mother in North Carolina asked. In Richmond, Virginia, in April 1865, just after the Confederate surrender that ended the Civil War, Garland H. White's mother also had questions for him. White, a Methodist minister, served as the chaplain of a regiment of the U.S. Colored Troops from Indiana. In a letter to the *Christian Recorder*, he described the scene in Richmond as African Americans realized that the war was over and that they were free. "A vast multitude assembled on Broad street," he wrote, "the slave pens were thrown open," and thousands gathered in the street thanking God and President Abraham Lincoln. Former slave Thomas Lewis Johnson, who was also in Richmond, described the celebrations as follows:

> The joy and rejoicing of the coloured people when the United States army marched into Richmond defies description. For days the manifestations of delight were displayed in many ways. The places of worship were kept open, and hundreds met for prayer and praise. Of the many songs of the Jubilee this was the chorus of one of them:
>
> Slavery's chain is broke at last,
> Broke at last, broke at last;
> Slavery's chain is broke at last,
> I'm going to praise God till I die.

According to Garland White, within the crowd, parents searched for their children who had been sold south, hoping to find their sons among the black soldiers. One old woman told soldiers that her children had been taken from her and sold to a lawyer in Georgia. She later got word that he was living in Ohio. The old woman told the soldiers that her son was named Garland H. White. According to White, some of the soldiers directed him to the old woman, with whom he had the following exchange:

> "What is your name, sir?"
> "My name is Garland H. White."
> "What was your mother's name?"
> "Nancy."
> "Where was you born?"
> "In Hanover County, in this state."

"Where was you sold from?"

"From this city."

"What was the name of the man who bought you?"

"Robert Toombs."

"Where did he live?"

"In the State of Georgia?"

"Where did you leave him?"

"At Washington."

"Where did you then go?"

"To Canada."

"Where do you now live?"

"In Ohio."

"This is your mother, Garland, whom you are now talking to; who has spent twenty years of grief about her son."[15]

White's mother's questions are reminiscent of the information that searchers packed into their ads—the small bits that they remembered or had uncovered. As mother and son stood face-to-face, neither knew the other. It was the facts, the names, the circumstances, and the details that enabled them to make the connection.

It was frightening to know that you could stand mere feet away from someone and not know that he was your child, so freedpeople told cautionary tales about the dangers of failing to recognize a relative. Former slave Henry Brown told an interviewer in South Carolina a story he had heard growing up:

A man once married his ma'am and didn't know it. He was sold from her when 'bout eight years old. When he grew to a young man, slavery then was over, he met this woman who he like and so they were married. They was married a month when one night they started to tell of their experience and how many times they was sold. The husband told how he was sold from his mother who liked him dearly. He told how his ma faint when they took him away and how his master then used to brand his baby slaves at a year old. When he showed her the brand she fainted cause she then realized that she had married her son.

True story or invented legend, this recitation that had circulated in Henry Brown's community warned that the confusion and pain of family separation in slavery could persist even long after the institution had been abolished.[16]

People who had been stunned and silenced by grief at the point of separation could be silenced again at reunification. It was difficult for them to put into words the emotions aroused when they found loved ones so many years after separation. Perhaps that is why Charles Chesnutt has Mr. Ryder identify himself to Liza Jane offstage, outside the text and beyond the gaze of the reader. Chesnutt gives no hint as to the emotions that either one expressed before the revelation at the ball, and readers do not share in their private, perhaps silent, expressions of feeling. Some who actually experienced reunification grappled with just how to convey those feelings. "I cannot express the joy I felt, at this happy meeting of my mother and other friends," Garland White wrote, "but suffice it to say, that God is on the side of the righteous, and will in due time reward them." Louis Hughes spoke of the quietness of his initial reunion with his brother, and he struggled with how to convey to readers the intensity of the emotions when his wife found her mother and sister. "The meeting was a joyful one to us all," he recalled. "No mortal who has not experienced it can imagine the feeling of those who meet again after long years of enforced separation and hardship and utter ignorance of one another's condition and place of habitation." Although they were all materially destitute, he said, the meeting again of mother and daughters "was an occasion of the profoundest joy." Long after that first evening with his wife's mother, he remembered and was moved by the scene. "I can see the old woman now," he wrote, "with bowed form and gray locks, as she gave thanks in joyful tones yet reverent manner, for such a wonderful blessing."[17]

Their initial silence broken, Hughes and his brother shared their life histories and expressed their feelings. Following the war, Billy had "returned to the old home in Virginia" in search of their mother and brothers but found no trace of them. "As we related our varied experiences," Hughes wrote, "the hardships, the wrongs, and sorrows which we endured and at last the coming of brighter days, we were sad, then happy." They were sad about their loss of each other for many years and the loss of their mother and brother, but they were happy, too, at having found each other against such great odds. "It seemed, and indeed was, wonderful that we should have met again after so long a separation. When I came to saying good-by to him, so close did I feel to him, the tie between us seemed never to have been broken. That week, so full of new experiences and emotions can never be erased from my memory."[18]

Although Hughes had a wife and was a new father to twin girls, he seemed to say that he had tapped into new emotions in meeting his brother once again. Though he barely knew him, he experienced with his brother and his brother's family a connection that he had not known before. "As I looked into the faces of his wife and children, I seemed to have entered a new and broader life," he wrote, "and one in which the joys of social intercourse had marvelously expanded." We generally think of family as the smallest, most insular sphere of relationship, but for Hughes, renewed contact with the only member of his family he had seen in many years opened up his life, expanded his world, gave him a sense of belonging, and made possible new depths of feeling.[19]

Renewed connections between parent and child or among siblings could be powerful, overwhelming, and even baffling. Louis Hughes had not even realized that he missed his brother until he found him, yet from their reunion he took a sense of greater belonging in the world. Anna Barker and Mingo White needed some time to know who their mothers were; they took their cues from the adults and responded to the parents' love with love. It is easy to imagine, though, that even the most loving reunion of parent and child would sometimes give way to conflict. Mingo White, for example, would have had to adjust to his mother's personality and would have noticed that she did some things differently and perhaps had rules for behavior that were different from those of his surrogate mother, Selina White.

Any meeting among family members after years of separation could bring tension, but none more so than between husbands and wives. Under the best conditions, marriage, with all its intricacies, could be a vulnerable relationship; slavery, with its forced couplings and enforced separations, presented its own particular complications. Living in the same home, a husband and wife could grow apart, but not knowing if the other was dead or alive for many years could create serious ruptures. For some couples, recommitment after separation came easily. Others had to make difficult choices.

Some who were children at emancipation recalled that their parents reunited and put their lives back together with ease. July Ann Halfen's parents were separated when mother and child were sold away. Her mother attempted to run back to her husband, but she was caught and punished. When the war ended, Halfen's mother announced that she was returning to Adams County to find her husband, but her former owner accused her of stealing a bale of cotton and put her in jail. According to Halfen, "My pappy who was left in Adams County come down there and he got some white men to get my mammy out of jail and then mammy and pappy stayed together till he died."[20] George Washington Miller said that after the war, his mother went and found his father and they married again.[21] Both Halfen and Miller could provide only snippets of information because as children they did not have full access to their parents' thoughts or their private, anxious moments together.

For the adults, reunification could be much more complicated and fraught with conflict. It had been expected in slavery that once they were separated, enslaved spouses would establish new relationships. John Beck married a "pretty yellow girl" and assumed that Malinda had remarried as well. And when James Tate wrote to his wife, he seemed to be giving serious consideration to doing what his owner said he should do: moving on to one of the "several colloured ladies" in West Point who were in love with him. As it happens, Tate and his wife found their way back together, and in 1870 they and their children were living in the same household in Fulton County, Georgia. They had been separated during the war and had been apart for a relatively short time, during which their relationship was able to survive. For other couples, time and distance created emotional entanglements and tested loyalties.[22]

The existence of more than one spouse could present a profound emotional challenge for people who had remarried during slavery. The Information Wanted ad that John Walker placed in the *Christian Recorder* in 1869 highlights this potential problem for formerly enslaved African Americans who searched for spouses after the war. In his ad, Walker searched for not one, but two wives.

INFORMATION WANTED

John Walker, a servant of Dr. E. M. Patterson, in 1850, wishes to know the whereabouts of his wife Peggie, and his three sons William, Samuel, and Miles, who were also slaves of Dr. E. M. Patterson, of Nashville, Tennessee. Dr. Patterson lived at a place called Flat Rocks, about three miles from Nashville. And also the whereabouts of my last wife, Cornelia, who was a slave of Lee Shoot, a negro trader, in Nashville, Tenn. Any information of the above persons will be gladly received by John Walker. Ministers in charge will please read this to their congregations. Address letters to JOHN WALKER, No. 114 P St., betw'n 4th and 5th Sts, Sacramento, Cal.[23]

The ad omits the details of Walker's marriages and separations, but his wording hints at a hierarchy of caring. He searched, first, for his wife Peggie and their sons and then, second, for his "last wife," who could have been either his second or the last of several. It was not likely that he would find either woman, but the ad prompts the question of what would happen if he were to find both.

Northern visitors to the antebellum South had been fascinated by the slave trade and had documented their observations at slave auctions. Following emancipation, northern whites found, among other things, African Americans' search for family and family reunification fascinating and poignant. Many whites would have read *Uncle Tom's Cabin* and the slave narratives that laid out family separation as one of the horrors of slavery. Some may even have attended abolitionist meetings where former slaves such as Henry Bibb recounted their personal losses. It is not surprising, then, that John Eaton in Washington, D.C., and Charles Day at Camp Hamilton, Virginia, took notice of scenes of reunification at contraband camps as well as parents' attempts to claim their children from owners. Eaton and Day observed group interactions from afar, but two women, Mary Ames and Elizabeth Botume, moved among African Americans and wrote down the stories they heard. The diaries of these northern white women in the South offer insights into some of the complicated situations some spouses faced and the choices they made in the face of reunification. Through the prism of their observations and interpretations we are able to see freedpeople's competing realities.

Mary Ames, who traveled from Springfield, Massachusetts, to Edisto Island, South Carolina, in 1865 to teach freedpeople, recounted the story of Sarah, a woman who, with her husband, Jim, worked for the teachers. "Sarah is a fine-looking woman, quiet and sensible," Ames wrote. "She has always been a house-servant, was born and reared in Richmond, was sold with three children to Dr. Leavitt of Charleston, leaving the father of her children in Richmond. Since that, she has had six children, having had five husbands, or men with whom she was obliged to live, as she was sold from one master to another. Jim was the last one." During the war, as Jim and Sarah prepared to abandon the plantation, "one Saturday Campbell, who had been one of Sarah's five husbands, and was the father of her child Anne, came and claimed Sarah. Jim fought and conquered him, thus winning Sarah and her children. They walked nearly a hundred miles, Sarah carrying Margery, a two-year-old child, in her arms. She kept the other children in front of her, for many lost their children." It may be that the conflict truly was resolved through physical confrontation between the two men; it may also be that Sarah chose to remain with Jim.[24]

Near Beaufort, South Carolina, Elizabeth Botume also heard of postwar marital conflicts that resulted from family separation during slavery. She had sailed from New York to South Carolina in the fall of 1864 and taught at Old

Fort Plantation, a contraband village that was home to more than 800 people who fled slavery and the Confederate army. "Writing letters," Botume said, "was one of the first duties that pressed upon us in the beginning of the winter. Women who had husbands and sons and lovers in the regiments were eager to communicate with them." These letters, Botume said, "were sent to every nook and corner of the Confederacy, hunting for lost members of scattered families." The people "had a marvelous way of tracing out the missing members of their families, and inflexible perseverance in hunting them up."[25]

But hunting up an old spouse could result in confusion and pain when there was a new spouse in the picture. A woman named Sarah brought a letter for Botume to read. When Sarah heard that the letter was from Martin, her son who had been sold, she began to rock back and forth and thank God. Martin, the letter said, had been in Charleston when the Union captured it, and according to Botume, he immediately "turned heart and soul to his wife and child and his mother." He encountered a man who had belonged to the same owner who told him where his family was. His wife, he said in the letter, was Jane, who Botume knew was married to a man named Ferguson. But Sarah assured her, "Jane belongs to Martin, and she'll go back to him." Jane soon confirmed her mother-in-law's assertion. "Martin Barnwell is my husband, ma'am," she said. "I got no husband but he. When the secesh [Confederates] sell him off we never expect to see each other no more. He said, 'Jane take good care of our boy, and when we get to heaven us will live together to never part no more.' You see, ma'am, when I come here I had no one to help me." Ferguson had proposed, and according to Jane, "I told him I never expects Martin could come back, but if he did he would be my husband above all others. And Ferguson said, 'That's right, Jane'; so he cannot say nothing ma'am." Jane reiterated, "Martin is my husband, ma'am, and the father of my child; and Ferguson is a man. He will not complain. And we had an understanding, too, about it."

Both mother-in-law and daughter-in-law were very clear that Jane's real husband was Martin Barnwell. Ferguson had only been a placeholder, someone to help Jane when she was alone, someone with whom Jane claimed she had been honest about her true commitment to Martin. She had married again only because she did not think Martin would ever return to her. She now dictated a letter to Ferguson, who was away serving in the Union army. Botume thought the letter "was clear and tender" but firm; however, Ferguson was not as understanding as Jane expected him to be and sent a letter pleading with her to remain his wife. He wanted her to come to him in Jacksonville rather than going to Martin in Charleston. "Martin has not seen you for a long time," he said. "He cannot think of you as I do." But Jane was determined. She replied that she prayed for him and wished him well but would no longer be his wife. Soon, according to Botume, "Martin came and claimed his wife and child, who gladly clung to him."[26]

The emotional lives of former slaves were complicated by the compromises that slavery had imposed on them, and Botume and her fellow teachers received appeals from freedpeople to help them disentangle these marital situations. They heard from Kit, a man whose wife spent months going from one plantation to the other between him and her first husband, who had been sold away but returned after the war. Kit implored her to return to him full time, and eventually she relented, staying with Kit because, she said, he had no one but her. The teachers also heard from Charlotte, whose husband had been sold and later enlisted in the army. "She took a second husband," Botume wrote. "When the regiment was disbanded number one returned and claimed his wife. She had two boys belonging to him, and a girl baby belonging to number two. The poor woman was in a sore strait. Both men claimed their offspring. She knew whatever way she turned she must give up part of her children."[27]

These situations with all their entanglements were vivid to Botume, who heard the details directly from the people involved. "We were often sorely perplexed," Botume confessed. "All our preconceived ideas of propriety and the fitness of things were set at naught." She was reluctant to overlay a template of middle-class marital rules and expectations of fidelity or to judge people whose fragile marriages had had neither legal recognition nor protection from owners who had disrupted their unions at will.[28]

Stories of reunification are scarce, and those that document what happened after the initial moments of joy are more rare still. Here again, the fiction of Twain and Chesnutt recapitulates the historical record as the authors end their stories at the moments of recognition and revelation, respectively. "A True Story" is over when Aunt Rachel scrutinizes her son and recognizes him, as he has recognized her. Chesnutt ends his story at the ball just after Mr. Ryder reveals his relationship to Liza Jane. The most optimistic of readers believe that Ryder will once again claim Liza Jane as his wife, but although he "acknowledges" her, it is difficult to believe that he will take as his wife this woman who has been presented in such contrast to him. Significantly, Ryder does not introduce Liza Jane as his wife, but as the "wife of my youth."

There is a distinct pastness to this characterization, an implicit discontinuity. Would Mr. Ryder humiliate Mrs. Dixon at a public event where their social group expected him to propose to her? Chesnutt leaves the reader perhaps at first pleased with Mr. Ryder's honesty but then unsettled, wondering, wanting to know what happened after the story ended.

Just as Chesnutt offers no clean resolution, most people who conveyed their experiences offered few details of how it all worked out. Louis Hughes, who participated in two reunification experiences, wrote about the aftermath of one but not the other: He wrote that his wife's mother and sister moved with him and his wife to Canada, but he did not disclose whether he and his brother maintained contact after Hughes left Cleveland. Garland H. White met his mother in Richmond after twenty years of separation. He recounted how she identified him, a little about how he felt, but nothing about what came next. White had to keep moving with his regiment. He wrote of this experience in the *Christian Recorder* shortly after it occurred, a time when he could not know what their interactions and relationship would be like, so we are left to wonder. Those who wrote narratives had a lifetime to cover, so just as they did not provide day-to-day accounts of their feelings regarding loss and separation, they tended not to engage in long narrations of how they reconciled the multiple feelings and competing circumstances of their lives once they found family members.

It must have been difficult, once the immediate moments of joy passed, for people to put their lives back together with loved ones. So much had changed for those who had long been separated; they had to adjust to the new people they found. One can imagine that as Mingo White spent more time with his mother, he would have begun to see reflections of himself in her—perhaps in the slight tilt of her head when she listened to him intently, or her laugh, or the shape of her hands. Louis Hughes looked so much like his brother that he, too, may have felt that he found a part of himself when they met in Cleveland. The sources give only a hint of how people adjusted to one another. Instead, the accounts of reunification focus on the loss and longing and on the singular moments of recognition and reunification. Far removed from the events, we are left to imagine what their experiences must have been like beyond the shock of recognition, beyond the initial enthrallment, and beyond the moments of "the profoundest joy."

EPILOGUE

My great grandmother Rose
mother of Ashley gave her this sack when
she was sold at age 9 in South Carolina
it held a tattered dress 3 handfulls of
pecans a braid of Roses hair. Told her
It be filled with my Love always
she never saw her again
Ashley is my grandmother
Ruth Middleton
1921

Ashley's sack: plain-weave cotton ground, cotton lockstitch fabrication, and three-strand cotton embroidery floss, backstitch embroidery; sack, ca. 1850; needlework, 1921
(Middleton Place Foundation, Charleston, S.C.)

Help Me to Find My People
Genealogies of Separation

Something of the past always remains, if only as a haunting presence.

DOMINICK LACAPRA

Please help me to find my people. I will be glad to hear from some of them.

LUCY SUDDS

The loss of their families during slavery weighed heavily on African Americans. It was wrenching. It was unthinkable. It was a violation of the inviolate. As some children learned, a large part of what made someone a slave was the vulnerability to being sold and the powerlessness to prevent the loss of parents, siblings, spouses, family. People did not forget the loss, and they did not forget the power of the individuals and the institution that caused such pain. First the possibility and then the reality of separation hung as a haunting presence in the lives of African Americans during slavery. The memories survived long after it had ended.

The pain and memory of loss took over the minds of some who experienced separation directly. Former slave William Wells Brown recounted the impact of separation on a woman he knew. "One of my neighbors," he wrote, "sold to a speculator a negro boy, about 14 years old. It was more than his poor mother could bear. Her reason fled, and she became a perfect *maniac*, and had to be kept in close confinement. She would occasionally get out and run off to the neighbors. On one of these occasions she came to my house. With tears rolling down her cheeks, and her frame shaking with agony, she would cry out, '*Don't you hear him—they are whipping him now, and he is calling for me!*'"[1]

In South Carolina, Elizabeth Botume met a woman whom she described as "young and strong—a 'prime hand.' She always kept to herself," Botume said, "and was the saddest person I ever saw. She had been sold to a 'trader' to pay 'a gambling debt.' Then she was brought from Virginia and sold again. She had also left a little child behind her. 'I cannot sleep nights,' she said. 'Every time I shut my eyes I hear my baby cry, "Take me wid you mammy;

take me wid you!" I put my fingers in my ears, but all the time I hear him just the same, crying, "Take me wid you, mammy; take me wid you!"""[2]

Lizzie Baker, only a child during slavery, recalled, "They sold my sister Lucy and my brother Fred in slavery time, an' I have never seen them in my life. Mother would cry when she was telling me 'bout it. She never seen them anymore. I just couldn't bear to hear her tell it without crying. They were carried to Richmond, and sold by old master when they were children," Baker recounted. "We tried to get some news of brother and sister. Mother kept enquiring about them as long as she lived and I have hoped that I could hear from them. They are dead long ago I recons, and I guess there ain't no use ever expecting to see them."[3]

These mothers could not shake the memories of children taken from them, children who needed them but whom they were powerless to help. One mother had apparently lost her mind, had ceased to function in society and could only think about her son. Another went about her work with a profound sadness that seemed to place distance between her and others in her sphere. Another told and retold the story to her remaining daughter, passing on her sorrow. They all replayed their children's voices over and over in their minds. For them, the haunting was not metaphorical at all. The actual memories, the pain, and the guilt would not fade.

Fanny Kemble, the actress who married an American slaveowner and became a slave mistress for a few years before she fled back to her home in England, thought she saw in the countenance of the people her husband owned in Georgia "a mixture of sadness and fear, the involuntary exhibition of the two feelings, which I suppose must be the predominant experience of their whole lives, regret and apprehension, not the less heavy, either of them, for being, in some degree, vague and indefinite—a sense of incalculable past loss and injury, and a dread of incalculable future loss and injury."[4] Enslaved people, of course, experienced a range of emotions over the course of a lifetime, but this sense of loss, both past and potential, would have been common within that constellation of feelings. The lingering, quiet sadness that only the most perceptive white person could recognize would have been a familiar presence.

Memories of separation did not fade for many people. Indeed, the search for family continued for decades after slavery ended. Today, long after there is any chance that actual people can be found, descendants who did not know them, who only know that they must have existed—a grandmother must have had a grandmother, a father must have had a grandfather—take up the search, hoping to find traces of their ancestors in the documents that individuals and institutions leave behind. They take on the role of genealogists, digging into the past in an effort to put their fingers on just who they came from and perhaps, too, who they are. These descendants, removed from the palpable and direct loss of those who lived during slavery, can still be haunted by the need to know, the desire to find out about those who were lost through sale or through the negligence of history.

Some descendants employ literature to call up the ghosts, to explore the memories, and to build their own written monuments to the people of the past. Far removed from the separations of slavery, they go back to probe, to imagine, and to write about what the pain may have felt like, how people may have coped, and what the consequences of separations may have been, all the while acknowledging that much of it can never be known.[5] For most contemporary people the haunting does not consume a life as it did for the mother whom William Wells Brown observed; rather, it is a simmering element that asserts itself in particular moments. And all the digging and probing and imagining is not only intended to find the history of an individual or of a particular family; it is also meant to help construct the history of a people.

In the last decade of the nineteenth century and the first decade of the twentieth, African Americans continued to place ads in newspapers seeking to find family members. The ads closely resembled those from the 1860s and 1870s, but many of them now included a phrase that had appeared only sporadically before: "my people." Not everyone used the term, but it stands out in numerous ads in the later time period. "Please help me to find my people," Lucy Sudds wrote in the *Southwestern Christian Advocate* in 1890; "I will be glad to hear from some of them."[6] Mag Brown began her 1890 ad, "Mr. Editor: I ask a little space in the columns of your valuable paper to inquire for my people. I left them before the war, when I was 11 years old." She went on to name and describe her parents, siblings, and former owner and ended the ad, "Any information regarding my people will be gladly received. My name used to be Mag Overton."[7] Mary Delaney used the term in her ad in the *Christian Recorder* in 1902. "Information wanted of my people. My mother was sold from me when I could but crawl." At age three, Delaney had been given away as a gift. She thought she was now about thirty-nine years old. She knew that she had two sisters and two brothers, and she knew her mother's name. But, she said, "I never saw any of my people."[8] Also in 1902, nearly forty years after slavery was abolished, Jerry Williams placed an ad in the *Christian Recorder*

that read, "Information wanted of my people—my father's name was Jerry Thompson, mother's name Sophia Thompson, sisters were Sallie and Mary Thompson, my brothers are Washington and Samuel Thompson, my name is Jerry Williams. I was sold by Mr. Storks at Lumkins [Lumpkin] traders yard. My master's name was John Storks and I was sold at Richmond, Virginia, to go to Mississippi. My Post Office is Dickerson, Miss. Any information will by gladly received by my pastor Rev. J. S. Campbell."[9] From the 1880s to 1902 several people also said they were searching for their kin, or kindred, or kins people, but the search for "my people" was far more frequent.

On November 10, 1898, in one of the longest ads of any time period and under the caption "EVERYBODY READ THIS," Mrs. Angie Lina K. Odom took two paragraphs to tell her family history in the *Star of Zion* newspaper. "I have not seen my relatives since the civil war," she began. "My people belonged to Dr. Billy Hall." She went on to give the details of her extended family: "My people were all living in South Carolina when I left—Aunt Violet lived at the White House Place, my Uncle Henry Johnson lived at Pea Ridge Place. Both of my grandmothers lived there." In the end she wanted there to be no mistake about who she was, so she made an assertion that tied her to the past and to the family for which she searched and at the same time established her current social standing. "I am Eton Coleman's daughter," she reiterated, even though she had already identified her father, and "I married Mr. J. L. Odum of Louisiana." Mrs. Angie Lina K. Odum was a respectable married woman, someone worthy of assistance from the readers of this African Methodist Episcopal Zion newspaper.[10]

Something had changed in the language and possibly in the sentiment of the searchers. Although they continued to name and describe individual family members, former owners, and the circumstances and location of their separation, their use of this term, "my people," seemed to make a broader possessive claim. The term staked out a mutual and reciprocal belonging: The family belonged to you, and you belonged to it. "My people" seemed bigger and more expansive than simply "my family," "my kin," or "my relatives," which refer to a more direct connection than the more encompassing term. Perhaps use of "my people" revealed a desire to connect to anyone with a common ancestry. Perhaps it was an assertion of a claim of having had people, even if, like Mary Delaney, you had never seen them. The term said, "My people who help to give me a sense of history and identity, a sense of having come from somewhere and someone." These searchers were four decades removed from slavery and even farther from the initial separations. Some were now legally married; perhaps some had attended the freedpeople's schools and even the colleges that African Americans created following slavery and had moved into the African American middle class as Chestnutt's Mr. Ryder had. Still, they remembered the past, and they made a public declaration: They had people![11]

Despite persistent and stubborn hope, the search for living family members could not go on forever. Forty, fifty, or sixty years after separation there was diminishing likelihood that parents, aunts, uncles, and even children would still be alive. And of course, time took its toll on those who might have searched as well. It is not possible to know how many people who placed ads in the decades following emancipation ever found their family members; however, the ads themselves were testimony to the fact that those missing people had once existed, and that they mattered. That is to say, the ads interacted with memory on two grounds. First, those who placed ads asked readers to remember the people and the circumstances described so that readers might recognize someone and enable reunification. This was not remembering to establish a historical record; it was remembering to bring about a very concrete end—reunification. Second, though not the intended result, the brief descriptions provided in those purchased spaces in the newspapers left a trace of the seekers and their loved ones for later generations to find. The ads provided the best genealogies that searchers such as Mrs. Angie Lina K. Odum could fashion. The pleas for help themselves become remembrances.

As slavery and its separations and disruptions passed farther into memory, the attempt to find family members and the effort to remember them and have them remembered took on new forms. When interviewed in the 1930s and 1940s, many decades after slavery ended, former slaves inscribed their own genealogies of separation into the historical record. It had been important to enslaved parents that their children know what slavery had cost them, and so they passed on stories of how parents and grandparents and siblings had been sold or given away. Aged and close to the end of life, those who had been raised with the stories often seemed eager to relate these histories of separation. "I don't remember my grandparents," Nep Jenkins told the woman who interviewed him in North Gulfport, Mississippi. "My mother was sold away from them when I was a baby. They lived in Virginia, and my mother was sold and brought to Alabama. She never saw them anymore. I was six months old when my mother was sold."[12] Virginia Harris, interviewed in Coahoma County, Mississippi, dictated her family's history of separation like this: "My father, Preston Howell, and my mother, Lucy, both came from Virginia. I never knowed my grandpa and grandma. They were not sold, so they stayed on in Virginia where they was at, and my mother and father came on to their new owners in Louisiana."[13] Lizzie Davis from South Carolina told her interviewer, "I remember, I hear my father tell bout that his mammy was sold right here to this courthouse on that big public square up there, and say that the man set her up in the wagon and took her to Georgetown with him. Sold her right there on the block. Oh I hear them talking bout the selling block plenty times. Pa say, when he see them carry his mammy off from there, it make his heart swell in his breast."[14] Even when they could not remember the name of a grandparent or parent, they could recount what they had heard about sale and movement and loss. And the pain felt by Lizzie Davis's father lived on in his daughter's memory.

The accounts of former slaves impart a sense of repeated tellings, and they convey across the years the memories of separation. These now elderly former slaves relied on the memories that had been passed to them from their mothers and fathers. Often they prefaced the genealogies with "Mammy said" or "my pa said":

Mammy said she belonged to a Mr. Long in Adams County one time and when I was a baby she was sold to Mr. Carter with some more slaves.[15]

When my pa was fourteen years old he was sold at a auction to Wane Anderson, by a slave trader. He say he was brung down here in a covered wagon. They would stop at points and sell some of the slaves but my pa was held till he got to Mississippi where he was sold to my old marse.[16]

Mammy said when I was just big enough to nurse and wash little children, I was sold to Marse Hiram Cassedy and that man give me to his daughter, Miss Mary, to be her maid. The Cassedy's was good people.[17]

Perhaps when they sat around at night after working, or while a mother quilted, or while a father hunted or fished, the parent passed the stories down to the children, assuring that even relatives not known would be remembered and that the separations of slavery would not be forgotten.

People held on to these memories because mixed in with the pain of separation was the love of the people who had been left behind. Some also wanted to be sure to remember the injustices and deprivations of slavery. At the Atlanta Cotton States and International Exposition of 1895, a world's fair best known for Booker T. Washington's compromise speech that struck a deal with practices of discrimination and segregation, the Negro Building included displays of black progress in education, industry, and agriculture. These displays were meant to show how far blacks had come since the end of slavery. But not everything at the exposition aimed to leave slavery in the past. The Memphis Exhibition of the Colored People included a remembrance of slavery and separation. The exhibit contained needlework made by elderly women who had been enslaved, but the item that caught a reporter's eye was an old newspaper clipping. The curator of the Memphis Exhibition, an African American schoolteacher, told the reporter, "My husband's mother was sold four times. She wanted to send something to the Exposition, and she brought out this old paper in which she was advertised for sale. 'Don't lose it,' she said to me, with tears in her eyes." According to the reporter, it was the *Kentucky Gazette* of 1822. "Here," the reporter wrote, "are advertisements for 'a man named Tom'; a reward of $100 for return of the runaway. Here in a column with houses for sale, 'light-colored girl' is also offered. These old newspapers are treasured and hoarded by the old grandmothers of the race—fallen to them as keepsakes when the family was sundered on a master's or mistress' death." This old woman, a former slave, wanted to make sure that the thousands of people, black and white, Americans and foreigners, who attend the exposition would remember slavery, the sale of people, and the inevitable family separations. She had not forgotten how sale had disrupted her life, and she wanted to make sure that others also knew of that history that had so profoundly affected her.[18]

In a later time period, a descendant embroidered a memory of the separation of her grandmother and great-grandmother onto a plain muslin sack to mark her family's history. Written in brown, red, and black threads in cursive on the sack are these words:

My great grandmother Rose
mother of Ashley gave her this sack when
she was sold at age 9 in South Carolina
it held a tattered dress 3 handfulls of
pecans a braid of Roses hair. Told her
It be filled with my Love always

she never saw her again
Ashley is my grandmother
Ruth Middleton
1921.

This story had evidently been passed down in Ruth Middleton's family. For that family, the sack was a repository for their memories of vulnerability and grief. In a new generation Ruth Middleton embroidered an inscription that carried the story beyond the immediate family. Her needlework rendered the sack a lasting monument to Rose and Ashley.[19]

People during slavery and even in the four or more decades afterward searched for and remembered relatives they had known directly, people they had touched and talked to—people they missed. They looked for a physical presence. Those in the 1930s and 1940s who told interviewers about their family members who had been sold may have had some direct memories, but they had often heard the stories from parents who had known the ancestors. By the mid-twentieth century, and now into the twenty-first, African Americans searched for something different. They have no direct memories but hope to fill in the spaces by finding vestiges of their people from the past.

The work of doing these searches serves multiple purposes. As contemporary African Americans pore over dusty government records in archives and troll Internet sites to pull out and reclaim traces of obscured family members, they want to have a record of their ancestors' existence, a record that can be found in censuses, in regimental records, and in other documents that identify and confirm the existence of people who, for them, have previously existed only in family memory. These searchers want something more concrete than family-generated oral histories; they want documents that have more currency in a world that puts stock in paper and in written words. They can take a document to a family reunion and point to Aunt Sarah's name on the page of the census record or to great-great-great-grandfather's in a Civil War military service record. She lived. He has been authenticated. It is a way of honoring the memory of people who are rarely part of any scholarly history. Genealogists look for individual members of particular families, and doing that work, they want to make sure that these people are remembered within their families.

Genealogy is personal, it is individual, and it is private; but it also contributes to a larger work of naming people, of recognizing their existence, and of saying that their existence is worthy of remembrance. At the same time, genealogists are doing something for themselves. By unearthing ancestors, they also document their own history, establish their own extended past, and establish a place for themselves. They may even derive some elevation of status for being able to name and document their ancestors when so many cannot.

Enslaved children were stunned when they found out they could be sold. In a sense, some people are still stunned by the blow, by the deprivation of family members in the first place and of a family history in the second. First there was separation of families; then there was separation from history. People cannot fathom it, and they want to reestablish and reclaim that history. In 1977, after viewing the television series *Roots*, social worker Dorothy Redford set out to name her ancestors and to reclaim a history that was only faintly remembered within her own family. In the book *Roots*, Alex Haley had written about his search for his family's history that he claimed led him back to a village in the Gambia in West Africa. Redford's search led her to the Somerset Plantation in eastern North Carolina. But instead of focusing on only her family line, Redford took on the task of searching out all the people who had been enslaved by the Collins family at Somerset. All the slaves on the plantation became her people as she pieced together the documents that could chronicle their lives.

When former slaves searched for family members in the years following the Civil War, they frequently named former owners and gave the location of their enslavement and sale as clues to identifying relatives. For Redford, too, the place on which her people had been enslaved served as an important channel for coming to know her ancestors. "The day I first stepped on the ground of Somerset," she wrote, "I felt a tangibility more intense than all the documents and records I'd collected. And I realized now that this would be the power of the homecoming—to bring others to that place and give us each other as living monuments, as touchable reminders of the legacy of our shared ancestors."[20] In 1986, with twenty-one African American family lines identified, Redford planned the first reunion of descendants of people who had been enslaved on the Somerset Plantation. She wanted to share with them a tangible sense of the past, and that meant using the plantation as the site of the reunion.

While Dorothy Redford was conducting genealogical research and planning the Somerset Homecoming, writer Toni Morrison became conscious that she, too, wanted an accounting—wanted black people in the past to be remembered. She wanted to assert that the ancestors of African Americans had been here and to compel recognition of people whom she believed had largely been forgotten. In a 1986 interview she remarked,

There is no place you or I can go, to think about or not think about, to summon the presences of, or recollect the absences of slaves; nothing that reminds us of the ones who made the journey and of those who did not make it. There is no suitable memorial or plaque or wreath or wall or park or skyscraper lobby. There's no three-hundred-foot tower. There's no small bench by the road. There is not even a tree score, an initial that I can visit in Charleston or Savannah, or New York or Providence, or, better still, on the banks of the Mississippi. And because such a place doesn't exist (that I know of), the book had to.

Morrison's monument came in the form of *Beloved*, a novel that has at its core an escaped slave who murdered her young daughter rather than allow her to be returned to slavery. By writing the novel, Morrison constructed her marker, her memorial to African Americans who had lived out their lives as slaves. She was haunted by a newspaper clipping of the story of Margaret Garner and the child she killed, and she wanted the impossible choice that one mother faced to enter the consciousness of people who may have forgotten that such choices could exist in America. In the novel, Sethe is haunted by the memory of her dead child, much as the women William Wells Brown and Elizabeth Botume knew who could not get the children they lost to slavery out of their heads. "I can see now what I was doing on the last page," Morrison said. "I was finishing the story, transfiguring and disseminating the haunting with which the book begins. Yes, I was doing that; but I was also doing something more. I think I was pleading. I think I was pleading for that wall or that bench or that tower or that tree when I wrote the book."[21]

Morrison wrote as Dorothy Redford planned. At the end of August 1986, 200 years after the first eighty enslaved people arrived at Somerset Plantation, more than 2,000 people returned to this significant site of their family's history. Alex Haley, who had inspired Redford's journey into the past, attended. "We were finding our roots here, connecting with family, celebrating strength and survival," Redford remarked. Although she had always known members of her nuclear family, she had long felt that something was missing. "I began as a woman alone," Redford has written, "drifting in both time and space. But now I had a past peopled with links as strong and solid as any family in this nation. I was anchored. And I had a present cluttered with relatives, with blood kin. Now there is no place I can go that I can't find somebody I'm connected to, someone I belong to. The need to belong. That's what this was all about. Not just my need, but the need of our entire people, whose destiny was out of our hands for so long and who are still struggling to shape our identity, our sense of place in a society that was not our making."[22] As she revealed the history of those who had been enslaved at Somerset, and connected with fellow descendants, Redford echoed the sentiments that former slaves implied when they searched for "my people."

Sam Poole, who attended the Somerset reunion from Maryland, used language similar to the words Louis Hughes had used to describe how it felt to find family after slavery ended. Hughes spoke of a sense of an expansion of his world and of feelings of the profoundest joy.[23] Poole told of "a feeling of warmth, of connection and an indescribable feeling of joy."[24] And Barbara Eason Gadson of Queens, New York, told a reporter that she had grown up about eight miles from Somerset but had never known of her relationship to its history. "Now, I don't feel bitterness," she said. "I feel we are found."[25]

Charlie Crump, former slave from North Carolina, and his granddaughter
(Library of Congress, Prints and Photographs Division)

Notes

Introduction

1. Nell Irvin Painter, *Southern History across the Color Line* (Chapel Hill: University of North Carolina Press, 2002).

2. William M. Reddy, *The Navigation of Feeling: A Framework for the History of Emotions* (New York: Cambridge University Press, 2001), 48–49. Other works that have helped me think about the history of emotions include Catherine Lutz, "Morality, Domination and Understandings of 'Justifiable Anger' among the Ifaluk," in *Everyday Understanding: Social and Scientific Implications*, ed. Gün R. Semin and Kenneth J. Gergen (London: Sage, 1990), 204–26; Carol Zisowitz Stearns and Peter N. Stearns, *Anger: The Struggle for Emotional Control in America's History* (Chicago: University of Chicago Press, 1986), 1–66; Stuart Airlie, "The History of Emotions and Emotional History," *Early Medieval Europe* 10, no. 2 (2001): 235–41; Jeffrey Steele, "The Gender and Racial Politics of Mourning in Antebellum America," in *An Emotional History of the United States*, ed. Peter N. Stearns and Jan Lewis (New York: New York University Press, 1998), 91–106; and Drew Gilpin Faust, *This Republic of Suffering: Death and the American Civil War* (New York: Vintage, 2008).

3. Albert Raboteau, *Slave Religion: The "Invisible Institution" in the Antebellum South* (New York: Oxford University Press, 1978), 212–19, 243–66.

4. Dominick LaCapra, *Writing History, Writing Trauma* (Baltimore: Johns Hopkins University Press, 2001), 12.

5. Ulrich Bonnell Phillips, *American Negro Slavery: A Survey of the Supply, Employment and Control of Negro Labor as Determined by the Plantation Regime* (Baton Rouge: Louisiana State University Press, 1966), 343.

6. E. Franklin Frazier, *The Negro Family in the United States* (Notre Dame, Ind.: University of Notre Dame Press, 2001), 46–56.

7. Stanley M. Elkins, *Slavery: A Problem in American Institutional and Intellectual Life* (Chicago: University of Chicago Press, 1976), 98.

8. Ibid., 81–82.

9. Ibid., 98–102.

10. Ibid., 101–2.

11. Ibid., 23; Kenneth M. Stampp, *The Peculiar Institution: Slavery in the Ante-bellum South* (New York: Vintage, 1956).

12. Frazier, *Negro Family in the United States*, 25.

13. A few examples include John Blassingame, *Slave Community: Plantation Life in the Antebellum South* (New York: Oxford University Press, 1979); Ira Berlin, *Many Thousands Gone: The First Two Centuries of Slavery in America* (Cambridge, Mass.: Harvard University Press, 1998); Deborah Gray White, *Ar'n't I a Woman? Female Slaves in the Plantation South* (New York: Norton, 1985); Thavolia Glymph, *Out of the House of Bondage* (Cambridge: Cambridge University Press, 2008); Walter Johnson, *Soul by Soul:*

Life inside the Antebellum Slave Market (Cambridge, Mass.: Harvard University Press, 1999); Sharla Fett, *Working Cures: Healing, Health, and Power on Southern Slave Plantations* (Chapel Hill: University of North Carolina Press, 2002); Shane White and Graham White, *Stylin': African American Expressive Culture from Its Beginnings to the Zoot Suit* (Ithaca: Cornell University Press, 1998); Heather Andrea Williams, *Self-Taught: African American Education in Slavery and Freedom* (Chapel Hill: University of North Carolina Press, 2005); and Raboteau, *Slave Religion* (1978).

14. Daniel Patrick Moynihan, *The Negro Family: The Case for National Action* (Washington, D.C.: U.S. Department of Labor, March 1965), n.p.

15. Brenda E. Stevenson, *Life in Black and White: Family and Community in the Slave South* (New York: Oxford University Press, 1996), 160–61.

16. Nell Irvin Painter, "Soul Murder and Slavery: Toward a Fully Loaded Cost Accounting," in Painter, *Southern History across the Color Line*, 15–39.

17. Michael Tadman, *Speculators and Slaves: Masters, Traders, and Slaves in the Old South* (Madison: University of Wisconsin Press, 1996), 5.

18. Frederic Bancroft, *Slave Trading in the Old South* (Columbia: University of South Carolina Press, 1996); Tadman, *Speculators and Slaves*; Robert H. Gudmestad, *A Troublesome Commerce: The Transformation of the Interstate Slave Trade* (Baton Rouge: Louisiana State University Press, 2003); Johnson, *Soul by Soul*.

19. For the movement of white American children from New York to the West, see Linda Gordon, *The Great Arizona Orphan Abduction* (Cambridge, Mass.: Harvard University Press, 1999), and Marilyn Irvin Holt, *The Orphan Trains: Placing Out in America* (Lincoln: University of Nebraska Press, 1992). For Aboriginal Australian children, see the film *Rabbit-Proof Fence* (2002). For Native American children, see David Wallace Adams, *Education for Extinction: American Indians and the Boarding School Experience, 1875–1929* (Lawrence: University Press of Kansas, 1995). For British children sent to Australia, see "Australia's Rudd Says Sorry to Orphans, Child Migrants," *Reuters*, November 16, 2009, accessed at http://www.reuters.com/assets/print?aid=USTRE5AF0DI20091116.

20. "Holocaust Siblings Meet after 66 Years," http://www.cnn.com/2008/WORLD/europe/07/11/holocaust.reunion/index.html.

21. Kumiko's sister later found her and took her in. I am grateful to Dr. Hayumi Higuchi of Senshu University, Tokyo, for making my trip to Hiroshima possible, and to Dr. Makiko Takemoto and Ayako Yoshida for being my guides at the Fukuromachi Municipal Elementary School Peace Museum as well as at the Hiroshima Peace Memorial Museum and the Hiroshima National Peace Memorial Hall for the Atomic Bomb Victims.

Chapter 1

1. Letter from N. A. Hinkle to William Crow, September 24, 1836, University of Virginia Special Collections Library, Charlottesville.

2. Note regarding provenance of the William Crow Letters, and Guide to the Slave Trade Letters to William Crow, 1835–1842, University of Virginia Special Collections Library. Charlestown was then part of Virginia and is now in the state of West Virginia.

3. See, for example, Steven Mintz, *Huck's Raft: A History of American Childhood* (Cambridge, Mass.: Harvard University Press, 2004), vii.

4. For works on children during slavery, see Wilma King, *Stolen Childhood: Slave Youth in Nineteenth-Century America* (Bloomington: Indiana University Press, 1997), and Marie Jenkins Schwartz, *Born in Bondage: Growing Up Enslaved in the Antebellum South* (Cambridge, Mass.: Harvard University Press, 2000). Monographs with substantial material regarding children include Herbert Gutman, *The Black Family in Slavery and Freedom, 1750–1925* (New York: Vintage, 1977), and Deborah Gray White, *Ar'n't I a Woman? Female Slaves in the Plantation South* (New York: Norton, 1985).

5. Kate Drumgoold, *A Slave Girl's Story, Being an Autobiography of Kate Drumgoold* (Brooklyn, N.Y., 1898), in *Six Women's Slave Narratives*, ed. William L. Andrews (New York: Oxford University Press, 1988), 4–5.

6. Jean Piaget, *The Child's Conception of Physical Causality* (Totowa, N.J.: Littlefield, Adams, 1930, 1975), 131–34; James A. Fogarty, *The Magical Thoughts of Grieving Children: Treating Children with Complicated Mourning and Advice for Parents* (Amityville, N.Y.: Baywood Publishers, 2000), 49–64. I would like to thank Thomas Jackson of the University of North Carolina, Greensboro, Department of History, for the connection to the concept of magical thinking.

7. Charles Ball, *Slavery in the United States: A Narrative of the Life and Adventures of Charles Ball, a Black Man* (New York: John S. Taylor, 1837), 16–18.

8. See B. F. French, ed., *Historical Collections of Louisiana Embracing Translations of Many Rare Documents Relating to the Natural, Civil and Political History of the State*, pt. 3 (New York: D. Appleton and Company, 1851), 94. Louisiana was ruled by France from 1699 to 1769 and by Spain from 1769 to 1803. It became part of the United States in 1803. See Thomas N. Ingersoll, "Slave Codes and Judicial Practice in New Orleans, 1718–1807," *Law and History Review* 13, no. 1 (Spring 1995): 23, and Judith Kelleher Schafer, *Slavery, the Civil Law, and the Supreme Court of Louisiana* (Baton Rouge: Louisiana State University Press, 1994).

9. Michael Tadman, *Speculators and Slaves: Masters, Traders, and Slaves in the Old South* (Madison: University of Wisconsin Press, 1996), 6, 171. Tadman includes the following states in the category of Upper South: Delaware, Maryland, Kentucky, Virginia, Tennessee, and North Carolina.

10. *Virginia Gazette*, October 24, 1829.

11. *Charleston Courier*, April 14, 1846.

12. Letter dated December 20, 1858, from Dickenson Hill & Co., Joseph Dickinson Papers, Duke University Rare Book, Manuscript, and Special Collections Library, Durham, N.C. (hereafter cited as Duke).

13. Appraisal dated April 6, 1860, Alexander Hamilton Stephens Papers, Duke.

14. Bill of sale dated August 14, 1852, African American Miscellaneous Slavery File, Duke.

15. Bill of sale dated December 13, 1855, Slavery Division Papers, 1757–1867, African American Miscellaneous Slavery File, Duke.

16. Betts and Gregory Auctioneers, Richmond, Virginia, "State of our Negro Market," July 20, 1860, African American Miscellaneous Slavery File, Duke.

17. Jim Allen interview, in *Born in Slavery: Slave Narratives from the Federal Writers' Project, 1936–1938*, Mississippi Narratives, vol. 9, http://memory.loc.gov.

18. Letter from Samuel R. Browning, Greenwood, Miss., to A. W. Boyd, Alamance County, N.C., dated June 4, 1849, Archibald Boyd Letters, 1841–1897, Duke.

19. Parthena Rollins interview, in *The American Slave: A Composite Autobiography*, ed. George P. Rawick, vol. 5, *Indiana Narratives* (Westport, Conn.: Greenwood, 1972), 167–68. "Nigger trader" is one of the many terms enslaved people used for "slave trader." This meant the person bought and sold blacks, not that he himself was black.

20. William Wells Brown, *Narrative of William W. Brown, a Fugitive Slave. Written by Himself* (Boston: The Anti-slavery Office, 1847), 49.

21. Regarding awareness of being a slave, see Lunsford Lane, *The Narrative of Lunsford Lane, Formerly of Raleigh, NC* (Boston, 1842), 7–8, and Henry Bibb, *Narrative of the Life and Adventures of Henry Bibb, an American Slave* (New York, 1850), 14–15. See also Thomas L. Webber, *Deep Like the Rivers: Education in the Slave Quarter Community, 1831–1865* (New York: Norton, 1978), 19, and Mintz, *Huck's Raft*, 104. Mintz sees the awareness of being slaves often coming in adolescence, but when family separation was involved, children came to the awareness much earlier.

22. Thomas Lewis Johnson, *Twenty-Eight Years a Slave, or the Story of My Life in Three Continents* (Bournemouth, London: W. Mate and Sons, 1909), 1–2, electronic ed., Documenting the American South, http://docsouth.unc.edu/neh/johnson1/johnson.html.

23. Ibid.

24. Thomas H. Jones, *The Experience of Rev. Thomas H. Jones, Who Was a Slave for Forty-Three Years* (Boston, 1862), 6–8, electronic ed., http://docsouth.unc.edu/fpn/jones/jones.html.

25. Josiah Henson, *The Life of Josiah Henson, Formerly a Slave, Now an Inhabitant of Canada, as Narrated by Himself* (Boston: Arthur D. Phelps, 1849), 3–5, electronic ed., http://docsouth.unc.edu/neh/henson49/henson49.html.

26. John Brown, *Slave Life in Georgia: A Narrative of the Life, Sufferings, and Escape of John Brown, a Fugitive Slave* (Savannah: Beehive Press, 1991). This image of children hiding from unknown white men recurs in other narratives. See, for example, William Parker, *The Freedman's Story, in Two Parts* (Boston: Ticknor and Fields, 1866), electronic ed., Documenting the American South, http://docsouth.unc.edu/neh/parker1/menu.html.

27. "Gang" was the term used to describe work groups in certain agricultural environments, such as tobacco and cotton. People in a gang worked under close supervision of a slave driver and/or an overseer and had to keep up with the pace of the gang, and they usually worked from early morning until evening. In contrast, people who worked in rice cultivation in South Carolina usually labored on a task system in which each person was expected to accomplish a particular task, such as hoeing half an acre of land, each day. When the task was completed, the person could stop working.

28. Brown, *Slave Life in Georgia* (1991), 3–8.

29. Brown's father belonged to a different owner who had moved so far away that Brown only recalled seeing his father once. His mother remarried, and this husband also belonged to a different owner, so that with this division of property she lost most of her children as well as her second husband. See ibid., 1–3.

30. Ibid., 13–15.

31. Ibid., 15.

32. Sam Broach interview, in Rawick, *American Slave*, vol. 6, pt. 1, *Mississippi Narratives*, supplement ser. 1, 222–23.

33. Nettie Henry interview, in Rawick, *American Slave*, vol. 8, pt. 3, *Mississippi Narratives*, supplement ser. 1, 975–76.

34. Henson, *Life of Josiah Henson*, 1.

35. Fanny Hodges interview, in Rawick, *American Slave*, vol. 8, pt. 3, *Mississippi Narratives*, supplement ser. 1, 1024.

36. Hannah Chapman interview, in Rawick, *American Slave*, vol. 7, pt. 2, *Mississippi Narratives*, supplement ser. 1, 383.

37. Robert Glenn interview, in *Born in Slavery*, North Carolina Narratives, vol. 11, pt. 1, http://memory.loc.gov.

38. Ball, *Slavery in the United States*, 25.

39. Tadman, *Speculators and Slaves*, 50; John Brown, *Slave Life in Georgia: A Narrative of the Life, Sufferings, and Escape of John Brown, a Fugitive Slave, Now in England* (London, 1855), 14.

40. King, *Stolen Childhood*, 22–41. Thomas Lewis Johnson drove flies away from the table at mealtime and got his owner's slippers at night. Booker T. Washington also fanned flies from his owner's table, while his mother worked in the kitchen. See Booker T. Washington, *Up from Slavery: An Autobiography*, ed. W. Fitzhugh Brundage (Boston: Bedford/St. Martin's Press, 2003), 9; Johnson, *Twenty-Eight Years a Slave*, 3–4; and Bibb, *Narrative*, 16. Bibb wrote of his mistress: "While I was at home she kept me all the time rubbing furniture, washing, scrubbing the floors; and when I was not doing this, she would often seat herself in a large rocking chair, with two pillows about her, and would make me rock her, and keep off the flies. She was too lazy to scratch her own head, and would often make me scratch and comb it for her. She would at other times lie on her bed, in warm weather, and make me fan her while she slept, scratch and rub her feet; but after awhile she got sick of me, and preferred a maiden servant to do such business." On walking white children to school, see Washington, *Up from Slavery*, 42. On nursing white children, see Peter Bruner, *A Slave's Adventures toward Freedom: Not Fiction, but the True Story of a Struggle*, 13, electronic ed., http://docsouth.unc.edu/neh/bruner/bruner.html, and Elizabeth Keckley, *Behind the Scenes, or Thirty Years a Slave, and Four Years in the White House* (New York, 1868), 19–20, electronic ed., http://docsouth.unc.edu/neh/keckley/menu.html. On sleeping at the foot of the bed, see Susie King Taylor, *Reminiscences of My Life in Camp* (Athens: University of Georgia Press, 2006), 2.

41. *Alexandria Gazette*, May 17, 1828.

42. Ethan Allen Andrews, *Slavery and the Domestic Slave Trade in the United States* (Boston, 1836), 135–53; Wendell Holmes Stephenson, *Isaac Franklin: Slave Trader and Planter of the Old South* (Gloucester, Mass.: Peter Smith, 1968), 22–93.

43. *American Beacon and Norfolk and Portsmouth Advertiser*, November 22, 1831.

44. For the figure of 1 million people sold, see Michael Tadman, "The Interregional Slave Trade in the History and Myth-Making of the U.S. South," in *The Chattel Principle: Internal Slave Trades in the Americas*, ed. Walter Johnson (New Haven: Yale University Press, 2004), 124. For a contemporary assessment of the domestic slave trade, see William Jay, *Miscellaneous Writings on Slavery* (Boston, 1853). For scholarly works on the

trade, see Frederic Bancroft, *Slave Trading in the Old South* (Columbia: University of South Carolina Press, 1931, 1996); Tadman, *Speculators and Slaves*; Robert H. Gudmestad, *A Troublesome Commerce: The Transformation of the Interstate Slave Trade* (Baton Rouge: Louisiana State University Press, 2003); and Johnson, *Chattel Principle*.

45. *Norfolk and Portsmouth Herald*, February 23, 1821.

46. *Charleston Courier*, April 27, 1846.

47. *Flag of '98* (Warrenton, Va.), November 30, 1844.

48. For a discussion of white men making their wealth and status out of slaves, see Walter Johnson, *Soul by Soul: Life inside the Antebellum Slave Market* (Cambridge, Mass.: Harvard University Press, 1999), 78–116.

49. *Hillsborough Recorder*, May 26, 1824.

50. Advertisement in the *Norfolk and Portsmouth Herald*, January 29, 1821.

51. *Norfolk and Portsmouth Herald*, January 15, 1821.

52. Letter dated August 20, 1845, from Charles A. Rice to Dr. James Gaines, James S. Gaines Papers, 1823–1876, Duke.

53. Bill of Sale, Guilford County, North Carolina, April 1, 1850, African American Miscellaneous Slavery Division Papers, 1757–1867, Duke.

54. William Henry Singleton, *Recollections of My Slavery Days*, ed. Katherine Mellen Charron and David S. Cecelski (Raleigh: Division of Archives and History, 1999), 32–35.

55. Bill of Sale, Pittsylvania County, Virginia, August 6, 1813, African American Miscellaneous Slavery Division Papers, 1757–1867, Duke.

56. Bill of sale, Alexander County, North Carolina, November 8, 1859, African American Miscellaneous Slavery Division Papers, 1757–1867, Duke.

57. Bill of sale, September 28, 1850, Duke.

58. Bill of Sale, Leake County, Mississippi, January 25, 1857, African American Miscellaneous Slavery Division Papers, 1757–1867, Duke.

59. See Johnson, *Soul by Soul*, 192–213.

60. Brown, *Slave Life in Georgia* (London, 1855), 15–16.

61. Old Elizabeth, *Memoir of Old Elizabeth, a Coloured Woman* (Philadelphia: Collins Printer, 1863), in Andrews, *Six Women's Slave Narratives*, 4.

62. Robert Glenn interview.

63. Ibid. Children sometimes did not have anyone to take care of them once they lost their family members. See Dylan C. Penningroth, "My People, My People: The Dynamics of Community in Southern Slavery," in *New Studies in the History of American Slavery*, ed. Edward E. Baptist and Stephanie M. H. Camp (Athens: University of Georgia Press, 2006).

64. Laura Clark interview, in Rawick, *American Slave*, vol. 6, *Alabama and Indiana Narratives*, 72.

65. Ibid., 73.

66. Ibid.

67. Louis Hughes, *Thirty Years a Slave: From Bondage to Freedom—The Institution of Slavery as Seen on the Plantation and in the Home of the Planter* (Milwaukee, 1897; reprint, Miami, Fla.: Mnemosyne Publishing, 1969), 10.

68. Ibid., 15.

69. Mingo White interview, in Rawick, *American Slave*, vol. 6, *Alabama and Indiana Narratives*, 413–14.

70. Ibid.

71. Laura Clark interview, 72.

72. Johnson, *Twenty-Eight Years a Slave*, 6.

73. She was known only as Elizabeth or Old Elizabeth, with no last name. See Old Elizabeth, *Memoir*.

74. Ibid., 3–7.

75. Thomas S. Kidd, *The Great Awakening: A Brief History with Documents* (Boston: Bedford/St. Martin's Press, 2008), 5–9.

76. Old Elizabeth, *Memoir*, 7.

77. Caleb Craig interview, in Rawick, *American Slave*, vol. 2, pt. 1, *South Carolina Narratives*, 230–31.

78. Interview of Sylvia Cannon in Florence, S.C., conducted August 4, 1937, by Annie Ruth Davis, in Rawick, *American Slave*, vol. 2, pts. 1 and 2, *South Carolina Narratives*. Former slaves frequently commented on how they had been treated like animals during slavery. See Mia Bay, *The White Image in the Black Mind* (New York: Oxford University Press, 2000), 119–20.

79. Singleton, *Recollections of My Slavery Days*, 33–34.

80. Susan Hamilton interview, in Rawick, *American Slave*, vol. 14, pt. 2, *South Carolina Narratives*, 235.

81. Dinah Hayes interview, in Rawick, *American Slave*, vol. 8, pt. 3, *Mississippi Narratives*, supplement series 1, 962.

Chapter 2

1. Henry Bibb, *Narrative of the Life and Adventures of Henry Bibb, an American Slave. Written by Himself* (New York, 1850), 38.

2. George M. Stroud, *Sketch of the Laws Relating to Slavery in the Several States of the United States of America* (1856; reprint, New York: Negro Universities Press, 1968), 41.

3. Laura F. Edwards, "'The Marriage Covenant Is at the Foundation of All Our Rights': The Politics of Slave Marriages in North Carolina after Emancipation," *Law and History Review* 14, no. 1 (Spring 1996): 80–86; Nancy F. Cott, *Public Vows: A History of Marriage and the Nation* (Cambridge, Mass.: Harvard University Press, 2000), 1–12; Margaret Burnham, "An Impossible Marriage: Slave Law and Family Law," *Law and Inequality* 5 (July 1987): 187–225; Michael Grossberg, *Governing the Hearth: Law and the Family in Nineteenth-Century America* (Chapel Hill: University of North Carolina Press, 1985), 24–27; Thomas R. R. Cobb, *An Inquiry into the Law of Negro Slavery in the United States of America* (Philadelphia, 1858; reprint, Athens: University of Georgia Press, 1999), 242. Regarding slaveholding women, see, for example, Kirsten E. Wood, *Masterful Women: Slaveholding Widows from the American Revolution through the Civil War* (Chapel Hill: University of North Carolina Press, 2004).

4. *Girod v. Lewis*, May Term 1819, in *The American Slave Code in Theory and Practice: Its Distinctive Features Shown by Its Statutes, Judicial Decisions, and Illustrative Facts*, ed.

William Goodell (New York: American and Foreign Anti-Slavery Society, 1853; reprint, New York: Negro Universities Press, 1968), 107.

5. Louisiana Code of 1824, in *Civil Code of the State of Louisiana Preceded by the Treaty of Cession with France, the Constitution of the United States of America and of the State* (published by a citizen of Louisiana, 1825), 92.

6. Ibid., 76–87.

7. Peter W. Bardaglio, *Reconstructing the Household: Families, Sex, and the Law in the Nineteenth-Century South* (Chapel Hill: University of North Carolina Press, 1995), 23–29.

8. *State v. Samuel*, 19 N.C. (2 Dev. & Bat.) 174; Bardaglio, *Reconstructing the Household*, 27.

9. *Howard v. Howard et al.*, 51 N.C. 237–38.

10. Ibid., 241.

11. Goodell, *American Slave Code*, 107–8. The book was published by the American Antislavery Society, of which Goodell was a founder.

12. Thomas H. Jones, *The Experience of Rev. Thomas H. Jones, Who Was a Slave for Forty-Three Years* (Boston, 1862), 31, electronic ed., http://docsouth.unc.edu/nc/jones85/menu.html.

13. Bibb, *Narrative*, 40–41.

14. Bethany Veney, *The Narrative of Bethany Veney, a Slave Woman* (Worcester, Mass., 1889), 18, electronic ed., Documenting the American South, http://docsouth.unc.edu/fpn/veney/veney.html.

15. Francis Fredric, *Slave Life in Virginia and Kentucky; of Fifty Years of Slavery* (London, 1863), 25.

16. Jones, *Experience*, 9.

17. Ibid. I would like to thank my former UNC student Rachel Allen for bringing Thomas Jones's narrative to my attention. The term "archive of memory" is from Diane Cole, *After Great Pain a New Life Emerges* (New York: Summit Books, 1992).

18. Jones, *Experience*, 29.

19. Ibid., 29–31.

20. Bibb, *Narrative*, 34.

21. Ibid., 33–34. Bibb included the following footnote when he referred to "the highest circles of slaves": "The distinction among slaves is as marked, as the classes of society are in any aristocratic community. Some refusing to associate with others whom they deem beneath them in point of character, color, condition, or the superior importance of their respective masters."

22. Of course, it is also possible that Malinda's owner wanted to reserve his own access to her. It seems unlikely, though, that Bibb would have agreed to that condition.

23. Bibb, *Narrative*, 40.

24. *State v. Samuel*, 171; Goodell, *American Slave Code*, 107.

25. Lunsford Lane, *The Narrative of Lunsford Lane—formerly of Raleigh* (1842), in *Flight from the Devil: Six Slave Narratives*, ed. William Loren Katz (Trenton, N.J.: Africa World Press, 1996), 10.

26. Ibid., 8.

27. Ibid., 6–8. See Bardaglio, *Reconstructing the Household*, 31–36, regarding the narrowly circumscribed rights of married white women in the antebellum South.

28. Letter from Ch. H. Locher to Capt. William Weaver, December 3, 1859, Mss1 W3798a11, Virginia Historical Society, Richmond.

29. Letter from J. O. Walker to William Middleton, January 27, 1847, Middleton Place Plantation, Charleston, S.C.

30. Letter from Fickling and Glen to Mrs. E. Kane, September 22, 1825, Jared Irwin Papers, Duke University Rare Book, Manuscript, and Special Collections Library, Durham, N.C. Billy may have been owned by Tyre Glen, a western North Carolina planter and slave trader.

31. For a discussion of the idea of paternalism, see Eugene D. Genovese, *Roll, Jordan, Roll: The World the Slaves Made* (New York: Pantheon, 1972), 3–7.

32. Nathan Bass, "Essay on the Treatment and Management of Slaves," in *Transactions of the Southern Central Agricultural Society of Georgia, 1846–1851* (Macon, Ga., 1852), 16.

33. H. N. McTyeire, "Plantation Life—Duties and Responsibilities," *De Bow's Review* 29 (September 1860): 362.

34. Sometimes also "broad."

35. Virginia planter William Byrd II captured this patriarchal and paternalistic ideal when he wrote, "I have a large Family of my own, and my Doors are open to Every Body. . . . Like one of the Patriarchs, I have my Flocks and my Herds, my Bond-men and Bond women, and ever Soart of trade amongs my own Servants, so that I live in a kind of Independence on everyone but Providence" (cited in Bardaglio, *Reconstructing the Household*, 25). And John Wilson expressed his notion of the paternalistic ideal as follows: "The *pater-familias*, or head of the family, should, in one sense, be the father of the whole concern, negroes and all. And while he allows no undue familiarity and companionship on the part of the latter, they should yet be convinced that he cares for them—that master is their best friend and that he will, to the best of his ability, redress all their grievances, settle their disputes on equitable principles, and protect them from all wrong from whatever quarter it may come" (John S. Wilson, M.D., "The Peculiarities and Diseases of Negroes," in *Advice among Masters: The Ideal in Slave Management in the Old South*, ed. James O. Breeden [Westport, Conn.: Greenwood, 1980], 59).

36. Herbert Gutman, *The Black Family in Slavery and Freedom, 1750–1925* (New York: Vintage, 1977), 88.

37. Southron, "The Policy of the Southern Planter," *American Cotton Planter and Soil of the South*, n.s. 1 (October 1857): 292–96, in Breeden, *Advice among Masters*, 243.

38. See Sally E. Hadden, *Slave Patrols: Law and Violence in Virginia and the Carolinas* (Cambridge, Mass.: Harvard University Press, 2001).

39. "On the Management of Slaves," *Southern Agriculturist, and Register of Rural Affairs* 6 (June 1833): 281–87.

40. Ibid.

41. Ibid.

42. Francis Boykin, "Management of Negroes," *Southern Field and Fireside* 1 (June 30, 1860): 406, in Breeden, *Advice among Masters*, 244–45.

43. Tattler, "Management of Negroes," *Southern Cultivator* 9 (November 1850): 162–64, in Breeden, *Advice among Masters*, 241.

44. William Geddy will. Virginia Historical Society.

45. Jones, *Experience*, 30.

46. Veney, *Narrative of Bethany Veney*, 18.

47. Letter from Charles J. McDonald, December 23, 1854, Farish Carter Papers, Ms 2230, Southern Historical Collection, University of North Carolina, Chapel Hill (hereafter cited as SHC). My thanks to former UNC student Warren Garris for finding this document. See also McDonald biographical information in *New Georgia Encyclopedia*, http://www.georgiaencyclopedia.org/nge/Article.jsp?id=h-2817&sug=y.

48. For an owner requesting a white minister to marry his slaves, see letter from Alan Rives to Rev. Mr. Timberlake, June 5, 1847, Walter Timberlake Papers, 1814–1849, Duke University Rare Book, Manuscript, and Special Collections Library.

49. The term "self-deification" was suggested by my 2011 undergraduate seminar student Matt Schaefer.

50. Francis Terry Leak Papers, Tippah County, Mississippi, Collection #1095, Plantation Book, vol. 4, SHC. For nineteenth-century wedding vows, see *The Constitution of the Presbyterian Church in the United States of America* (Philadelphia, 1850), 441–44, and Protestant Episcopal Church, *The Book of Common Prayer and Other Rites and Ceremonies of the Church According to the Use of the Protestant Episcopal Church in the United States of America* (Philadelphia, 1848), 316–18. Regarding weddings among enslaved people, see Thomas E. Will, "Weddings on Contested Ground: Slave Marriage in the Antebellum South," *Historian* 62 (1999): 99–117; Patrick W. O'Neil, "Tying the Knots: The Nationalization of Weddings in Antebellum America" (Ph.D. diss., University of North Carolina, Chapel Hill, 2009), 186–232.

51. Regarding slaves who taught themselves to read and write, see Heather Andrea Williams, *Self-Taught: African American Education in Slavery and Freedom* (Chapel Hill: University of North Carolina Press, 2005).

52. Rice Carter Ballard Papers, 1822–1888, Collection no. 04850, SHC; Wendell Holmes Stephenson, *Isaac Franklin: Slave Trader and Planter of the Old South* (Gloucester, Mass.: Peter Smith, 1968), 56; William Kauffman Scarborough, *Masters of the Big House: Elite Slaveholders of the Mid-Nineteenth-Century South* (Baton Rouge: Louisiana State University Press, 2003), 125. Regarding Ballard and "fancy girls," see Edward E. Baptist, "'Cuffy,' 'Fancy Maids,' and 'One-Eyed Men': Rape, Commodification, and the Domestic Slave Trade in the United States," in *The Chattel Principle: Internal Slave Trades in the Americas*, ed. Walter Johnson (New Haven: Yale University Press, 2004), 165–203. Regarding slave sales in Louisiana to avoid Mississippi law, see Michael Tadman, *Speculators and Slaves: Masters, Traders, and Slaves in the Old South* (Madison: University of Wisconsin Press, 1996), 88–89.

53. Letter from Delia, Louisville, Kentucky, October 22, 1854, Rice C. Ballard Papers, SHC. Henry would not ordinarily have had any say in who purchased him, but in this situation, where Ballard was only doing Delia a favor, Henry would have been able to decline.

54. Ibid.

55. Letter from Henry Tatterson, October 18, 1845, Holladay Family Papers, 1753–1961, Virginia Historical Society. Regarding African Americans purchasing themselves and their families, see Glenda Elizabeth Gilmore, *Gender and Jim Crow: Women and the Politics of White Supremacy in North Carolina, 1896–1920* (Chapel Hill: University of North Carolina Press, 1996), 5–6. Information regarding the value attached to enslaved women

is from Daina Ramey Berry Slave Value Database in Berry, "The Price for Their Pound of Flesh: The Value of Human Chattels" (forthcoming).

56. Moses Grandy, *Narrative of the Life of Moses Grandy, Late a Slave in the United States of America*, 1843, 15–16, http://docsouth.unc.edu/fpn/grandy/menu.html. A dram is a coin.

57. Brownrigg Family Papers, Genealogical Material, SHC. For Choctaw removal, see Kenneth H. Carleton (Tribal Historic Preservation Officer/Archaeologist, Mississippi Band of Choctaw), "A Brief History of the Mississippi Band of Choctaw Indians," 2002, http://www.msarchaeology.org/maa/carleton.pdf.

58. Letter from Sarah Sparkman, October 20, 1835, Brownrigg Family Papers, SHC.

59. Letter from Sarah Sparkman to John H. Brownrigg, November 4, 1835, Brownrigg Family Papers, SHC. I have not included here two notes from daughters to their mothers.

60. Regarding plans for more slaves to go to Mississippi in the spring, see letter from Phebe Brownrigg, September 13, 1835, in *Slave Testimony: Two Centuries of Letters, Speeches, Interviews and Autobiographies*, ed. John Blassingame (Baton Rouge: Louisiana State University Press, 1977), 22.

61. Letter from R. T. Hoskins, November 6, 1835, Brownrigg Family Papers, SHC.

62. Letter from William Sparkman to Richard Brownrigg, November 6, 1835, Brownrigg Family Papers, SHC.

63. Ibid., December 15, 1835.

64. Letter from Thomas L. Brownrigg to Richard Brownrigg, December 20, 1835, Brownrigg Family Papers, SHC.

65. Letter from Sarah Sparkman to her sister Mary Brownrigg, January 4, 1836; letter from R. T. Hoskins to Richard Brownrigg, January 18, 1836; and letter from Thomas Brownrigg to Richard Brownrigg, March 11, 1836, Brownrigg Family Papers, SHC.

66. Letter from Richard Brownrigg to John Brownrigg, February 5, 1836, and letter from Thomas Brownrigg to Richard Brownrigg, January 17, 1836, Brownrigg Family Papers, SHC.

67. Letter from Thomas Brownrigg to Richard Brownrigg, March 11, 1836, Brownrigg Family Papers, SHC.

68. Mississippi State and Territorial Census, Lowndes County, 1837.

69. For the most thorough treatment of resilience among African American families, see Gutman, *Black Family in Slavery and Freedom*. Gutman's research found, for example, that despite family separations during slavery, "upon their emancipation most Virginia ex-slave families had two parents, and most older couples had lived together in long-lasting unions" (9).

70. Letter from James Tate, February 4, 1863, Berry Family Collection, Schomburg Center for Research in Black Culture, New York, N.Y. Tate's letter is dated one month after President Abraham Lincoln issued the Emancipation Proclamation, but Tate and his wife were still enslaved, as were most African Americans in the South. Regarding the limits of the Emancipation Proclamation, see Ira Berlin, Joseph P. Reidy, and Leslie S. Rowland, eds., *Freedom's Soldiers: The Black Military Experience in the Civil War* (New York: Cambridge University Press, 1982).

My thanks to Adriane Lentz-Smith for bringing James Tate's letter to my attention.

71. *Report of the Special Committee Appointed by the Protestant Episcopal Convention, at Its Session in 1858, to Report on the Duty of Clergymen in Relation to the Marriage of Slaves* (Charleston, S.C.: Walker, Evans, 1859), in *Defending Slavery: Proslavery Thought in the Old South*, ed. Paul Finkelman (New York: Bedford/St. Martin's Press, 2003), 114–21. But see contrary finding by a church, R. L. Ryburn, *Sketches, Historical and Biographical, of the Broad River and King's Mountain Baptist Associations from 1800–1882* (1887), 38.

72. This is the resilience of which historian Herbert Gutman wrote in *Black Family in Slavery and Freedom*.

73. Letter from John E. Beck to Elick Farer, July 22, 1856, in *Records of Ante-Bellum Southern Plantations from the Revolution through the Civil War*, ed. Kenneth Stampp, series 1, pt. 3, reel 7 (Frederick, Md.: University Publications of America, 1995).

74. Henry Box Brown, *Narrative of Henry Box Brown, Who Escaped from Slavery Enclosed in a Box 3 Feet Long and 2 Wide. Written from a Statement of Facts Made by Himself. With Remarks Upon the Remedy for Slavery by Charles Stearns*, 55, electronic ed., Documenting the American South, http://docsouth.unc.edu/neh/boxbrown/boxbrown.html.

75. Ibid., 57.

76. Ibid., 58–64; Jeffrey Ruggles, *The Unboxing of Henry Brown* (Richmond: Library of Virginia, 2003).

Brown went to the train station and figured out the dimensions of the largest shipping boxes. He paid a carpenter to build a box to match that size. He enlisted the help of another man, who sealed him in the box and delivered him to the train station. He traveled in the box to Philadelphia, where the box was retrieved, taken to the home of an antislavery Quaker, and opened in front of several men. The incident garnered a great deal of publicity.

77. John Hope Franklin and Loren Schweninger, *Runaway Slaves: Rebels on the Plantation* (New York: Oxford University Press, 1999), 52–74. See Freddie Parker, *Stealing a Little Freedom: Slave Runaways in North Carolina, 1775–1840* (New York: Garland Publishing, 1994), for a collection of runaway ads.

78. *Flag of '98* (Warrenton, Va.), January 5, 1850.

79. *Charleston Courier*, January 4, 1830.

80. *Norfolk and Portsmouth Herald*, December 29, 1820.

81. *Charleston Courier*, January 1, 1836.

82. *Richmond Enquirer*, September 9, 1831.

83. *Charleston Courier*, October 19, 1836.

84. Ibid., August 6, 1836.

85. Ibid., January 4, 1830.

86. Ibid. Ads generally called for the runaway to be captured and turned over to a local jail or workhouse. The jailer then placed an ad in the paper announcing that he had a slave fitting a particular description, and the owner paid the jailer's fees and picked up the enslaved person.

87. Veney, *Narrative of Bethany Veney*, 18–24.

88. Ibid.

89. Jones, *Experience*, 31–32.

90. Kenneth J. Doka, ed., *Disenfranchised Grief: Recognizing Hidden Sorrow* (Lexington, Mass.: Lexington Books, 1989), 3–7.

91. "Speech by freedman Bayley Wyatt, December 1866. Published by Friends' Association of Philadelphia and this vicinity for the Relief of Colored Freedmen," Virginia Freedmen's Bureau, RG105, M1048, roll 21, National Archives and Records Administration, Washington, D.C. "Hollow silence" is from the book's opening epigraph taken from Elizabeth Nunez, *Beyond the Limbo Silence* (New York: Ballantine Books, 1998), 7.

Chapter 3

1. Quotes from Chaplin's journal are taken from the original Journal of Thomas B. Chaplin, South Carolina Historical Society, Charleston (hereafter cited as Chaplin Journal), and from Theodore Rosengarten, *Tombee: Portrait of a Cotton Planter* (New York: McGraw-Hill, 1987). I am indebted to Rosengarten for his extensive research on Thomas Chaplin and his family. Excerpts from the journal also appear in Willie Lee Rose, ed., *A Documentary History of Slavery in North America* (Athens: University of Georgia Press, 1999), 375–77.

2. Rosengarten, *Tombee*, 92–93.

3. Ibid., 100, 111.

4. Chaplin Journal, January 13, 1845.

5. Ibid., January 13, March 19, 1845.

6. Rosengarten, *Tombee*, 327.

7. All citations are to Chaplin Journal: beef for market, January 15; fifth hog, January 20; Rose's baby, January 25; deer hunting, January 24; fishing, April 24; trial, January 18; militia, February 22 and March 25; cotton, January 17; sickness of enslaved children, February 20; sugarcane, March 3; planting cotton, March 27; potatoes, April 1; talk with Isabella Chaplin Baker, February 11.

8. Ibid., May 3, 1845.

9. Ibid.

10. See Chap. 1 text at n. 17.

11. Regarding debt, see Rosengarten, *Tombee*, 131–32; regarding honor, see Bertram Wyatt-Brown, *Southern Honor: Ethics and Behavior in the Old South* (New York: Oxford University Press, 2007), and Peter W. Bardaglio, *Reconstructing the Household: Families, Sex, and the Law in the Nineteenth-Century South* (Chapel Hill: University of North Carolina Press, 1995), 20–23.

12. All references to individual slaves are from Chaplin Journal. Regarding Robert's ownership, see Rosengarten, *Tombee*, 31.

13. According to Theodore Rosengarten, prime field hands sold for $550 each at this time; see *Tombee*, 331 n. 53.

14. William B. Fickling was a Charleston magistrate and lawyer; see Rosengarten, *Tombee*, 336.

15. Jacob Stroyer, *Sketches of My Life in the South* (1879), 30, electronic ed., http://docsouth.unc.edu/neh/stroyer/stroyer.html.

16. Author's observation of Chaplin's home on St. Helena, S.C.

17. Letter from Catherine Percy to Barnard Elliott, October 5, 1778, Baker-Grimke Papers, 11-537-29/45, South Carolina Historical Society.

18. Percy wrote "senseably," probably intending "sensibly," which, according to the *Oxford English Dictionary*, would have meant keenly felt; acutely, intensely felt.

19. Chaplin Journal, May 5, 1845.

20. Thomas Jefferson, *Notes on the State of Virginia*, ed. David Waldstreicher (New York: Bedford/St. Martin's Press, 2002), 177.

21. Thomas R. R. Cobb, *An Inquiry into the Law of Negro Slavery in the United States of America to which is prefixed, An Historical Sketch of Slavery* (Philadelphia: J. & J. W. Johnson, 1858), 1:39.

22. Letter from Judge Walton, February 26, 1792, Addressed to His Excellency Edward Telfair, Edward Telfair Papers, 1791–1841, Duke University Rare Book, Manuscript, and Special Collections Library, Durham, N.C. Regarding Walton's professional history, see http://www.ushistory.org/declaration/signers/walton.htm.

23. *Charleston Courier*, May 10, 1845.

24. Rosengarten, *Tombee*, 350 n. 173. Regarding destinations of people sold in Charleston, see Michael Tadman, *Speculators and Slaves: Masters, Traders, and Slaves in the Old South* (Madison: University of Wisconsin Press, 1996), 253.

25. By 1856, as the abolition movement intensified, city officials were concerned enough with the overflow crowds and the public display of selling human beings that they forbade the sale of slaves near the Exchange. Most auctions eventually moved into Ryan's Auction Mart on Chalmers Street. Regarding slave auctions in Charleston and destinations of slaves sold in the Charleston market, see Frederic Bancroft, *Slave Trading in the Old South* (Columbia: University of South Carolina Press, 1931, 1996), 166–70; Tadman, *Speculators and Slaves*; and Robert H. Gudmestad, *A Troublesome Commerce: The Transformation of the Interstate Slave Trade* (Baton Rouge: Louisiana State University Press, 2003). Regarding slaves intervening in their own sales, see Walter Johnson, *Soul by Soul: Life inside the Antebellum Slave Market* (Cambridge, Mass.: Harvard University Press, 1999), 163–72. See also Steven Deyle, *Carry Me Back: The Domestic Slave Trade in American Life* (New York: Oxford University Press, 2005).

26. Bancroft, *Slave Trading in the Old South*, 178.

27. Johnson, *Soul by Soul*.

28. Nehemiah Adams, *South-side View of Slavery; or Three Months at the South in 1854* (Boston, 1854).

29. Thomas F. Gossett, *Uncle Tom's Cabin and American Culture* (Dallas: Southern Methodist University Press, 1985), 164.

30. The deck of cards with instructions provided on the "Justice" card can be viewed at http://utc.iath.virginia.edu/tomituds/game3f.html. Regarding the wide range of products inspired by the novel, see Louise L. Stevenson, "Virtue Displayed: The Tie-Ins of *Uncle Tom's Cabin*," http://utc.iath.virginia.edu/interpret/exhibits/stevenson/stevenson.html.

31. *National Era*, March 24, 1853.

32. *Frederick Douglass' Paper*, February 2, 1855.

33. *Liberator*, April 20, 1833.

34. *Frederick Douglass' Paper*, February 16, 1855. Reprinted from the *Vermont Caledonian*.

35. *National Era*, July 8, 1847.

36. Reprinted in *Frederick Douglass' Paper* from the *National Era*, February 25, 1853.

37. *Frederick Douglass' Paper*, February 2, 1855 (editorial correspondence of the *Utica Herald*).

38. C. Abner, letter, November 18, 1859, Mss2Ab722a1, Virginia Historical Society, Richmond.

39. Letter from Charles Barrow, Charleston, S.C., November 11, 1839, University of South Carolina, South Caroliniana Library, Columbia.

40. Letter from Edwin T. Evans, Charleston, S.C., March 2, 1851, University of South Carolina, South Caroliniana Library.

41. Slave auction in Richmond, Virginia, *National Era*, March 24, 1853.

42. Frederick Douglass, *Narrative of the Life of Frederick Douglass*, ed. David W. Blight (New York: Bedford Books, 1993), 14–15. Walter Johnson suggests that the songs enslaved people sang on coffles were memorials to the communities that the slave trade destroyed; see Johnson, *Soul by Soul*, 69. See also George M. Fredrickson, *The Black Image in the White Mind: The Debate on Afro-American Character and Destiny, 1817–1914* (Hanover, N.H.: University Press of New England, 1971), 57–58.

43. Letter from Obadiah Fields to Jane Fields, November 29, 1822, Obadiah Fields Papers, Duke University Rare Book, Manuscript, and Special Collections Library, Durham, N.C.

44. Ethan Allen Andrews, *Slavery and the Domestic Slave Trade in the United States* (New York: Books for Libraries Press, 1971) 97, 135. Andrews prepared his series of letters from the South for the American Union for the Relief and Improvement of the Colored Race.

45. See Johnson, *Soul by Soul*, regarding people attempting to choose their purchasers.

46. Article reprinted on March 15, 1850, in the *North Star*, a newspaper published by Frederick Douglass in Rochester, New York. The article had first appeared in a St. Louis, Missouri, newspaper. See Johnson, *Soul by Soul*, for a discussion of slaves internalizing the monetary value owners attached to them.

47. Mary Boykin Chesnut, *A Diary from Dixie* (Cambridge, Mass.: Harvard University Press, 1980), 38.

48. Veney transposed two lines from the third verse with two from the fourth. My thanks to Andrew E. Williams for helping me to identify the tune for this hymn.

49. Bethany Veney, *The Narrative of Bethany Veney, a Slave Woman* (Worcester, Mass., 1889), 29–30, electronic ed., Documenting the American South, http://docsouth .unc.edu/fpn/veney/veney.html.

50. Albert J. Raboteau, *Slave Religion: The "Invisible Institution" in the Antebellum South* (New York: Oxford University Press, 2004), 209, 311–12.

51. Veney, *Narrative of Bethany Veney*, 30.

52. Austin Bearse, *Reminiscences of Fugitive-Slave Law Days in Boston* (Boston, 1880), 8–9.

53. Gerda Lerner, *The Grimké Sisters from South Carolina: Pioneers for Women's Rights and Abolition* (Chapel Hill: University of North Carolina Press, 2004).

Chapter 4

1. Peter Randolph, *From Slave Cabin to the Pulpit: The Autobiography of Rev. Peter Randolph. The Southern Question Illustrated and Sketches of Slave Life* (Boston, 1893), Documenting the American South, http://docsouth.unc.edu/neh/randolph/menu.html.

2. Jacob Stroyer, *Sketches of My Life in the South* (1879), 30, electronic ed., http://docsouth.unc.edu/neh/stroyer/stroyer.html.

3. William Parker, *The Freedman's Story, in Two Parts* (Boston: Ticknor and Fields, 1866), 154, electronic ed., Documenting the American South, http://docsouth.edu/parker/parker.htm1.

4. Edwin Morris Betts, ed., *Thomas Jefferson's Farm Book* (Princeton, N.J.: Princeton University Press, 1953), 19. In 1774 Thomas Jefferson owned 187 slaves, some of whom he purchased and some who came to him through marriage.

5. Pauline Boss, *Ambiguous Loss: Learning to Live with Unresolved Grief* (Cambridge, Mass.: Harvard University Press, 1999), 5–6.

6. C. R. Snyder and Shane J. Lopez, *Positive Psychology: The Scientific and Practical Explorations of Human Strengths* (Thousand Oaks, Calif.: Sage, 2007), 34.

7. Friedrich Nietzsche, *Human, All Too Human*, trans. Marion Faber, with Stephen Lehman (Lincoln: University of Nebraska Press, 1984), 58; Snyder and Lopez, *Positive Psychology*, 24.

8. John Sella Martin autobiographical essay, 1867, in *Slave Testimony: Two Centuries of Letters, Speeches, Interviews and Autobiographies*, ed. John Blassingame (Baton Rouge: Louisiana State University Press, 1977), 703–35.

9. Ibid., 711–13. For anthropological and archaeological findings of blue glass beads in excavation of slave sites, see Theresa A. Singleton in *Before Freedom Came: American Life in the Antebellum South*, ed. Edward D. C. Campbell Jr. (Charlottesville: University of Virginia Press, 1991); Linda France Stine et al., "Blue Beads as African-American Cultural Symbols," *Historical Archaeology* 30, no. 3 (1996): 49–75; B. W. Higman, *Montpelier Jamaica: A Plantation Community in Slavery and Freedom, 1739–1912* (Kingston, Jamaica: University of the West Indies Press, 1998), 252–57, 323–27; Jerome S. Handler and Frederick W. Lange, *Plantation Slavery in Barbados* (Cambridge, Mass.: Harvard University Press, 1978), 144–50, 274–81; and Leland Ferguson, *Uncommon Ground* (Washington, D.C.: Smithsonian Institution Press, 1992), 116–17.

10. Walter Johnson, *Soul by Soul: Life inside the Antebellum Slave Market* (Cambridge, Mass.: Harvard University Press, 1999), 167–69.

11. Martin essay, 719.

12. Moses Roper, *A Narrative of the Adventures and Escape of Moses Roper, from American Slavery* (1848), in *North Carolina Slave Narratives: The Lives of Moses Roper, Lunsford Lane, Moses Grady, and Thomas H. Jones*, ed. William L. Andrews (Chapel Hill: University of North Carolina Press, 2003).

13. See Chap. 2 text at nn. 70 and 73.

14. Letter from Charles, formerly Joseph Greenhill, to William Greenhill, July 31, 1825, Mss1B6108a221, Virginia Historical Society, Richmond.

15. Letter from Vilet Lester to Miss Patsy, August 29, 1857, Duke University Rare Book, Manuscript, and Special Collections Library, Durham, N.C.

16. Ibid.

17. *Voice of the Fugitive*, June 18, 1851.

18. Ibid.

19. http://new.oberlin.edu/events-activities/black-history/at-oberlin.dot.

20. *Palladium of Liberty*, May 20, 1844. For a history of the *Palladium of Liberty*, see Ohio Historical Society, The African-American Experience in Ohio, 1850–1920, http://dbs.ohiohistory.org/africanam/nwspaper/liberty.cfm.

21. *Palladium of Liberty*, April 17, 1844.

22. Ibid., August 14, 1844.

23. Henry Bibb, *Narrative of the Life and Adventures of Henry Bibb, an American Slave. Written by Himself* (New York, 1850), 185.

24. Ibid., 187.

25. Johnson, *Soul by Soul*, 113–15; Deborah Gray White, *Ar'n't I a Woman? Female Slaves in the Plantation South* (New York: Norton, 1985).

26. Bibb, *Narrative*, 189–90.

27. Ibid., 190.

28. Ibid., 191–92.

Chapter 5

1. Journal of Thomas B. Chaplin, South Carolina Historical Society, Charleston.

2. Willie Lee Rose, *Rehearsal for Reconstruction: The Port Royal Experiment* (New York: Bobbs-Merrill, 1964), 11–12; Theodore Rosengarten, *Tombee: Portrait of a Cotton Planter* (New York: McGraw-Hill, 1987), 219.

3. Regarding reasons for secession, see, for example, Mississippi Declaration of Secession, 1861, http://avalon.law.yale.edu/19th_century/csa_missec.asp. For Lincoln's intentions, see Ira Berlin, Joseph P. Reidy, and Leslie S. Rowland, eds., *Freedom's Soldiers: The Black Military Experience in the Civil War* (New York: Cambridge University Press, 1982), 1–20.

4. Charles P. Day to S. S. Jocelyn, August 11, 1862, American Missionary Association Archives, Virginia Records, Amistad Research Center, Tulane University, New Orleans, La.

5. Berlin, Reidy, and Rowland, *Freedom's Soldiers*, 1–20. About 179,000 black men from the North and the South served in the Union army during the course of the war. Regarding the Confederate massacre of surrendered black soldiers at Fort Pillow, Tennessee, for example, see David Eicher, *The Longest Night: A Military History of the Civil War* (New York: Simon and Schuster, 2001), 656–57, and Andrew Ward, *River Run Red: The Fort Pillow Massacre in the American Civil War* (New York: Viking, 2005). Regarding threats, see Berlin, Reidy, and Rowland, *Freedom's Soldiers*, 18.

6. *Christian Recorder*, August 25, 1866. The text of the ad read, "INQUIRY FOR FRIENDS. Madison Medley, who was formerly owned by a man by the name of Burtis,

is living about ten miles from Raleigh, Wake Co., North Carolina. Any of his friends wishing to hear from him can do so by addressing his sister, NANCY ANN THOMAS, Richmond, Ind."

7. William H. Robinson, *From Log Cabin to the Pulpit, or, Fifteen Years in Slavery* (Eau Claire, Wisc., 1913), http://docsouth.unc.edu/fpn/robinson/robinson.html, 117.

8. 39th Congress, 1st Session, Senate Executive Documents, vol. 2, document 27, *Reports of the Assistant Commissioners of the Freedmen's Bureau made since December 1, 1865* (Washington, D.C.: Government Printing Office, 1866), 151.

9. Nettie Henry interview, in *The American Slave: A Composite Autobiography*, ed. George P. Rawick, vol. 8, pt. 3, *Mississippi Narratives*, supplement ser. 1 (Westport, Conn.: Greenwood, 1972), 975–76.

10. John Richard Dennett, *The South as It Is* (New York: Viking, 1965), 130–31.

11. For more about the work of the Freedmen's Bureau, see George R. Bentley, *A History of the Freedmen's Bureau* (New York: Octagon Books, 1974); Paul A. Cimbala, *Under the Guardianship of the Nation: The Freedmen's Bureau and the Reconstruction of Georgia, 1865–1870* (Athens: University of Georgia Press, 1997); and Mary Farmer-Kaiser, *Freedwomen and the Freedmen's Bureau* (New York: Fordham University Press, 2010). The bureau also provided rations and other help to whites.

12. Bentley, *History of the Freedmen's Bureau*, 72.

13. Ibid., 74.

14. Circular no. 3 issued by the Freedmen's Bureau, February 2, 1867, Virginia Freedmen's Bureau Archives, M1048, roll 29, National Archives and Records Administration, Washington, D.C. (hereafter cited as NA).

15. John William De Forest, *A Union Officer in the Reconstruction* (New Haven: Yale University Press, 1948), 36–37.

16. Ibid., 37.

17. Letter from Sherwood to Bvt. Brig. General O. Brown, November 18, 1866, Virginia Freedmen's Bureau Archives, M1048, roll 19, NA.

18. December 1, 1866; undated letter from Sherwood that appears to be in response to the December 1 inquiry; letter from Bvt. Major Genl. Schofield, December 7, 1866; letter from J. H. Remington, December 10, 1866; undated endorsement from Sherwood, Virginia Freedmen's Bureau Archives, M1048, roll 19, NA.

19. North Carolina Freedmen's Bureau, M4493, roll 8, NA.

20. October 13, 1866, North Carolina Freedmen's Bureau Archives, M4493, roll 8, NA; Mary J. Farmer, "'Because They Are Women': Gender and the Virginia Freedmen's Bureau's 'War on Dependency,'" in *The Freedmen's Bureau and Reconstruction: Reconsiderations*, ed. Paul A. Cimbala and Randall M. Miller (New York: Fordham University Press, 1999), 166. Farmer found that the policy of discouraging dependency applied not just to assistance with transportation but to food rations and other forms of assistance as well.

21. Hawkins Wilson to Freedmen's Bureau, Richmond, May 11, 1867, Virginia, Bowling Green, Caroline County, Letters Received, M1913, roll 58, NA. See also Ira Berlin and Leslie Rowland, eds., *Families and Freedom: A Documentary History of African-American Kinship in the Civil War Era* (New York: New Press, 1997), 17–20.

22. Johnson endorsements, dated January and February 1868, and Wood endorsements, dated April 1868, RG105, M1483, roll 1, New Orleans Field Office, NA. The Rich-

mond Field Office of the Freedmen's Bureau also enlisted black churches in the search for former slaves. See, for example, correspondence regarding the children of Leah Lancaster, January 1866, Virginia Freedmen's Bureau, M1048, roll 18, NA.

23. Endorsements dated February 27, March 21, 24, 1868, New Orleans Freedmen's Bureau, RG105, M1483, roll 1, NA.

24. Regarding Baltimore traders and their connections to New Orleans, see Frederic Bancroft, *Slave Trading in the Old South* (Columbia: University of South Carolina Press, 1996), 122, and Stanton Tierman, "Baltimore's Old Slave Markets," reprinted from the *Baltimore Sun* (n.d.) at http://www.nathanielturner.com/baltimoreslavemarkets.htm.

25. "Freedmans Association for the Restoration of Lost Friends," no. 343, Pennsylvania Avenue, Washington, D.C., June 1, 1867, Virginia Freedmen's Bureau, RG105, M1048, roll 24, NA. The circular was printed on the stationery of Kendall and Harlan.

26. *Boston Daily Advertiser*, June 14, 1867.

27. *Black Republican*, Saturday, April 29, 1865.

28. *South Carolina Leader* (Charleston), May 12, 1866; Leon Litwack, *Been in the Storm So Long: The Aftermath of Slavery* (New York: Knopf, 1979), 411–12; Ira Berlin, *Slaves without Masters: The Free Negro in the Antebellum South* (New York: Pantheon, 1974), 216–28; Tommy L. Bogger, *Free Blacks in Norfolk, Virginia, 1790–1860: The Darker Side of Freedom* (Charlottesville: University Press of Virginia, 1997), 53; James Oliver Horton and Lois E. Horton, *In Hope of Liberty: Culture, Community, and Protest among Northern Free Blacks, 1700–1860* (New York: Oxford University Press, 1997), 114; Leslie M. Harris, *In the Shadow of Slavery: African Americans in New York City, 1626–1863* (Chicago: University of Chicago Press, 2003), 96, 265.

29. Some ads were placed so close to emancipation in April 1865 that the searchers must have been in the free states or Canada during slavery. But sometimes a year or two had elapsed between emancipation and the appearance of the ad, time in which someone could have moved north.

30. Advertisers in the church-sponsored *Christian Recorder* were particularly aware that the paper had the potential to reach large numbers of people. The African Methodist Episcopal Church, founded in resistance to the insults of a white Methodist Episcopal congregation in Philadelphia in 1816, had been allowed to exist in Baltimore and New Orleans until exposure of the Denmark Vesey conspiracy in 1822, in Charleston. With emancipation came expansion into southern states, along with broader distribution of the newspaper. Black Baptist congregations had also existed in some areas of the South during slavery; some operated fairly independently, while others were under the watchful eyes of white ministers. These churches also multiplied following emancipation. See Reginald Hildebrand, *The Times Were Strange and Stirring: Methodist Preachers and the Crisis of Emancipation* (Durham: Duke University Press, 1995), xxiii, and Albert Raboteau, *Slave Religion: The "Invisible Institution" in the Antebellum South* (New York: Oxford University Press, 2004), 204–7, 196–204.

31. Frederick Douglass, *My Bondage and My Freedom* (New York: Dover Publications, 1855, 1969), 341–48.

32. Regarding name change due to escape, see ibid. (1855), 342.

33. Walter Johnson, *Soul by Soul: Life inside the Antebellum Slave Market* (Cambridge, Mass.: Harvard University Press, 1999), 41–42.

Chapter 6

1. Tines Kendricks (male), Georgia—Born in Crawford County, Georgia, in *Lay My Burden Down: A Folk History of Slavery*, ed. B. A. Botkin (Chicago: University of Chicago Press, 1945), 74.

2. G. M. McClellan, "The Negro as Writer," in *Twentieth Century Negro Literature; or, a Cyclopedia of Thought on the Vital Topics Relating to the American Negro*, ed. Daniel Wallace Culp (Atlanta, 1902), 284–85. Thanks to Michelle Lanier for bringing this source to my attention.

3. Fred Kaplan, *The Singular Mark Twain: A Biography* (New York: Anchor Books, 2005), 9–10; Mark Twain House and Museum, http://www.marktwainhouse.org/man/biography_main.php.

4. Helen M. Chesnutt, *Charles Waddell Chesnutt: Pioneer of the Color Line* (Chapel Hill: University of North Carolina Press, 1952), 1–7; Charles W. Chesnutt, *The Wife of His Youth and Other Stories*, ed. Earl Schenck Miers (Ann Arbor: University of Michigan Press, 1968), v–vii; Richard Brodhead, ed., *The Journals of Charles Chesnutt* (Durham: Duke University Press, 1993), 2–4.

5. Charles Chesnutt, "The Wife of His Youth," *Atlantic Monthly* 82 (1989): 1–6, 55–61 (also published as the title story in *The Wife of His Youth, and Other Stories of the Color Line* [Boston: Houghton, Mifflin, 1899]).

6. Ibid., 12–14.

7. Ibid., 14–15.

8. Ibid., 21–22.

9. Mark Twain, "A True Story, Repeated Word for Word as I Heard It," *Atlantic Monthly* 34 (November 1874): 591–94.

10. Anna Barker interview, in *The American Slave: A Composite Autobiography*, ed. George P. Rawick, vol. 6, pt. 1, *Mississippi Narratives*, supplement ser. 1 (Westport, Conn.: Greenwood, 1972), 90–95.

11. Mingo White interview, in Rawick, *American Slave*, vol. 6, *Alabama and Indiana Narratives*, 415. For earlier discussion of Mingo White, see Chap. 1 text at nn. 69 and 70.

12. Louis Hughes, *Thirty Years a Slave: From Bondage to Freedom—The Institution of Slavery as Seen on the Plantation and in the Home of the Planter* (Milwaukee, 1897; reprint, Miami, Fla.: Mnemosyne Publishing, 1969), 203.

13. Ibid., 203–4.

14. Robert Glenn interview, in Rawick, *American Slave*, vol. 11, pt. 1, *North Carolina Narratives*. For earlier discussion of Robert Glenn, see Chap. 1 text at nn. 37 and 62.

15. *Christian Recorder*, April 22, 1865.

16. Henry Brown, in South Carolina interviews, in Rawick, *American Slave*, vol. 2, pts. 1 and 2, *South Carolina Narratives*, 125.

17. *Christian Recorder*, April 22, 1865; Hughes, *Thirty Years a Slave*, 192–94.

18. Hughes, *Thirty Years a Slave*, 204.

19. Ibid. Thanks to Hayumi Higuchi for her insights about Hughes's emotions.

20. July Ann Halfen, Osyka, Mississippi, in Rawick, *American Slave*, vol. 8, pt. 3, *Mississippi Narratives*, supplement ser. 1.

21. Rawick, *American Slave*, vol. 9, pt. 4, *Mississippi Narratives*, 1483.

22. Ninth U.S. Census, 1870. For John Beck, Malinda, and James Tate, see Chap. 2.

23. *Christian Recorder*, February 28, 1869.

24. Mary Ames, *From a New England Woman's Diary in Dixie in 1865* (Springfield, 1906), 16, electronic ed., http://docsouth.unc.edu/church/ames/ames.html.

25. Elizabeth Botume, *First Days amongst the Contrabands* (Boston: Lee and Shepard, 1893), 143, 154. See also Dorothy Sterling, *We Are Your Sisters* (New York: Norton, 1984, 1997), 314–17.

26. Botume, *First Days amongst the Contrabands*, 154–55.

27. Ibid., 160–61, 163.

28. Ibid., 160.

Epilogue

1. William Wells Brown, *Narrative of William W. Brown, a Fugitive Slave. Written by Himself* (Boston: The Anti-slavery Office, 1847), 139 (emphasis in original).

2. Elizabeth Botume, *First Days amongst the Contrabands* (Boston: Lee and Shepard, 1893), 164.

3. George P. Rawick, *The American Slave: A Composite Autobiography*, vol. 14, pt. 1, *North Carolina Narratives* (Westport, Conn.: Greenwood, 1972), 69.

4. Fanny Kemble, *Fanny Kemble's Journals*, ed. Catherine Clinton (Cambridge, Mass.: Harvard University Press, 2000), 128.

5. Toni Morrison, *Beloved* (New York: Penguin, 1987); Edward P. Jones, *The Known World* (New York: Amistad, 2003); J. California Cooper, *Family* (New York: Random House, 1992).

6. *Southwestern Christian Advocate*, May 22, 1890.

7. Ibid., January 16, 1890.

8. *Christian Recorder*, September 12, 1901.

9. Both ads appeared in the *Christian Recorder* on July 17, 1902.

10. *Star of Zion*, November 10, 1898.

11. Working in a much later time period, historian Barbara Ransby recounts the story of civil rights activist Ella Baker repeatedly asking an interviewer, "Now, who are your people?" Ransby interpreted the question as "an attempt to locate an individual as part of a family, a community, a region, a culture, and a historical moment" (Barbara Ransby, *Ella Baker and the Black Freedom Movement: A Radical Democratic Vision* [Chapel Hill: University of North Carolina Press, 2003], 13–14).

12. Nep Jenkins interview, in Rawick, *American Slave*, vol. 8, pt. 3, *Mississippi Narratives*, supplement ser. 1, 1149–50.

13. Virginia Harris interview, in Rawick, *American Slave*, vol. 8, pt. 3, *Mississippi Narratives*, supplement ser. 1, 937.

14. Lizzie Davis interview, in Rawick, *American Slave*, vol. 2, pt. 1, *South Carolina Narratives*, 293.

15. July Ann Halfen interview, in Rawick, *American Slave*, vol. 8, pt. 3, *Mississippi Narratives*, supplement ser. 1., 897–98.

16. Wash Hayes interview, in Rawick, *American Slave*, vol. 8, pt. 3, *Mississippi Narratives*, supplement ser. 1.

17. Fanny Hodges interview, in Rawick, *American Slave*, vol. 8, pt. 3, *Mississippi Narratives*, supplement ser. 1, 1024.

18. Louise Dunham Goldsberry, "The Negro in the Atlanta Exposition," *Zion's Herald* (1868–1910), Oct. 9, 1895. I am grateful to Theda Perdue for bringing this article to my attention. Booker T. Washington, a former slave and president of Tuskegee Institute in Alabama, gave a speech at the exposition in which he seemed to endorse the developing concept of separate but equal. "In all things that are purely social," Washington said, "we can be as separate as the fingers, yet one as the hand in all things essential to mutual progress" (reprinted in Booker T. Washington, *Up from Slavery: An Autobiography*, ed. W. Fitzhugh Brundage [Boston: Bedford/St. Martin's Press, 2003], 142–45).

19. Ashley's sack from Middleton Place. The provenance is not known. The woman who donated it to Middleton Place purchased it at a yard sale in Tennessee. Information obtained from Barbara Doyle, historian and research consultant, and Mary Edna Sullivan, curator, Middleton Place Plantation, Charleston, S.C.

20. Dorothy Spruill Redford with Michael D'Orso, *Somerset Homecoming: Recovering a Lost Heritage* (New York: Doubleday, 1988; reprint, Chapel Hill: University of North Carolina Press, 2000), 140. In the 1980s only the former owners' house was still standing at Somerset Plantation. Dorothy Redford convinced the North Carolina Department of Cultural Resources Office of Archives and History to build replicas of several buildings, including slave cabins, an overseer's house, and a hospital. Redford directed the Somerset Plantation Historical Site until her retirement in 2008. The site remains open to the public. See http://www.nchistoricsites.org/somerset/main.htm.

21. "'A Bench by the Road': *Beloved* by Toni Morrison," in *Toni Morrison: Conversations*, ed. Carolyn C. Denard (Jackson: University of Mississippi Press, 2008), 44–50.

22. Redford with D'Orso, *Somerset Homecoming*, 158. In the twenty-first century the search has taken on added dimension through the use of DNA evidence. See, for example, Henry Louis Gates Jr., *In Search of Our Roots: How Nineteen Extraordinary African Americans Reclaimed Their Past* (New York: Crown, 2009).

23. For Louis Hughes, see Chap. 6.

24. Redford with D'Orso, *Somerset Homecoming*, 153.

25. Ibid., 151.

Bibliography

Primary Sources

Archives

NEW YORK
Schomburg Center for Research in Black Culture, New York

NORTH CAROLINA
Duke University, Durham
    Divinity School Library
    Rare Book, Manuscript, and Special Collections Library
University of North Carolina, Chapel Hill
    North Carolina Collection
    Southern Historical Collection

SOUTH CAROLINA
Avery Research Institute, Charleston
Middleton Place Plantation, Charleston
South Carolina Historical Society, Charleston
University of South Carolina, South Caroliniana Library, Manuscripts Division, Columbia

VIRGINIA
Afro-American Historical Association of Fauquier County, Warrenton
Library of Virginia, Richmond
University of Virginia Special Collections Library, Charlottesville
Virginia Historical Society, Richmond
Warrenton Public Library, Warrenton

WASHINGTON, D.C.
National Archives and Records Administration

Newspapers and Periodicals

Alexandria Gazette
American Beacon and Norfolk and Portsmouth Advertiser
Atlantic Monthly
Black Republican (New Orleans)
Boston Daily Advertiser
Charleston Courier
Christian Recorder (Philadelphia)
Colored Citizen (Cincinnati)

Colored Tennessean (Nashville)

Flag of '98 (Warrenton, Va.)

Frederick Douglass' Paper (Rochester, N.Y.)

Free Man's Press (Galveston)

Harper's Weekly

Hillsborough Recorder (Hillsborough, N.C.)

The Liberator (Boston)

Loyal Georgian, a.k.a. *The Colored American* (Augusta, Ga.)

National Era (Washington, D.C.)

Norfolk and Portsmouth Herald

Palladium of Liberty

Richmond Enquirer

South Carolina Leader (Charleston)

Southwestern Christian Advocate (New Orleans)

Star of Zion (Charlotte, N.C.)

Virginia Gazette (Warrenton)

Voice of the Fugitive (Ontario, Canada)

Slave Narratives

Ball, Charles. *Slavery in the United States: A Narrative of the Life and Adventures of Charles Ball, a Black Man*. New York: John S. Taylor, 1837.

Bibb, Henry. *Narrative of the Life and Adventures of Henry Bibb, an American Slave. Written by Himself*. New York, 1850.

Brown, Henry Box. *Narrative of Henry Box Brown, Who Escaped from Slavery Enclosed in a Box 3 Feet Long and 2 Wide. Written from a Statement of Facts Made by Himself. With Remarks Upon the Remedy for Slavery by Charles Stearns*. Documenting the American South. http://docsouth.unc.edu/neh/boxbrown/boxbrown.html.

Brown, John. *Slave Life in Georgia: A Narrative of the Life, Sufferings, and Escape of John Brown, a Fugitive Slave*. Savannah: Beehive Press, 1991.

Brown, William Wells. *Narrative of William W. Brown, a Fugitive Slave. Written by Himself*. Boston: The Anti-slavery Office, 1847.

Bruner, Peter. *A Slave's Adventures Toward Freedom: Not Fiction, but the True Story of a Struggle*. Electronic ed. http://docsouth.unc.edu/neh/bruner/bruner.html.

Douglass, Frederick. *My Bondage and My Freedom*. New York: Dover Publications, 1855, 1969.

———. *Narrative of the Life of Frederick Douglass*. Edited by David W. Blight. New York: Bedford Books, 1993.

Drumgoold, Kate. *A Slave Girl's Story, Being an Autobiography of Kate Drumgoold*. Brooklyn, N.Y., 1898. In *Six Women's Slave Narratives*, edited by William L. Andrews. New York: Oxford University Press, 1988.

Fredric, Francis. *Slave Life in Virginia and Kentucky; of Fifty Years of Slavery*. London, 1863.

Grandy, Moses. *Narrative of the Life of Moses Grandy, Late a Slave in the United States of America, 1843*. http://docsouth.unc.edu/fpn/grandy/menu.html.

Henson, Josiah. *The Life of Josiah Henson, Formerly a Slave, Now an Inhabitant of Canada, as Narrated by Himself*. Boston: Arthur D. Phelps, 1849. http://docsouth.unc.edu/neh/henson49/henson49.html.

Hughes, Louis. *Thirty Years a Slave: From Bondage to Freedom—The Institution of Slavery as Seen on the Plantation and in the Home of the Planter*. Milwaukee, 1897. Reprint, Miami, Fla.: Mnemosyne Publishing, 1969.

Johnson, Thomas Lewis. *Twenty-Eight Years a Slave: The Story of My Life in Three Continents*. Bournemouth, England: W. Mate and Sons, 1909. http://docsouth.unc.edu/neh/johnson1/johnson.html#john2.

Jones, Thomas H. *The Experience of Rev. Thomas H. Jones, Who Was a Slave for Forty-Three Years*. Boston, 1862. http://docsouth.unc.edu/fpn/jones/jones.html.

Keckley, Elizabeth. *Behind the Scenes, or Thirty Years a Slave, and Four Years in the White House*. New York, 1868.

Lane, Lunsford. *The Narrative of Lunsford Lane, Formerly of Raleigh, NC*. Boston, 1842.

Old Elizabeth. *Memoir of Old Elizabeth, a Coloured Woman*. Philadelphia: Collins Printer, 1863. In *Six Women's Slave Narratives*, edited by William L. Andrews. New York: Oxford University Press, 1988.

Parker, William. *The Freedman's Story, in Two Parts*. Boston: Ticknor and Fields, 1866. http://docsouth.unc.edu/neh/parker1/menu.html.

Randolph, Peter. *From Slave Cabin to the Pulpit: The Autobiography of Rev. Peter Randolph. The Southern Question Illustrated and Sketches of Slave Life*. Boston, 1893. http://docsouth.unc.edu/neh/randolph/menu.html.

Roper, Moses. *Narrative of the Adventures and Escape of Moses Roper, from American Slavery*. 1848. In *North Carolina Slave Narratives: The Lives of Moses Roper, Lunsford Lane, Moses Grandy, and Thomas H. Jones*, edited by William L. Andrews. Chapel Hill: University of North Carolina Press, 2003.

Singleton, William Henry. *Recollections of My Slavery Days*. Edited by Katherine Mellen Charron and David S. Cecelski. Raleigh: Division of Archives and History, 1999.

Stroyer, Jacob. *Sketches of My Life in the South*. 1879. http://docsouth.unc.edu/neh/stroyer/stroyer.html.

Taylor, Susie King. *Reminiscences of My Life in Camp*. Athens: University of Georgia Press, 2006.

Veney, Bethany. *The Narrative of Bethany Veney, a Slave Woman*. Worcester, Mass., 1889. http://docsouth.unc.edu/fpn/veney/veney.html.

Washington, Booker T. *Up from Slavery: An Autobiography*. Edited by W. Fitzhugh Brundage. Boston: Bedford/St. Martin's Press, 2003.

Published Works

Adams, Nehemiah. *South-side View of Slavery; or Three Months at the South in 1854*. Boston, 1854.

Ames, Mary. *From a New England Woman's Diary in Dixie in 1865*. Springfield, 1906. http://docsouth.unc.edu/church/ames/ames.html.

Andrews, Ethan Allen. *Slavery and the Domestic Slave Trade in the United States*. Freeport, N.Y.: Books for Libraries Press, 1971.

Bearse, Austin. *Reminiscences of Fugitive-Slave Law Days in Boston*. Boston, 1880.

Berlin, Ira. *Slaves without Masters: The Free Negro in the Antebellum South*. New York: Pantheon, 1974.

Berlin, Ira, Joseph P. Reidy, and Leslie S. Rowland, eds. *Freedom's Soldiers: The Black Military Experience in the Civil War*. New York: Cambridge University Press, 1982.

Berlin, Ira, et al. *Freedom: A Documentary History of Emancipation, 1861–1867*. Ser. 1, vol. 3, *The Wartime Genesis of Free Labor: The Lower South*. Cambridge: Cambridge University Press, 1990.

Betts, Edwin Morris, ed. *Thomas Jefferson's Farm Book*. Princeton, N.J.: Princeton University Press, 1953.

Blassingame, John, ed. *Slave Testimony: Two Centuries of Letters, Speeches, Interviews, and Autobiographies*. Baton Rouge: Louisiana State University Press, 1977.

Botkin, B. A., ed. *Lay My Burden Down: A Folk History of Slavery*. Chicago: University of Chicago Press, 1945.

Botume, Elizabeth. *First Days amongst the Contrabands*. Boston: Lee and Shepard, 1893.

Breeden, James O., ed. *Advice among Masters: The Ideal in Slave Management in the Old South*. Westport, Conn.: Greenwood, 1980.

Chesnut, Mary Boykin. *A Diary from Dixie*. Cambridge, Mass.: Harvard University Press, 1980.

Chesnutt, Charles W. *The Wife of His Youth and Other Stories*. Edited by Earl Schenck Miers. Ann Arbor: University of Michigan Press, 1968.

Civil Code of the State of Louisiana Preceded by the Treaty of Cession with France, the Constitution of the United States of America and of the State. Published by a citizen of Louisiana, 1825.

Cobb, Thomas R. R. *An Inquiry into the Law of Negro Slavery in the United States of America*. Philadelphia, 1858. Reprint, Athens: University of Georgia Press, 1999.

De Forest, John William. *A Union Officer in the Reconstruction*. New Haven: Yale University Press, 1948.

Dennett, John Richard. *The South as It Is*. New York: Viking, 1965.

Donnnan, Elizabeth. *Documents Illustrative of the History of the Slave Trade in America*. Washington, D.C.: Carnegie Institution of Washington, 1935.

Eaton, John. *Grant, Lincoln and the Freedmen: Reminiscences of the Civil War*. New York: Longmans, Green, 1907.

———. *Report of the General Superintendent of Freedmen, Department of the Tennessee and State of Arkansas for 1864*. Memphis, Tenn., 1864.

French, B. F., ed. *Historical Collections of Louisiana Embracing Translations of Many Rare Documents Relating to the Natural, Civil and Political History of the State*. Pt. 3. New York: D. Appleton and Company, 1851.

Goodell, William, ed. *The American Slave Code, in Theory and Practice*. New York: American and Foreign Anti-Slavery Society, 1853. Reprint, New York: Negro Universities Press, 1968.

Jay, William. *Miscellaneous Writings on Slavery*. Boston, 1853.

Jefferson, Thomas. *Notes on the State of Virginia*. Edited by David Waldstreicher. New York: Bedford/St. Martin's Press, 2002.

Kemble, Fanny. *Fanny Kemble's Journals*. Edited by Catherine Clinton. Cambridge, Mass.: Harvard University Press, 2000.

Morrison, Toni. *Beloved*. New York: Penguin, 1987.

Moynihan, Daniel Patrick. *The Negro Family: The Case for National Action*. Washington, D.C.: U.S. Department of Labor, March 1965.

Nunez, Elizabeth. *Beyond the Limbo Silence*. New York: Ballantine Books, 1998.

Parker, Freddie. *Stealing a Little Freedom: Advertisements for Slave Runaways in North Carolina, 1791–1840*. New York: Garland Publishing, 1994.

Protestant Episcopal Church. *The Book of Common Prayer and Other Rites and Ceremonies of the Church According to the Use of the Protestant Episcopal Church in the United States of America*. Philadelphia, 1848.

Rawick, George P. *The American Slave: A Composite Autobiography*. 19 vols. Westport, Conn.: Greenwood, 1972.

Rose, Willie Lee, ed. *A Documentary History of Slavery in North America*. Athens: University of Georgia Press, 1999.

Rosengarten, Theodore. *Tombee: Portrait of a Cotton Planter*. New York: McGraw-Hill, 1987.

Snethen, Worthington G. *Black Code of the District of Columbia in Force September 1, 1848*. New York, 1848.

Stampp, Kenneth, ed. *Records of Southern Plantations from Emancipation to the Great Migration*. Bethesda, Md.: Lexis Nexis, 2002.

Starobin, Robert S. *Blacks in Bondage: Letters of American Slaves*. New York: New Viewpoints, 1974.

Sterling, Dorothy. *We Are Your Sisters*. New York: Norton, 1984, 1997.

Still, William. *Still's Underground Rail Road Records*. Philadelphia: William Still, 1883.

Stowe, Harriet Beecher. *Uncle Tom's Cabin*. New York: Norton, 1994.

Stroud, George M. *Sketch of the Laws Relating to Slavery in the Several States of the United States of America*. 1856. Reprint, New York: Negro Universities Press, 1968.

Secondary Sources

Adams, David Wallace. *Education for Extinction: American Indians and the Boarding School Experience, 1875–1929*. Lawrence: University Press of Kansas, 1995.

Bancroft, Frederic. *Slave Trading in the Old South*. Columbia: University of South Carolina Press, 1996.

Bardaglio, Peter W. *Reconstructing the Household: Families, Sex, and the Law in the Nineteenth-Century South*. Chapel Hill: University of North Carolina Press, 1995.

Bentley, George R. *A History of the Freedmen's Bureau*. New York: Octagon Books, 1974.

Berlin, Ira, and Leslie Rowland, eds. *Families and Freedom: A Documentary History of African-American Kinship in the Civil War Era*. New York: New Press, 1997.

Bogger, Tommy L. *Free Blacks in Norfolk, Virginia, 1790–1860: The Darker Side of Freedom*. Charlottesville: University Press of Virginia, 1997.

Boss, Pauline. *Ambiguous Loss: Learning to Live with Unresolved Grief*. Cambridge, Mass.: Harvard University Press, 1999.

Brigham, Johnson. *James Harlan*. Iowa City: State Historical Society of Iowa, 1913.

Brodhead, Richard, ed. *The Journals of Charles W. Chesnutt*. Durham: Duke University Press, 1993.

Chesnutt, Helen M. *Charles Waddell Chesnutt, Pioneer of the Color Line*. Chapel Hill: University of North Carolina Press, 1952.

Cimbala, Paul A. *Under the Guardianship of the Nation: The Freedmen's Bureau and the Reconstruction of Georgia, 1865–1870*. Athens: University of Georgia Press, 1997.

Cimbala, Paul A., and Randall M. Miller, eds. *The Freedmen's Bureau and Reconstruction: Reconsiderations*. New York: Fordham University Press, 1999.

Cole, Diane. *After Great Pain a New Life Emerges*. New York: Summit Books, 1992.

Cott, Nancy F. *Public Vows: A History of Marriage and the Nation*. Cambridge, Mass.: Harvard University Press, 2000.

Denard, Carolyn C., ed. *Toni Morrison, Conversations*. Jackson: University of Mississippi Press, 2008.

Deyle, Steven. *Carry Me Back: The Domestic Slave Trade in American Life*. New York: Oxford University Press, 2005.

Dixon, Chris. *Perfecting the Family: Antislavery Marriages in Nineteenth-Century America*. Amherst: University of Massachusetts Press, 1997.

Doka, Kenneth J., ed. *Disenfranchised Grief: Recognizing Hidden Sorrow*. Lexington, Mass.: Lexington Books, 1989.

Edwards, Laura F. *The People and Their Peace*. Chapel Hill: University of North Carolina Press, 2009.

Eicher, David. *The Longest Night: A Military History of the Civil War*. New York: Simon and Schuster, 2001.

Elkins, Stanley M. *Slavery: A Problem in American Institutional and Intellectual Life*. Chicago: University of Chicago Press, 1976.

Faust, Drew Gilpin. *This Republic of Suffering: Death and the American Civil War*. New York: Vintage, 2008.

Ferguson, Leland. *Uncommon Ground*. Washington, D.C.: Smithsonian Institution Press, 1992.

Finkelman, Paul, ed. *Slavery and the Law*. Madison, Wisc.: Madison House Press, 1997.

Finley, Randy. *From Slavery to Uncertain Freedom: The Freedmen's Bureau in Arkansas, 1865–1869*. Fayetteville: University of Arkansas Press, 1996.

Fogarty, James A. *The Magical Thoughts of Grieving Children: Treating Children with Complicated Mourning and Advice for Parents*. Amityville, N.Y.: Baywood Publishers, 2000.

Foner, Eric. *A Short History of Reconstruction*. New York: Harper and Row, 1988.

Franklin, John Hope, and Loren Schweninger. *Runaway Slaves: Rebels on the Plantation*. New York: Oxford University Press, 1999.

Frazier, E. Franklin. *The Negro Family in the United States*. Chicago: University of Chicago Press, 1966.

Fredrickson, George M. *The Black Image in the White Mind: The Debate on Afro-American Character and Destiny, 1817–1914*. Hanover, N.H.: University Press of New England, 1971.

Gillespie, Carmen. *Critical Companion to Toni Morrison: A Literary Reference to Her Life and Work*. New York: Facts on File, 2008.

Gilmore, Glenda Elizabeth. *Gender and Jim Crow: Women and the Politics of White Supremacy in North Carolina, 1896–1920*. Chapel Hill: University of North Carolina Press, 1996

Gordon, Linda. *The Great Arizona Orphan Abduction*. Cambridge, Mass.: Harvard University Press, 1999.

Gossett, Thomas F. *Uncle Tom's Cabin and American Culture*. Dallas: Southern Methodist University Press, 1985.

Greenwood, Janette Thomas. *First Fruits of Freedom: The Migration of Former Slaves and Their Search for Equality in Worcester, Massachusetts, 1862–1900*. Chapel Hill: University of North Carolina Press, 2009.

Grossberg, Michael. *Governing the Hearth: Law and the Family in Nineteenth-Century America*. Chapel Hill: University of North Carolina Press, 1985.

Gudmestad, Robert H. *A Troublesome Commerce: The Transformation of the Interstate Slave Trade*. Baton Rouge: Louisiana State University Press, 2003.

Gutman, Herbert G. *The Black Family in Slavery and Freedom, 1750–1925*. New York: Vintage, 1976.

Hadden, Sally E. *Slave Patrols: Law and Violence in Virginia and the Carolinas*. Cambridge, Mass.: Harvard University Press, 2001.

Handler, Jerome S., and Frederick W. Lange. *Plantation Slavery in Barbados*. Cambridge, Mass.: Harvard University Press, 1978.

Harris, Leslie M. *In the Shadow of Slavery: African Americans in New York City, 1626–1863*. Chicago: University of Chicago Press, 2003.

Harvey, John H. *Embracing Their Memory: Loss and the Social Psychology of Storytelling*. Needham Heights, Mass.: Simon and Schuster, 1996.

Higman, B. W. *Montpelier Jamaica: A Plantation Community in Slavery and Freedom, 1739–1912*. Kingston, Jamaica: University of the West Indies Press, 1998.

Hildebrand, Reginald. *The Times Were Strange and Stirring: Methodist Preachers and the Crisis of Emancipation*. Durham: Duke University Press, 1995.

Holt, Marilyn Irvin. *The Orphan Trains: Placing Out in America*. Lincoln: University of Nebraska Press, 1992.

Horton, James Oliver, and Lois E. Horton. *In Hope of Liberty: Culture, Community, and Protest among Northern Free Blacks, 1700–1860*. New York: Oxford University Press, 1997.

Hudson, Larry E., Jr. *To Have and to Hold: Slave Work and Family Life in Antebellum South Carolina*. Athens: University of Georgia Press, 1997.

Iyasere, Solomon O., and Marla W. Iyasere. *Understanding Toni Morrison's* Beloved *and* Sula: *Selected Essays and Criticisms of the Works by the Nobel Prize–Winning Author*. Troy, N.Y.: Whitston, 2000.

Johnson, Walter. *Soul by Soul: Life inside the Antebellum Slave Market*. Cambridge, Mass.: Harvard University Press, 1999.

———, ed. *The Chattel Principle: Internal Slave Trades in the Americas*. New Haven: Yale University Press, 2004.

Jordan, Winthrop D. *White over Black: American Attitudes Toward the Negro, 1550–1812*. Chapel Hill: University of North Carolina Press, 1968.

Kaplan, Fred. *The Singular Mark Twain: A Biography*. New York: Anchor Books, 2005.

Kidd, Thomas S. *The Great Awakening: A Brief History with Documents*. Boston: Bedford/St. Martin's Press, 2008.

King, Wilma. *Stolen Childhood: Slave Youth in Nineteenth-Century America*. Bloomington: Indiana University Press, 1997.

LaCapra, Dominick. *Writing History, Writing Trauma*. Baltimore: Johns Hopkins University Press, 2001.

Lerner, Gerda. *The Grimké Sisters from South Carolina: Pioneers for Women's Rights and Abolition*. Chapel Hill: University of North Carolina Press, 2004.

Litwack, Leon. *Been in the Storm So Long: The Aftermath of Slavery*. New York: Knopf, 1979.

Martinez-Alier, Verena. *Marriage, Class and Colour in Nineteenth-Century Cuba: A Study of Racial Attitudes and Sexual Values in a Slave Society*. London: Cambridge University Press, 1974.

Mintz, Steven. *Huck's Raft: A History of American Childhood*. Cambridge, Mass.: Harvard University Press, 2004.

Mitchell, Mary Niall. *Raising Freedom's Child*. New York: New York University Press, 2008.

Nietzsche, Friedrich. *Human, All Too Human*. Translated by Marion Faber, with Stephen Lehman. Lincoln: University of Nebraska Press, 1984.

O'Neil, Patrick W. "Tying the Knots: The Nationalization of Weddings in Antebellum America." Ph.D. diss., University of North Carolina, Chapel Hill, 2009.

Outhwaite, R. B., ed. *Marriage and Society: Studies in the Social History of Marriage*. New York: St. Martin's Press, 1982.

Painter, Nell Irvin. *Southern History across the Color Line*. Chapel Hill: University of North Carolina Press, 2002.

Phillips, Ulrich Bonnell. *American Negro Slavery: A Survey of the Supply, Employment and Control of Negro Labor as Determined by the Plantation Regime*. Baton Rouge: Louisiana State University Press, 1966.

Piaget, Jean. *The Child's Conception of Physical Causality*. Totowa, N.J.: Littlefield, Adams, 1930, 1975.

Raboteau, Albert. *Slave Religion: The "Invisible Institution" in the Antebellum South*. New York: Oxford University Press, 2004.

Rainwater, Lee, and William L. Yancey. *The Moynihan Report and the Politics of Controversy*. Cambridge, Mass.: MIT Press, 1967.

Ransby, Barbara. *Ella Baker and the Black Freedom Movement: A Radical Democratic Vision*. Chapel Hill: University of North Carolina Press, 2003.

Reddy, William M. *The Navigation of Feeling: A Framework for the History of Emotions*. New York: Cambridge University Press, 2001.

Redford, Dorothy Spruill, with Michael D'Orso. *Somerset Homecoming: Recovering a Lost Heritage*. New York: Doubleday, 1988. Reprint, Chapel Hill: University of North Carolina Press, 2000.

Reevy, Gretchen M., ed. *Encyclopedia of Emotion*. Vols. 1 and 2. Santa Barbara, Calif.: Greenwood, 2010.

Rose, Willie Lee. *Rehearsal for Reconstruction: The Port Royal Experiment*. New York: Bobbs-Merrill, 1964.

Scarborough, William Kauffman. *Masters of the Big House: Elite Slaveholders of the Mid-Nineteenth-Century South*. Baton Rouge: Louisiana State University Press, 2003.

Schafer, Judith Kelleher. *Slavery, the Civil Law, and the Supreme Court of Louisiana*. Baton Rouge: Louisiana State University Press, 1994.

Schwartz, Marie Jenkins. *Born in Bondage: Growing Up Enslaved in the Antebellum South*. Cambridge, Mass.: Harvard University Press, 2000.

Sellers, James Benson. *Slavery in Alabama*. Birmingham: University of Alabama Press, 1950.

Semin, Gün R., and Kenneth J. Gergen, eds. *Everyday Understanding: Social and Scientific Implications*. London: Sage, 1990.

Smith, John David, and John C. Inscoe. *Ulrich Bonnell Phillips: A Southern Historian and His Critics*. New York: Greenwood, 1990.

Snyder, C. R., ed. *Handbook of Hope: Theory, Measures, and Applications*. New York: Academic Press, 2000.

Snyder, C. R., and Shane J. Lopez. *Positive Psychology: The Scientific and Practical Explorations of Human Strengths*. London: Sage, 2007.

Stanley, Amy Dru. *From Bondage to Contract: Wage Labor, Marriage, and the Market in the Age of Slave Emancipation*. New York: Cambridge University Press, 1998.

Stearns, Carol Zisowitz, and Peter N. Stearns. *Anger: The Struggle for Emotional Control in America's History*. Chicago: University of Chicago Press, 1986.

Stearns, Peter N., and Jan Lewis, eds. *An Emotional History of the United States*. New York: New York University Press, 1998.

Stephenson, Wendell Holmes. *Isaac Franklin: Slave Trader and Planter of the Old South*. Gloucester, Mass.: Peter Smith, 1968.

Stevenson, Brenda E. *Life in Black and White: Family and Community in the Slave South*. New York: Oxford University Press, 1996.

Tadman, Michael. *Speculators and Slaves: Masters, Traders, and Slaves in the Old South*. Madison: University of Wisconsin Press, 1996.

Tally, Justine, ed. *The Cambridge Companion to Toni Morrison*. Cambridge: Cambridge University Press, 2007.

Ward, Andrew. *River Run Red: The Fort Pillow Massacre in the American Civil War*. New York: Viking, 2005.

Webber, Thomas L. *Deep Like the Rivers: Education in the Slave Quarter Community, 1831–1865*. New York: Norton, 1978.

White, Deborah Gray. *Ar'n't I a Woman? Female Slaves in the Plantation South*. New York: Norton, 1985.

Williams, Heather Andrea. *Self-Taught: African American Education in Slavery and Freedom*. Chapel Hill: University of North Carolina Press, 2005.

Wood, Kirsten E. *Masterful Women: Slaveholding Widows from the American Revolution through the Civil War*. Chapel Hill: University of North Carolina Press, 2004.

Wyatt-Brown, Bertram. *Honor and Violence in the Old South*. New York: Oxford University Press, 1986.

———. *Southern Honor: Ethics and Behavior in the Old South*. New York: Oxford University Press, 2007.

Acknowledgments

I have so many people to thank. I begin with Glenda Gilmore, whose reading of the first draft of the manuscript helped me tremendously. I am grateful to Glenda for reading so carefully and for all her support and advice over the years. Throughout the process of writing this book, Jerma Jackson listened and got excited, made suggestions, and listened some more. She read the manuscript as I neared the end, and her comments buoyed my belief in the book and helped me to know that I could send it out into the world. I could not ask for a more caring and encouraging colleague and friend.

My research took place in a number of archives, and I am thankful to the archivists and librarians who took the time to work with me. At the University of North Carolina, Laura Clark Brown has always offered cheerful assistance at the Southern Historical Collection, and when research librarian Robert Dalton teaches my students, he is also teaching me. I am once again appreciative of Reginald Washington's willingness to share his deep knowledge of the collections at the National Archives. I also received help at the National Archives from Norman Peters. Nelson Lankford and the staff at the Virginia Historical Society helped me to make the best use of my time during my Andrew Mellon Research Fellowship. I have never done research in a more efficiently run archive. I am also grateful to Brent Tarter at the Library of Virginia. Barbara Doyle, historian and research consultant, and Mary Edna Sullivan, curator, at the Middleton Place Plantation in Charleston, S.C., gave me access to Ashley's sack. Karen White generously shared the collections of the Afro-American Historical Association of Fauquier County, Va., with me. I offer my thanks to the staff at the following archives as well: University of Virginia Special Collections Library; Avery Research Institute, Charleston, S.C.; South Carolina Historical Society, Charleston; the Manuscripts Division of the South Caroliniana Library, Columbia; Duke University Special Collections Library, Durham, N.C.; Warrenton Public Library, Warrenton, Va.; and the Schomburg Center for Research in Black Culture, New York, N.Y.

I was pleased to receive input from my colleagues during a semester's fellowship at the Institute for Arts and Humanities at UNC early in the life of the book. I began writing during my year at the National Humanities Center with the support of the John Medlin Fellowship, which is endowed by the C. D. Spangler Foundation. I am grateful to Sandy Darity for encouraging me to apply to the NHC, and I would like to thank several staff members at the Center for their help during that year: Lois Whittington, Kent Mullikin, Sarah Payne, Marianne Wason, and especially librarians Eliza Robertson and Jean Houston.

I greatly appreciate my interactions with people who offered ideas and sometimes just listened as I worked through my sources. I would like to thank Cheryl Hicks, Dorothy Rice, and Jerma Jackson for a week of thinking and writing in the mountains of North Carolina. I thank the members of the Emotions Working Group at the National Humanities Center, including Ellen Garvey and Kathleen Jones. My conversations with Hayumi Higuchi influenced my analysis. I thank her, too, for making my visit to Japan and my interactions with Japanese historians in both Japan and the United States possible.

Over the years several people were drawn to this project and thought of me as they conducted their own research. I am grateful to Theda Perdue, Matt Harper, Hilary Green, Adriane Lentz Smith, Gordon Golding, Yolonda Wilson, and Michelle Lanier, each of whom led me to very valuable sources.

At UNC I have had the privilege of teaching wonderful undergraduates who shared my enthusiasm for this book and whose ideas and feedback informed my thinking about the material. Students in my research seminar for history majors and my African American history survey course have been particularly helpful over the years. They include Joseph Long, Warren Garris, Mallory Todd, and Marlin Earp. My colleagues at UNC have contributed a great deal to my general quality of life and to my thinking about this project as well. I can't name everyone, but I would like to offer special thanks to Jacquelyn Dowd Hall, Genna Rae McNeil, Theda Perdue, Peter Filene, John Kasson, Reginald Hildebrand, Joseph Jordan, Harry Watson, Joy Kasson, and Melissa Bullard. The staff members in the History Department, including Nadine Kinsey, LaTissa Davis, Joyce Loftin, Joy Jones, Violet Anderson, and Wanda Wallace, help to make my life better in so many ways. I am grateful to them for helping to create a warm and inviting work environment. I would like to thank William L. Andrews for his profound contribution to the study of African American history through the work he has done to make slave narratives accessible. Lloyd Kramer, chair of the History Department, has been enormously important to my development as a scholar and faculty member. I deeply appreciate his support of my work as well as his leadership of our department.

Once again it has been a pleasure working with Chuck Grench and the talented and patient staff at UNC Press. I am particularly grateful to Stephanie Ladniak Wenzel, project editor for the book. I appreciate the time and attention that the outside readers for the press committed to my manuscript. Their input made a great deal of difference.

I am thankful for the many friendships that sustain me. With my Chapel Hill/Durham community of friends, Karolyn Tyson, Tanya Shields, Lyneise Williams, Yolonda Wilson, Danielle Eliott, Karla Slocum, and Marlyn Allicock, I share food, ideas, warmth, and lots of laughter. Nia-Malika Henderson gives wise counsel at moments when I really need it. Qiana Whitted, Brenda Jones Harden, Mark McClain, and Joyce Swagerty listen and encourage.

Some people offer encouragement and support that is more significant than they ever realize. During a chance conversation many years ago, Joan L. Bryant gave me just the challenge I needed to begin to conceptualize this book. My sister Sonia read every word of my first book; it helps a writer tremendously to know that at least one person will read her words. J. D. Livingston called me periodically to check on the status of the book. There were days when I wondered if anyone would notice if I never finished, so it was always good to hear from J. D. and to know that he was waiting for the book. My father helped me with my research on the song "How Firm a Foundation" and gave me design feedback as I made the quilt for the book cover. My mother is still always in the background encouraging me. My little cousin Ariadne Frank brought her unique energy into my home as I was revising one more time. My nieces Sheena and Nicole and my nephew Christopher continue to be the loving and funny souls who keep me connected. My brother-in-law, Errol, feeds me Jamaican food and lifts my spirits with his welcoming, "Hi Doc." And my nephew Clay has mastered the art of lovingly, yet firmly, pushing me to get back to work. He has also made me proud by producing the photography for the jacket of this book.

While I worked on this book about family and loss, my own family experienced its share of joy and sadness. Just as I began writing, my sister Patricia was diagnosed with breast cancer. We are all incredibly grateful that she has now been in remission for four years. I am continually in awe of her courage and her unceasing generosity. My niece Nicole graduated from college, and my nephew Derrick graduated from high school. Clay married Tammi and made her a beautiful part of our family. And while the book was at press, my father lost his courageous fight against lung cancer. All of these experiences of sadness, anxiety, and happiness have connected me even more deeply to my family and make me appreciate every moment and every conversation with them. These bonds have also given me insight into what it must have been like to suddenly lose family members and have no idea where they had gone.

Index

response to separation from children, 190–91; Phillips on, 6–7, 9, 10; in the presence of white people, 4, 111–12; retelling of sorrowful stories, 191; to reunification, 143; silenced responses to separation, 86–88; uncontrollable emotion, 190. *See also* Despair; Grief; Hope; Longing; Loss; White attitudes

Empathy, 3, 12, 97, 115–16

Enslaved people: awareness of enslaved status, 206 (n. 21); freedom of movement and, 61–63; and internalization of monetary value attached to themselves, 111, 217 (n. 46); legal institution of marriage and, 49–51; resilience of, 2–3, 9, 10, 173, 213 (n. 69); value of family for, 54; values attached to enslaved women, 134–36

Escapes: to enlist in Civil War efforts, 142; harboring of escaped slaves, 83, 84–85; name changes due to, 222 (n. 32); recent sale as impetus for, 83; role of marriage in prevention of, 60–62; after spousal separation, 81–86

Esther (wife of Thos Simmons), 168

Evangelicalism, 43–44

Evans, Edwin T., 106–7

Evans, James, 167

Family separation: creation of new families and, 11–12; escape after, 81–86; of father and children, 144; marriage as emotional response to, 54–55; resilience in the face of, 2–3, 9, 10, 173, 213 (n. 69); surrogate caretakers and, 40–42, 208 (n. 63); universality of, 14–16. *See also* Childhood separation; Marriage; Parents; Spouses

Famuluk, Irene, 15

Farer, Elick, 80

Farmer, Mary J., 220 (n. 20)

Farrar, Alexander K., 81

Ferguson (husband of Jane), 186

Fickling, William B., 59 (ill.), 94, 95, 99, 100, 215 (n. 14)

Fickling and Glen letter of permission, 59 (ill.), 211 (n. 30)

Fiction, use of for understanding history, 5–6, 172–73, 187

Fields, Jane M., 109–10, 151

Fields, Obadiah, 109–10, 151

Finney, Starling, 31, 39

Fisher, T., 132–33

Fitzpatrick, Sarah, 140

Fleming, Anthony (Anthony Terrill), 166

Flora (spouse of Billy), 59 (ill.), 211 (n. 30)

Frances (son of Viney), 37

Franklin, Isaac, 67

Franklin and Armfield (slave traders), 34–35, 67, 72, 110

Frazer, Fanny, 160

Frazier, E. Franklin, 7, 9–10, 11

Fred (brother of Lizzie Baker), 191

Fredric, Francis, 52, 53–54, 55, 56

Freedmans Association for the Restoration of Lost Friends, 151–52, 153

Freedmen's Bureau, 145–51, 153, 220 (n. 20), 220 (n. 11)

Freedom: marriage vs., 53, 55–56, 137–38; of movement, 61–63; search for family and, 143–45, 156; separation from family in search of, 134–36; at Union Camps, 142

French, James, 1–2, 156

Gadson, Barbara Eason, 200

Gangs, defined, 206 (n. 27)

Garlic, Delia, 21

Garner, Margaret, 199

Garris, Warren, 212 (n. 47)

Geddy, Edward, 64

Gender: gendered responses to separation, 87; gendered values for sale of children, 25, 26, 37; patriarchy and, 50, 57

Genealogical searches, 194–200

George (brother of Jim Allen), 27

George (of Hampton, Va.), 83–84

Gibson, John, 36–37

Gilchrist, J. M., 99

Gilchrist, Samuel, 166

79–80, 126, 127–28, 130–31; Fickling
and Glen letter of permission, 59 (ill.),
211 (n. 30); Vilet Lester letters, 120,
127–31, 129 (ill.), 138, 149; letters to
Freedmen's Bureau, 148–51; privacy of,
80–81; James Tate letters, 77–80, 81,
126, 184, 213 (n. 70); Hawkins Wilson
letters, 149–50
Levy, William, 84–85
Lewis, Bearty, 164
Lewis, George William, 164
Lewis & Jordan (slave traders), 35
Lidbaugh, Josiah, 162
Lincoln, Abraham, 141
Lindsey, Elizabth, 64
Literacy, 4–5, 125, 153
Litwack, Leon, 1
Locher, Charles, 58–59
Long, Henry, 33
Long, Mr. (Adams County), 195
Longing, 2, 55, 80–81, 98, 122–23, 146, 153,
167–68. *See also* Despair; Hope
Loss: acceptance of permanence of, 77–80;
ambiguous, 3, 122; and ambivalence of
hope/despair, 120, 122–23, 146, 154, 156,
167–68, 194; disenfranchised grief and,
3, 88; as haunting presence, 190–92,
199; of hope, 112; remembrances of, 77–
80; and sense of past/potential, 191–92;
universality of, 14–16
Lost Friends ads, 152, 154, 160, 174–75, 177
Louisa (of St. Helena Island), 94, 95, 99
Lowery, Lucinda, 162
Lowndes, Edward, 161
Lucy (sister of John Brown), 30–32
Lucy (sister of Lizzie Baker), 191
Lumsden, James, 162
Lyons, Thomas, 164

Madison, Dibsy, 163
Magical thinking, 24, 156
Malinda (former wife of John E. Beck),
80–81, 88, 126, 184
Malinda (wife of Henry Bibb), 53, 56–57,
133–38

Marcus (of St. Helena Island), 94, 99,
100
Margery (daughter of Sarah), 185
Marriage: escapes to freedom and, 52,
56, 133–34; exogamous marriages, 61;
freedom of movement and, 61–63; at
home/abroad marriages, 60–62, 75,
77–79; impermanence of, 64–65; legal
institution of, 49–51; marriage vows,
64–65; ownership of slaves through
marital contract, 91; as preventing escape, 60–62; remarriage, 136, 184–97;
as response to family separation, 53–54,
54–55; reunification conflicts, 184–97;
rights of married white women, 210
(n. 27); separation of partners through
movement of slaveowners, 75; slaveowner approval for, 57–64, 59 (ill.),
66–67, 211 (n. 30), 212 (n. 48); slaveowners' contradictions concerning
marriage laws, 51–52, 60; slaveowner
tolerance for emotional responses to
spousal separation, 87–88; soul preservation and, 52; and spousal privilege,
50; value of for enslaved people, 52–56;
white people as officiants for, 65–66,
211 (n. 30). *See also* Spouses
Martha (mother of Caleb Craig), 44
Martin (son of Sarah), 186
Martin, John Sella, 123–26
Martin, Mr., 164
Mary (sister of Martin Scott), 167
Mary Ann (friend of John Beck), 81
Mary Olivia (daughter of James Tate), 79
Mason, Catherine, 165
Mason, Kate, 165
Mason, Lewis, 165
Mason, Lizzie, 165
Matthew 19:5–6, 48
McClellan, G. M., 173
McCord, Mary Ann, 173
McDermitt, Elias Lowery, 164
McDermitt, Martha, 163, 164
McDonald, Charles J., 65, 88, 212 (n. 47)
McDonald, Hugh, 38

McDonald, W., 38

McTyeire, H. N., 60

Medley, Madison, 219 (n. 6)

Memory. *See* Remembering

Memphis Exhibition of the Colored People, 196

Methodology, 3–6, 13–14, 17–18, 23

Middleton, Ruth, 197

Middleton Place Plantation (S.C.), 189, 224 (n. 1), 224 (n. 19)

Miller, George Washington, 183–84

Miller, Thomas S. P., 161

Milles, Mary, 136

Mintz, Steven, 206 (n. 21)

Miss Patsy, 128, 129 (ill.), 130, 149

Mitchell, Alice, 159

Morrison, Toni, 139, 198–99

Moses (husband of Pal), 66

Moses (of St. Helena Island), 94, 99

Moss, Charity, 2

Moss, David, 2

Mourning rituals, 24

Moynihan, Daniel Patrick, 9–11

Murdock, William, 131–32

Music: coffle songs, 217 (n. 42); as response to isolation and loss, 5, 112–14; songs of reunification, 120–21; songs of separation, 120–21; use of for remembering people, 5–6

"My people" phrase, 192–94, 198, 223 (n. 11)

Nagles, Frances, 166

Nagles, Harriet, 166

Nagles, Lucy, 166

Nagles, Martin, 166

Nagles, Mary, 166

Nagles, Richard, 166

Native Americans, 71

Nelson, George, 83

Newspaper advertisements: in black and church-sponsored newspapers, 153–54, 193, 221 (n. 25); of children for sale, 38 (ill.); costs of, 154; of display at Atlanta Cotton States and International Ex-

position, 196; of display at Memphis Exhibition of the Colored People, 196; emancipation and, 221 (n. 25); emotional impact of, 1–3; to enable reunification, 5, 194; of escaped slaves, 5; Kendall and Harlan circulars, 221 (n. 25); literacy and, 153; Lost Friends ads, 1–2, 152, 154, 160, 174–75, 177; as remembrances, 194; and shift to "my people" language, 192–94, 198, 223 (n. 11). *See also* Information Wanted ads

Nietzsche, Friedrich, 122–23

North Carolina: marriage laws in, 50–51

Notes on the State of Virginia (Jefferson), 97

Nottingham, Mrs., 164

Nunez, Elizabeth, xii, 88

Odom, Angie Lina K., 193, 194

Odum, J. L., 193

Old Curry (of St. Helena Island), 92

Oliver, Sidney, 166

O'Neal, Sam, 27

O'Neile, John, 112

Outlaw, Cherry, 157

Outlaw, Eli, 157

Outlaw, Hagar, 157

Outlaw, Hugh, 157

Outlaw, Joseph, 157

Outlaw, Mills, 157

Outlaw, Noah, 157

Outlaw, Thomas Rembry, 157

Outlaw, Viny, 157

Overton, Mag (Mag Brown), 192

Paine, Elvira (Puss), 160

Paine, John C., 160

Paine, Leonard, 160

Paine, Levi, 160

Paine, Warren, 160

Paine, William, 160

Painter, Nell Irvin, 3, 12

Pal (wife of Moses), 66

Palladium of Liberty (newspaper), 132, 133, 219 (n. 20)

Parents: emotional response of to separation from their children, 23, 190; father/child relations, 32–34; gendered responses of to separation, 87; mother/child relations, 23–32, 199; powerlessness of over separation from children, 28–32; and purchase attempts of children, 33–34; refusal of to let children live within slavery, 199

Paris, Martha, 163

Parker, William, 119, 121

Parker, Willis, 36

Paternalism, 60–61, 211 (n. 35)

Patriarchy, 50, 57

Patterson, E. M., 184

Patton, Mr., 161

Paul (of Goose Creek), 84

Paul (of St. Helena Island), 94, 95, 96, 99, 107

Pearson, C. J., 51, 58

Peculiar Institution (Stampp), 8

Peggy (of St. Helena Island), 94

Percy, Catherine, 96–97, 115, 216 (n. 18)

Perdue, Theda, 224 (n. 18)

Person, Hannah, 167

Person, Hannah (Hannah Cole), 167

Person, John, 167

Phillips, Ulrich Bonnell, 6–7, 9, 10

Phillis (sister of Martha Smith), 161

Phoebe (mother of Emeline Hodge), 166

Pinckney, H. L., 84

Pointer, Thomas, 165

Poole, Sam, 200

Powell, Julie, 40–41

Powell, Maybell, 40

Power, 28, 31, 50, 57

Preston, William, 37

Prince (of St. Helena Island), 94, 95, 96, 99, 100, 107

R., Isaac, 29

Rachel (daughter of Esther), 168

Randolph, Peter, 120

Randolph, Thomas Mann, 122

Ransby, Barbara, 223 (n. 11)

Ratlif, Eliza Ann, 163, 164

Recognition: childhood separation and, 124–26, 177–78, 179–80, 181; failures of, 181; physical attributes that trigger, 177–79; remembering as enabling reunification, 194; reunification challenges, 172, 176–78, 179; use of detailed ads to trigger, 156–57; use of material objects for, 124–25

Redford, Dorothy, 198, 199–200, 224 (n. 20)

Religious organizations: church aid in reunification efforts, 158–59; church-sponsored newspapers and, 153–54, 193, 221 (n. 25); as comforting spaces, 42–44, 112–14

Remembering: coffle songs as, 217 (n. 42); contemporary responses to, 191–92; as enabling recognition/reunification, 194; as mixture of sadness and fear, 191–92; as recognition of those forgotten, 198–99; as remembrances themselves, 194; as way to feel better after separation, 54–55

Remington, J. H., 148

Resilience, 2–3, 9, 10, 173, 213 (n. 69)

Resistance, 8–9, 52

Reunification: accounts of by Mark Twain, 5–6, 173, 176, 187; at Camp Hamilton, 141–42; challenges of due to naming conventions for enslaved people, 159–62; challenges of for spouses, 183–87; after childhood separation, 176–80; church aid in, 153–54, 158–59, 162–63, 168, 193, 221 (n. 25); complexity of, 172; emotional responses to, 143; emotional silence and, 182–84; escapes in hopes of, 83–86, 120, 125–26, 131–32; fictional accounts of by Charles Chesnutt, 173–76; and Freedmans Association for the Restoration of Lost Friends, 151–52; Freedmen's Bureau and, 145–51; in heaven, 120; letter writing and, 120, 126–32, 149–50; material objects as tokens of remembrance, 124, 125; prob-

lems of recognition, 175–76; recon-
ciliation of past with present, 173–76;
remembering as enabling recognition,
194; resources for enlisted freedmen,
152–53; return to old places, 143–44;
scarcity of, 187; songs of, 120–21; and
word-of-mouth searches, 120. *See also*
Newspaper advertisements

Rhodes, Catherine, 165

Rhodes, Jeremiah, 165

Rhodes, William, 165

Rice (of Nashville), 132–33

Rives, Alan, 212 (n. 48)

Robert (of St. Helena Island), 94

Robinson, William, 143

Rogers, Robert, 1, 156

Rollins, Parthena, 27–28

Roots (Haley), 198

Roots (television series), 198

Roper, Moses, 125–26

Rosanna (sister of Anthony Terrill), 166

Roscoe, Ann, 161

Roscoe, Thos., 161

Rose (great-grandmother to Ruth Middleton), 196–97, 224 (n. 19)

Rose (mother of Ashley), 196–97, 224
(n. 19)

Rose (of St. Helena Island), 92, 94

Rose (wife of Hardy), 73–74, 77, 108

Rosengarten, Theodore, 215 (n. 1)

Roundfield, Henry, 168

Ruffin, Thomas, 50, 58

Rumbo, George, 75

Runaways. *See* Escapes

Ryan, Thomas, 99

Sale, James, 38

Salley (of Orangeburg, S.C.), 26

Sancter, Alexander, 167

Sandy (husband of Anis), 74, 76

Sarah (mother of Martin), 186

Sarah (wife of Jim), 185

Savoie, Leigh, 15

Sawyer, Enoch, 70

Schaefer, Matt, 212 (n. 49)

Schiller, James, 37

Scott, Martin, 167

Search for families: abolitionist aid in,
134; church aid in, 153–54, 158–59,
162–63, 168, 193, 221 (n. 25); duration
of separations, 165–68; Freedmen's
Bureau and, 143; freedom and, 143–45,
156; long-term tracking of sales and
movements, 163–64; post–Civil War,
1–2, 141–43, 198; rhetorical challenges
to institution of slavery through,
164–65; through place of separation,
162–63; through slaveowners and
slave traders, 160–65

Secession, 141, 219 (n. 3)

Separation: abroad marriages, 63–64;
attempts to intervene in, 66–69;
awareness of enslaved status and, 206
(n. 21); and awareness of impending
loss, 11; contemporary family dysfunction as response to, 11; creation
of new families and, 11–12; as death,
120–23; through death of slaveowner,
64, 73; economic self-interests of
slaveowners in, 98; and happiness at
leaving, 95; across historical moments
and nation-states, 14–16, 204 (n. 19);
through movement of owners, 70–77;
nonsurvivors of emotional torment,
12; for payment of slaveowner debt, 27,
37, 76, 85, 91–92, 93, 94–95, 98, 123–24,
144, 149, 190; resistance against, 11;
through sales, 70–71; songs of, 120–21;
universality of, 14–16. *See also* Childhood separation; Family separation;
Spouses

Shaw, Amanda (Amanda Allison), 161

Shepherd, Ben, 163

Shepherd, Caroline, 163

Shepherd, Louisa, 163

Shepherd, Mandy, 163

Shepherd, Martha, 163

Shepherd, Mary, 163

Shepherd, Paten, 163

Shepherd, Virginia, 163

as embodied property, 151; toward spectacle of slave markets, 100–110; tolerance for emotional responses of enslaved people, 87–88, 94. *See also* Slaveowners; Slaveowning women

"Wife of His Youth" (Chesnutt), 173–76, 187

Wilford, Robert R., 172

Williams, Andrew E., 217 (n. 48)

Williams, Jerry, 192–93

Williams, Sarah, 167

Williams, Sarah (formerly Bailey), 160

Williams, Thomas, 127

Wilson, Hawkins, 149–50

Wilson, John, 211 (n. 35)

Wilson, Jonathan M., 151

Wilson and Hines slave traders, 150–51

Winnie (mother of Sella Martin), 123–25

Women: gendered responses of to separation, 87; rights of married white women, 210 (n. 27) *See also* Gender; Slaveowning women

Wood, Martha Ann, 150

Wood, Robert, 150

Wood, Sophia, 150

Wyatt, Bayley, 47, 88

Yoshida, Ayako, 204 (n. 21)

Young, Dock, 160

Young, Henry, 163

Young, Martha, 163

Young, Milzes, 160

Young, Milzes (Milzes Arbet), 160

Young, Nancy, 161